W9-APU-250

personal construct systems in psychotherapy

personal construct systems in psychotherapy

A. W. LANDFIELD university of missouri, columbia, missouri

rand mcnally & company, chicago

Rand McNally Psychology Series
Lloyd Humphreys, Advisory Editor

Printed in U.S.A. by Rand McNally & Company
Library of Congress Catalog Card Number 79-149985

To my wife, Susan Jean,
and to our children,
Megan Elizabeth and Kent Bevan

PREFACE

EVERY PROGRAM OF INVESTIGATION HAS A POINT OF ORIGIN. THE rather complex data shared with you in the ensuing chapters originated in the context of my commitment to the study of "internal" man. Specifically, I was intrigued by the possibilities of applying a theory called the *Psychology of Personal Constructs* to a particular mode of human interaction called *psychotherapy*. Psychotherapy represents a professional commitment to helpfully understand the personal and individual natures of man. Personal construct theory represents a theoretical and scientific approach to man's thinking and behavior, an approach ideally suited for investigations of psychotherapy.

Psychotherapy was chosen as a vehicle within which to comprehend certain aspects of personal construct theory. Conversely, personal construct theory was selected as a way of systematically illuminating the nature of the psychotherapeutic relationship. No attempt was made to validate a particular school of psychotherapy. However I did make the experimental assumptions that the psychotherapy relationship can have impact on the client, for better or worse, and that maladjustment, improvement, and change are useful constructions. Making these assumptions did allow us to proceed with the study.

The core of the more formal investigation is comprised of seven hypotheses which focus on the congruency of the client and his therapist as measured by the content and organization of their *personal construct systems*. Since very little is known about the clinical uses of personal construct information, two chapters are devoted to a discussion of illustrative case material.

ACKNOWLEDGMENTS

Many persons and organizations contributed to the completion of this project. First and most importantly, I am grateful to the psychologists and clients of the Mental Hygiene Clinic, Student Health Service, University of Missouri. The therapists who participated in both parts of the study gave many long hours, taking and retaking Rep Tests as well as filling out rating scales and dictating on their clients. The cooperation of the clients did not lag until the follow-up and a certain amount of foot dragging at this stage of the investigation can be understood.

Special thanks are due to Dr. Lynn Ourth who engineered the project and conducted the intake and terminal research interviews. The very difficult task of rating improvement and change was assigned to external judges: Dr. George A. Kelly, Dr. Janet Lyon, and Dr. Loretta Cass. Their careful judgments constitute the bedrock of the research. Certain agencies contributed funds at various times, namely, the National Institute of Mental Health, The Greater Kansas City Mental Health Foundation, and the University of Missouri Graduate Research Council. I gratefully acknowledge permission from the W. W. Norton Company to quote from the volume, *The Psychology of Personal Constructs;* the American Psychological Association for the right to reprint sections of two articles from the *Journal of Counseling Psychology,* 1964, 11, 336–341, and 1965, 12, 336–371; and Dr. Don Bannister for sharing his "Exercise in Paradox."

Colleagues Robert Dolliver, Ruth Allee, Walter Danforth, and Carlton Paine made many helpful suggestions in the writing phase. And above all, I am indebted to the late Dr. George A. Kelly who created the psychology of personal constructs. Dr. Kelly often remarked to his students, "Try it out and see what happens." It was with this spirit of exploration that the present study was undertaken.

CONTENTS

INTRODUCTION

THE PRESENT INVESTIGATION IS AN EXPLORATION OF CLIENT-THERAPIST congruency in the context of psychotherapeutic relationships. It is a study of how therapists understand their clients and how this understanding is related to conceptual congruence in the therapy dyad. It highlights the relationship between client-therapist congruence in the content and structure of their conceptual systems and premature termination and improvement. The implications of client-therapist dyadic meaningfulness also are explored. It is a study of the impact a therapist may have on his client. Primarily and most importantly, it is a more systematic investigation done within a particular theory—*the Psychology of Personal Constructs.*

One does not have to be a devotee of personal construct theory to find something of value in this research. Many reported observations and relationships should be of interest to anyone with involvements in clinical practice, psychotherapy, and personality theory. However, personal construct theory does provide new vistas for understanding human nature, and there may be sections of the manuscript which will require the reader to suspend, for the moment, his preoccupation with other conceptions. It is hoped that the reader will not suspend his critical judgment at these moments. However, if critical judgment is tied to a particular theory very different from the present one, the reader should approach the volume as science fiction. It is all good fun, and there just might be a bit of truth in it. Why not approach it this way. Scientific writing is partly science fiction, as each older generation *may* discover and as each new generation *does* discover. Moreover, sometimes science fiction may serve as a cultural base for later profound discovery.

A particular conception of man can become a roadblock to the understanding of other theories. The awareness of this possibility by social scientists leads to interesting behavior. It is not unusual to find a commentator on the state of psychological research urging his colleagues to agree upon certain limited dimensions and areas of research and to create a science on empirical grounds. In the same breath this commentator points to certain empirically oriented investigators and states that they need to know more about psychoanalysis, existential thought, or a theory of learning. His behavior could be construed as inconsistent. He tells us that we should be empirical; then he places our empirical findings within a broader framework of meaning and criticizes us for not having done the same. This paradoxical behavior might be given the following interpretation. The commentator has become disenchanted with some theory and cannot find a satisfactory substitute. Now he is looking for the facts of life which he hopes will give him meaning. However, he discovers that the facts do not make much sense without resorting to a more general framework.

This illustration points up an important aspect of man. Man wants to know and to feel certain he knows; yet his understanding is at least one step removed from the facts. This is another way of saying that meaning is obtained through the process of abstraction and high order generalization. *Man is theoretical* whether the limits of his interests are broad or narrow. Man is theoretical even though he may assume that his life is only factual. Man creates theories within which he may understand the events of his life. His theorizing is not restricted to scientific events but also encompasses the more personal happenings in his everyday living. To understand man one must investigate the nature of these theories, both scientific and personal, in all their variations and with their many implications. This is the essence of the psychology of personal constructs.

A STATEMENT OF PURPOSE

The present volume is addressed to those clinicians, psychotherapists, counselors, researchers, and personality theorists who assume (1) that drawing inferences about man's thinking, values, and life plans is a necessary part of a science of psychological man, and (2) that speculation, highly exploratory investigation, and clinical observation all have a place in formal scientific discourse. The volume is addressed particularly to those who are curious about how a psychologist has used personal construct theory as a vehicle of both research in psychotherapy and clinical practice. It covers a wide range of topics, including formal research hypotheses and methods of investigation, as well as a discussion of several individuals who were assessed by methods derived from personal construct theory. Since I feel strongly that a theory should not be identified exclusively with a particular method of measurement, a new method called the *Pyramid Procedure* is described in a later section. This method, although not used in the primary investigation, can be viewed as an outgrowth of experiences with the more traditional method.

A colleague suggested that a research volume is a way of getting something out of one's system, or a way of clearing the decks prior to the next adventure. It may also be a way of trying to assert the eternal validity of one's ideas. Whatever the underlying purpose *really* may be, I want to raise several questions about the nature of psychotherapeutic relationships and demonstrate the fertility of a personal construct approach to research and clinical practice.

PROBLEMS OF DOING RESEARCH

I encountered innumerable choices in the planning, execution, and analysis stages of the investigation. First, what theoretical or methodological framework should one employ? Not only is it difficult to use multiple theoretical approaches, but the investigator soon discovers that it is impossible to do all the things he wishes, even within a more limited framework. Choice of a setting within which to do research creates even more problems. Why should an investigator attempt a study of psychotherapy? The number of unknown and uncontrolled variables which conceivably could affect processes of psychotherapy are infinite.

At some point an investigator must make a commitment, as I did, to theory, method, and setting on a rather simple basis: *This is an interesting way of doing it.* It cannot be otherwise, unless one wishes to be caught in the Miller's dilemma.

> A Miller and his Son were driving their Ass to a neighbouring fair to sell him. They had not gone far when they met a troop of girls returning from the town, talking and laughing. "Look there!" cried one of them, "did you ever see such fools, to be trudging along the road on foot, when they might be riding!" The old Man, hearing this, quietly bade his Son get on the Ass, and walked along merrily by the side of him. Presently they came up to a group of old men in earnest debate. "There!" said one of them, "it proves what I was saying. What respect is shown to old age in these days? Do you see that idle young rogue riding, while his old father has to walk?—

> Get down you scapegrace and let the Old Man rest his weary limbs." Upon this, the Father made his Son dismount, and got up himself. In this manner they had not proceeded far when they met a company of women and children. "Why, you lazy old fellow!" cried several at once, "how can you ride upon the beast, while that poor little lad there can hardly keep pace by the side of you." The good-natured Miller stood corrected, and immediately took up his Son behind him. They had now almost reached the town. "Pray, honest friend," said a townsman, "is that Ass your own?" "Yes," says the old Man. "Oh! One would not have thought so," said the other, "by the way you load him. Why, you two fellows are better able to carry the poor beast than he you!" "Anything to please you," said the old Man; "we can but try." So, alighting with his Son, they tied the Ass's legs together, and by the help of a pole endeavoured to carry him on their shoulders over a bridge that led to the town. This was so entertaining a sight that the people ran out in crowds to laugh at it; till the Ass, not liking the noise nor his situation, kicked asunder the cords that bound him, and, tumbling off the pole, fell into the river (Aesop's Fable from Rhys, 1913).

THE SIGNIFICANCE OF CLIENT-THERAPIST CONGRUENCE

The concept of interpersonal congruence and incongruence is receiving increased attention. A growing interest in this dimension as a clinical and explanatory variable is related to certain ethical concerns and to the possibility that congruence may be a basis for communication as well as a source of therapist influence. That the variable of client-therapist personality congruence may be a controversial issue is raised by Weisskopf-Joelson (1968).

> Likewise, when discussing the dichotomy between "being" and "doing" I felt an antagonism in my students when I stated that in psychotherapy "being" is more important than "doing"; i.e., what kind of person the therapist is will affect the patient more than the methods he uses. The students did not like to hear that. These efficient and energetic young men wanted to be taught definite and objective techniques.

Investigations of client-therapist congruence, even as they may seem contradictory and sometimes unsystematic, do suggest that some clients identify with their therapists' values and that initial congruence or similarity of client-therapist values may have important implications for improvement.

Rosenthal (1955), working within a psychoanalytic framework, administered tests of valuing to twelve patients and their therapists. Although Rosenthal did not comment on the relationship between initial congruence of the therapy dyads, tabular data suggest that he did not find any relationship between initial congruence and later improvement. However, he did report that improved patients tend to identify more closely with the values of their therapists at the end of therapy. Farson (1961), using the Butler-Haigh Q Sort in a study of client-centered therapy, found increasing congruence over a period of therapy to be negatively correlated with therapist competence as judged by peer-group therapists. This result is in direct opposition to the findings of Rosenthal. Tuma and Gustad (1957) found some evidence that client-counselor similarities on selected personality traits are related to specific types of client learning. Gerler (1958) hypothesized that a medium similarity between client and counselor as obtained on personality inventory ratings is better for outcome than high or low similarity. This hypothesis was only partially confirmed in that medium- and high-similarity dyads could be differentiated but not medium and low dyads. Halpern and Lesser (1960), in a study of empathy, report a significant correlation between predictive accuracy of an acquaintance's self-ratings and personality similarity between predictor and predictee. Welkowitz, Cohen, and Ortmeyer (1967), using the Ways To Live Scale and the Strong Vocational Interest Blank, found that the patients rated most improved by their therapists in two psychoanalytic training centers were closer to their therapists in values than those patients rated least improved.

The classic study by Hollingshead and Redlich (1958) on social class bias in psychiatric treatment certainly gives some support for the proposition that a lack of shared social language affects treatment. Class similarities, suggesting language congruence, resulted in greater emphasis by the psychiatrist on the patient-therapist relationship. Dissimilarities were linked to a greater emphasis on the symptoms and a more manipulative treatment. Hunt (1961) found the staff and lower-class clients differing on codes which may introduce noise into the communication system leading ultimately to dissolution of the therapy dyad.

Heilbrun (1961), in a study of personality correlates of early termination in student counseling, found that non-stay clients, male or female, tend to conform more closely to the cultural stereotype appropriate to their sex. If Heilbrun's conclusions can be generalized and if counselors do not adhere closely to cultural sex-role stereotypes, then non-stay clients may well be less congruent with their counselors than those who remain in counseling.

Mendelsohn (1968), in an unpublished report, concludes that marked dissimilarity between client and counselor leads almost always to shorter-term counseling. Furthermore, similarity, which may lead to short- or long-term counseling is a necessary condition for longer-term work and bears no consistent relationship to counseling effectiveness. Sex matching per se was not found to be related to outcome; however, client-counselor similarity is more important when the client is a female. Pepinsky and Karst (1964) took the position that convergence is an important phenomenon in psychotherapy, and Persons and Pepinsky (1966) discuss a therapy study done with delinquent boys in which successfully treated delinquents become more like their therapists on such measures as the Taylor Manifest Anxiety Scale and the Minnesota Multiphasic Personality Inventory (MMPI).

Curvilinear relationships were found in two interesting but contradictory studies. Runkle (1956), using a theory of colinearity, presented evidence that students who rank order value statements in ways similar to or opposite of their teachers earn higher grades. Carson and Heine (1962), using MMPI statements from clients and inexperienced therapists, found very high and very low statement congruence related to less improvement. The contrasting nature of these studies, one focusing more on organization and the other on content, did suggest the importance of defining our own data at different levels of abstraction, i.e., content and structure.

These studies of congruence are interesting and raise many questions. For example, what is the relationship between initial congruence and convergence? Do initial congruence and convergence both relate to improvement in therapy? Is the congruency-improvement relationship curvilinear or direct? What happens if prematurely terminating clients, those unable to sustain a therapy relationship, are analyzed separately from clients who are able to sustain such a relationship? What happens if client-therapist congruence is defined at different levels of abstraction? Finally, what happens when a more systematic theoretical-methodological approach, employed in the context of a personality theory, is applied to an investigation of client-therapist congruence?

CONGRUENCY-INCONGRUENCY AS AN ETHICAL ISSUE

A psychotherapist may teach, either by design or unintentionally, his own personal values. To do so might be considered a sign of incompetence or even an index of unethical behavior. Moreover, some experienced psychotherapists would feel that a therapist's continual assertion of his specific values could restrict, unwisely and unnecessarily, the independence and freedom of his patients. The helpless and dependent patient or the externally oriented and tropistic client might be particularly vulnerable in the hands of a professional who knows exactly how another person should live.

To take advantage of the helplessness of another human being is a matter of ethical concern. But how does one help another human being in psychological distress without projecting his own particular values and problems onto the patient? That we cannot escape the moral dilemma is succinctly stated by London (1964):

> . . . psychotherapy is a moralistic as well as a scientific undertaking to such an extent that it cannot be properly understood as the latter unless it is also thoroughly evaluated as the former. Therapists use theoretical and technical skills and scientific opinions as the basis for studying and treating their patients, but it is in terms of moral concern that they decide the ultimate goals and objectives of their treatment (Preface, p. V).

Therapists of various schools employ interesting devices to avoid or lessen the moral dilemma. Proper theoretical training, self-analysis, situations which maximize the freedom of self-expression, mirror feelings, and therapy aimed at specific behaviors are all ways of lessening the moral problem. Within the psychology of personal constructs, Kelly offers advice about how to stay within the client's language system. He also urges the therapist to provide the client with methodological construction rather than content construction. To assist a client in the ways of learning, focusing on personal exploration and experimentation is more important than telling the client what contents he should specifically learn.

Although Kelly emphasizes creative processes which are defined at higher levels of generality, his focus is no less value laden than a minutely detailed prescription of how one must live since there are people and patients who do not want freedom. Structures of freedom may be value laden and possibly even coercive for some individuals, as value laden and coercive as structures of authoritarianism. Although not a palatable conception, it is one with which we must contend.

Apparently there is no simple solution to the ethical dilemma. The best we can do is to be aware of the issue and to maintain our concern about our clients and ourselves in relation to it. Part of our concern can lead to scientific questioning. What are the personal values of therapists and their clients? What are the implications of placing together clients and therapists of similar and different values? In the context of the present investigation, I will pursue the implications of client-therapist congruence in the content and structure of their personal construct systems.

Kessel and McBrearty (1967), in their review of the literature on values in psychotherapy, conclude that "the ratio of theoretical to empirical literature . . . highlights the need for further research . . . , particularly with regard to similarity in values of therapist and patient and its effect on outcome in therapy" (p. 683). In agreement with this statement, I would like to emphasize even further the need for more empirical investigations of a programmatic nature, studies which fit clearly within theoretical models.

OVERVIEW OF CHAPTERS

In Chapter 1, general hypotheses are presented together with selected methods, corollaries, and concepts of personal construct theory. Specifically, the individuality, commonality, sociality, organization, and dichotomy corollaries are considered along with the concept of methodological construction. This latter construction is given special emphasis by Kelly as a key to understanding the most effective therapist role. Chapter 1 also includes an introduction to certain measurements of personal construct content and structure. Each of these measures will be given more detailed consideration in later sections. The research design is described in Chapter 2. The measurements of construct meaningfulness, content, and organization are elaborated in Chapter 3.

Several measures of client-therapist congruency are related to premature termination, improvement, and attributed pathology in Chapters 4, 5, and 6. Chapter 7, entitled "Clinical Appraisal and Other Explorations," gives the reader some idea about how one may employ personal construct information in understanding the individual. This chapter also includes statistical explorations not encompassed by our formal hypotheses. A new procedure, one having both diagnostic and therapeutic implications which was derived from personal construct theory, is described in Chapter 8. Some of the fragments and pieces are fitted together in the final chapter in ways that, hopefully, will be thought-provoking, if not eternally valid. A note on reflexiveness of theory, a vital issue for the personal construct psychologist, also is included in this chapter.

CHAPTER ONE

A THEORETICAL POSITION

CERTAIN ASSUMPTIONS AND CONCEPTS OF PERSONAL CONSTRUCT THEORY which are most relevant to the research are described in this chapter. The reader interested in a fuller account of the general theory is referred to Kelly's *The Psychology of Personal Constructs* (1955) and to a volume of his manuscripts, *Clinical Psychology and Personality,* edited by Brendan Maher (1969). A review of current research done within the theory is provided by Bannister and Mair (1968) and Bonarius (1965).

PERSONAL CONSTRUCT THEORY

The Author of Personal Construct Theory. Personality theories do not spring full blown from just anywhere. They are created by men, men of broad experience, keen powers of observation, and a deep involvement in the affairs of their fellow man. Professor George A. Kelly, author of the *Psychology of Personal Constructs,* was such a man.

Although his education in psychology followed the traditions of his day, Dr. Kelly did not cling to these traditions. His destiny lay in questioning them and doing so from a base within science itself. As important ideas tend to be, his central thesis is amazingly simple. As important ideas tend to have, his thesis has far reaching implications.

Professor Kelly was curious about what would happen if ordinary men were construed as having something in common with their scientific brethren. Do curiosity and fear of change mark the lives of both layman and scientist? Is a willingness to treat an event from different points of view important to layman and scientist alike? Are assumption and hypothesis the tools of the scientist alone? Does man create his own theory of life just as the scientist creates his theory and for the same reasons?

That scientist and layman may bear resemblance was an exciting idea for Dr. Kelly. The psychology of personal constructs was his attempt to formulate a science of man's theories, a theory of theories—highly abstract, but with intriguing ramifications for how we do and can understand and interact with our fellow man.

Models of Man. Psychology begins by assuming certain models of man. Today there are psychologies of the thinking man; the empty, mindless man; the emotional man; the hedonistic, pleasure-seeking man; and the man who is primarily searching for relief from pain. There is the organic and physiological man. There are psychologies of the self-actualizing man and creative man. There is man, the helpless respondent. There is the computerized man and even the loving man. There is a psychology for men who believe they think like rodents. And there is also a psychology of the rodent who is forced to behave like a human. There is a psychology suited for each of us, if we can find it or create it.

What can we learn from this vast array of psychologies? It is obvious that psychologists vary across the spectrum—in the content of their interests, in the ways they think, organize, and learn this content, as well as in the assumptions they make about the nature of life. These assumptions are all too often about the other man's life, not their own. Men do have theories about other men's lives. Men do vary in the theories they have about other men's lives. And psychologists are men applying their own personal ideas about the nature of *other* men's lives.

Scientist and Subject. The psychology of personal constructs represents a kind of reformation within psychology since it assumes that scientists are human, just as human beings are intrinsically scientists. Viewing all men as scientists trying to make sense of, and predict, life, removes the psychologist from a specialized priesthood and elevates all men to a position of greater importance, giving them a personal role in their own development.

The psychology of personal constructs assumes that man theorizes, although his theorizing may not always be evident, highly verbal, or related to the rules of formal logic. Not only does man erect structures of meaning, referred to as personal construct systems, but man uses his theories in the anticipation of life events. And his behavior can be plotted within his own language system.

Even though the validity of many details of this theory may be, and undoubtedly will be, questioned, the theory will stand as a significant protest against certain high priests of psychology, a priesthood unwilling to seriously consider the reflexive potentialities of its own theorizing. What would happen if a psychologist seriously tried to explain his own theorizing within his own theory? What would happen if a psychologist turned his own theory back upon himself and pondered the broader implications of his theory for himself as well as for others? But scientists are not required to turn their theories back upon themselves. The whole idea of being objective is to avoid such personal confrontations.

Assuming that all men theorize, it is possible to study both the scientist and his subjects as creators of theories. The major studies which will be described in this volume focus on both the scientist and his subject. However, we chose to study that special type of scientist, the psychotherapist, and his subject, the client or patient, and to devote our energies to pursuing the personal theories of scientist and subject, specifically the implications of client-therapist congruency in the content and structure of their personal construct systems.

Personal Constructs. Psychologists, in their attempts to be scientific, may avoid concepts of the inner man and focus only on external behavior. In contrast, Kelly established a theory about how man concerns himself with meaning. Within this theory, the central unit of meaning is the *personal construct* and it is defined by the contrasting ways of understanding life events employed by the individual as he tries to make sense of his experience. Specifically, a personal construct is defined as the way in which a person understands two things as being alike and different from a third. The personal construct is not just an object, event, or group of objects and events, but rather it is defined by inclusion, exclusion, and antithesis. The placing of personal constructions upon life events defines a major characteristic of man and has profound implications for his behavior.

The personal construct approach is not just a phenomenology. Certain "outer world" assumptions are made about the contrasting nature of man's thinking, the ways in which he organizes his thinking, the methods by which he employs his system of thinking in the anticipation of events, and the implications his ways of thinking may have for his behavior. Starting from a clearly nomothetic position, a variety of methods may be derived from the theory which are useful in eliciting information about an individual's personal language system. These methods, together with certain formal structures of the theory, do allow the clinician or research worker to group people together, to make generalizations, and to be scientifically respectable. Personal construct psychologists do have an interest in predicting behavior. However, it is assumed that truly adequate predictions of future behavior will be made by those willing to make inferences about the nature of man's thinking processes, ideas, and values. This assumption about the importance of man's ideas in understanding his behavior may account for the time that I have devoted to this investigation. Likewise, certain contrasting ideas about man may account for the time that other investigators have expended on projects where man's thinking has been avoided.

Although the hypotheses and methods employed in this investigation are related, as much as possible, to statements of personal construct theory, some analyses are more closely tied to the theory than others. Some methods, quite obviously, have been derived from explicit theory; others have not been so derived. However, it is believed that the project, as a whole, does catch the spirit of the psychology of personal constructs.

The Personal Construct System. A personal construct system is comprised of dimensions of meaning which are organized within contexts of relationship, and any appreciation of the personal construct system must take into account many levels of measurement. Bannister and Mair (1968) make this same point when they observe that the use of content and structural measures of personal construct systems is a convention. Content and structure do not refer to separate entities but rather are convenient ways of talking about different levels of interpretation. Some knowledge of structure, or the ways in which construct dimensions are related within the individual, enhances our appreciation of the meaning of the individual dimensions, their relative importance within the system, and the implications the use of one dimension may have for that of another dimension.

Content and Organization of Personal Construct Systems. This investigation focuses on the contents of personal constructs and the degree to which an individual's construct dimensions are interrelated or organized. Measures of content and organization are used to highlight important aspects of the personal construct systems of therapists and clients engaged in a human interaction called psychotherapy. Inferences about the meanings of particular personal construct descriptions are emphasized at the specific content level of analysis. The interrelationships between constructs are emphasized at the abstract organization level of analysis. A modification of the Role Construct Repertory Test (Rep

Test), a derivation from personal construct theory, is used to elicit constructs. The Rep Test is described in Chapter 3 and in Appendix A.

Content, as used in the present study, refers to the implied meanings of particular descriptions. For example, an acquaintance is described on the Rep Test as *harsh;* This description is postcoded by the author as "low tenderness." *Friendly* is categorized as "high social interaction"; *gregarious* is considered "high social interaction" and "high forcefulness"; *inactive* is assigned to "low forcefulness"; *indecisive* is scored as "low forcefulness," "low organization," and "low self-sufficiency"; and *enthusiasm* becomes "high forcefulness," "emotional arousal," and "high involvement." The Content Scoring Manual is described in Chapter 3 and in Appendix B.

Organization, as used in the present study, refers to the degree to which an individual's construct dimensions are interrelated as measured within a particular Rep Test grid. The grid is comprised of rating patterns established by asking a subject to describe all acquaintances used on the Rep Test within each construct dimension. Grid relationships may be inferred from overlapping or inverse rating patterns associated with any two construct dimensions. If Tom, Dick, and Harry are described as deadbeats and also as interesting people, a positive or direct relationship may be inferred between deadbeat and interesting. In this example, relationships are inferred between descriptive dimensions. Now, it is also possible to infer relationships between the people described. If Tom and Dick are both described as deadbeats, interesting, and intelligent, while Harry is described as deadbeat, interesting, and dull, Tom and Dick have more in common. The essential nature of grid inferred relationships is illustrated in Figures 1.1, 1.2 and 1.3.

Turning first to Figure 1.1, assume that a particular subject is

FIGURE 1.1

	Acquaintances				Columns		
	I	II	III	IV	Rating 1	Rating 2	
Row 1	grid ratings 1	2			Honest	Dishonest	Construct 1
Row 2			grid ratings 1	2	Open	Closed	Construct 2

asked to write the first names of four acquaintances in cells I, II, III, and IV. He then is asked to state one way in which Acquaintances I and II are different. His description of I as *honest* is recorded in the columns under Rating 1, and his description of II as *dishonest* is recorded under Rating 2. The subject has formed a personal construct.

Next, represent *honest* by the rating 1 and *dishonest* by the rating 2 and place these ratings under Acquaintances I and II in Row 1. Now assume that this subject differentiates his Acquaintances III and IV along the dimension of *open* vs. *closed* (Row 2). Represent *open* by the rating 1 and *closed* by the rating 2 and record these ratings under Acquaintances III and IV in Row 2, as shown in Figure 1.1. Finally, the subject rates the *honesty* and *dishonesty* of Acquaintances III and IV in Row 1, then rates the open or closed qualities of Acquaintances I and II in Row 2, as shown in Figure 1.2.

FIGURE 1.2

	Acquaintances				Columns		
	I	II	III	IV	Rating 1	Rating 2	
Row 1	1	2	1	2	Honest	Dishonest	Construct 1
Row 2	1	2	1	2	Open	Closed	Construct 2

Observe that the rating patterns of constructs 1 and 2 are the same in Figure 1.2. We may infer a positive or direct relationship between the dimensions of *honesty* and *openness. Honest* people are *open* and *dishonest* people are *closed.* If the ratings in the two rows are in contrast, as in Figure 1.3, an inverse relationship is inferred, i.e., *honest* people are *closed,* and *dishonest* people are *open.* Anyone who has given Rep Tests will not be astounded when he encounters such a strange relationship.

Our primary measurement of construct organization which will be elaborated in Chapter 3 is the Functionally Independent Construction (FIC) score, and it is defined as *the number of functionally different dimensional units of meaning inferred from a Rep Test grid.* A low FIC score means that a person's construct dimensions are highly

FIGURE 1.3

Acquaintances

	I	II	III	IV	
Row 1	1	2	1	2	Construct 1
Row 2	2	1	2	1	Construct 2

integrated and organized. A high FIC score means that his construct dimensions are used more independently of one another and constructs may not have implications for one another. Some investigators might describe a person using many different units of unrelated meanings as complex. However, I maintain that when complexity, defined in this way, is maximized, the person might better be described as confused or fragmented.

Cognitive complexity has been defined as the degree to which one's construct system is differentiated. This definition can imply that a person using his large repertoire of concepts will construe an event in many different ways, i.e., complexly. In contrast, a person lacking a large repertoire of concepts will construe the same event in a few ways, perhaps in only one way, i.e., simply. Now, using complexity in this context can be highly misleading since complex functioning assumes "a relatively large number of elements" which are "integrated hierarchically by relatively extensive bonds of relationship" (Crockett, 1965, p. 49). This statement by Crockett may appear somewhat paradoxical; nonetheless, it is a clear description of complex scientific thinking. The scientist must rely upon both integrative and differentiating skills if he is to make any sense of a variety of observations.

Having employed the same type of logic—one which seems consistent with personal construct theory—I have carefully avoided designating our organizational score as a measure of cognitive complexity, a term which might carry the erroneous implications that a high FIC score denotes the ability to encompass complexity and a low FIC score denotes an inability to encompass complexity. This careful avoidance of a particular definition of complexity, of course, does not reflect any desire to avoid the issue of complex functioning, and even though our hypotheses do not require us to label an FIC score as either good or bad, we believe that moderate FIC scores may be related to more effective functioning, whereas very high FIC scores may imply confusion and very low scores may imply simplicity.

COROLLARIES OF PERSONAL CONSTRUCT THEORY

Six corollaries of personal construct theory have particular relevance for the study: those pertaining to individuality of construction, the ways in which man's constructions are organized, the contrasting nature of man's thinking, the finiteness of constructions, the similarity of constructions across persons, and the nature of social role processes.

> [1.] *Individuality:* Persons differ from each other in their constructions of events.
> [2.] *Organization:* Each person characteristically evolves for his convenience in anticipating events a construction system embracing ordinal relationships between constructs.
> [3.] *Dichotomy:* A person's construction system is composed of a finite number of dichotomous constructs.
> [4.] *Range:* A construct is convenient for the anticipation of a finite range of events only.
> [5.] *Commonality:* To the extent that one person employs a construction of experience which is similar to that employed by another, his psychological processes are similar to those of the other person.
> [6.] *Sociality:* To the extent that one person construes the construction processes of another he may play a role in a social process involving the other person (Kelly, 1955, vol. II, pp. 561–562).

These formal statements of personal construct theory have particular implications for the present investigation. The first implication is that some commonality is necessary for the development of interpersonal communication between client and therapist. Kelly, in his discussion of the commonality corollary, states that some "I to eyeness" is important in a social relationship. Then he comments:

> Commonality between construction systems may make it more likely that one construction system can subsume a part of another, but that fact is incidental rather than essential in those cases where roles are played between people who think alike and understand each other (Kelly, 1955, vol. I, p. 99).

Nowhere does Kelly state that commonality will assure the development of a productive social process. Productive social interaction, as defined by the sociality corollary, depends on some commonality, but the critical factor in the development of productive role interaction or sociality lies in the ability of one or both participants in a dyadic relationship to subsume the points of view of the other person. The relationship between commonality and sociality is clarified when he states:

> Moreover, commonality can exist between two people who are in contact with each other without either of them being able to understand the other well enough to engage in a social process with him. The commonality may exist without those perceptions of each other which enable the people to understand each other or to subsume each other's mental processes. As in the case in psychotherapy in which the clinician identifies himself too closely with his client's way of seeing things that he cannot subsume the client's mental processes, the role the clinician plays becomes impoverished and the social process or the productive outcome of the clinician-client relationship comes to a standstill (Kelly, 1955, vol. I, p. 99).

Sociality presumes that a person has the ability to construe certain personal meanings or points of view of the other person. Another way of saying this is that sociality depends on some ability of one person to subsume certain aspects of the other person's construction system, and this ability should be correlated with efficiency in predicting behaviors which are implications of the other person's ways of thinking. This process of subsuming is central to the understanding of relationships which are most constructive and rewarding for the participants.

What is involved in the subsuming process? Kelly points out that subsuming may not take place if persons have identical construction systems. Apparently, the subsuming process depends on differences as well as commonalities between construction systems. Kelly comments:

> Let us make sure, further that we have not slighted the point that there is a difference between two people's holding the same construction system and two people's understanding each other so that they can play roles in relation to each other. Consider the differences in the characteristic approaches to life of men and women. None of us would claim, we believe, that men and women construe all aspects of life in the same way. And yet nature has provided us with no finer example of role relationships and constructive social interaction than in the sexes . . . (Kelly, 1955, vol. I, p. 100).

Kelly's discussion of the commonality and sociality corollaries suggests the following ideas about therapy relationships: (1) Although some degree of commonality between the construct systems of a client and his therapist is an underlying factor in developing lines of communication between them, the key to a successful relationship, i.e., improvement, is the ability of one or both members of a therapy dyad to encompass aspects of the construct system of the other person. (2) Highly similar client-therapist construct systems will not enhance the development of a successful relationship since encompassing some aspects of the other person's system involves an abstracting process which is impossible if two people are highly similar in the ways they think.

Starting from this theoretical base, it seemed reasonable that the initiation and maintenance of a therapy relationship, as differentiated from improvement, would require a particular type of commonality—that which is most related to establishing lines of discourse and communication. This reasonable idea raised two questions: what kind of commonality would most likely sustain a relationship, and how much commonality is a sufficient amount?

The decision was made to treat the question of sufficient commonality as an exploratory one to be considered more fully in future research, and to focus on hypotheses from which predictions of a relative nature are made, i.e., which group of client-therapist pairs will be associated with greater dyadic commonality. For example, premature terminators in psychotherapy were expected to have less commonality with their therapists than nonpremature terminators.

The decision was made to employ content congruency as the most appropriate measure of an ability to maintain a relationship. *Content,* i.e., the areas of focus inferred from personal construct description, is differentiated from *organization,* i.e., the degree to which construct dimensions are interrelated. Inability to maintain a relationship was associated with premature termination as defined by length of stay or by the unsatisfactory nature of the relationship inferred at the point of termination. The assessments of content, organization, and premature termination will be clarified in Chapters 2 and 3; however, the following illustration may give more meaning, at this point, to the concepts of content and organization.

Imagine that a therapy client employs personal construct dimensions, the contents of which point to high status, self-sufficiency, low tenderness, and future orientation. In contrast, his therapist emphasizes content which suggests concerns and interests in the areas of high social interaction, openness to experience, emotional arousal, and a sense of humor. According to our method of scoring the content of these two languages of social description, this client and his therapist would be incongruent in the content of their personal constructions. Expanding the illustration, imagine that this client and his therapist are similar in the degree to which each of them interrelates his own construct dimensions, i.e., organizes his dimensions. This congruency in the similarity of organization would not be as important a predictor of premature termination as would be the difference in content.

If content incongruence has important implications for premature termination, what is the significance of organizational incongruence? At this point, a discussion of Kelly's methodological construction, therapist role, and system organization will help clarify our position on the significance of organizational incongruency.

Methodological construction includes those more general ways in which a person goes about solving his problems. Kelly maintained that a therapist's methodological constructions have greater potential benefit for his client than intimate, concrete revelations by the therapist about his own life, overly specific solutions provided by rote, or fixed interpretations of behavior.

The *therapist's role,* as outlined within personal construct theory, is most complex and includes the therapist's careful and continuing evaluations of the client's construct system along certain axes suggested by the fundamental assumptions of the theory. One critical axis of transition and new learning is that of *system organization.* Kelly noted that some people have more tightly organized construction systems while others have more loosely organized construction systems. Bieri (1955) first tried to capture this difference in organization by a measure which he called cognitive complexity-simplicity. A cognitively complex person is one who uses many unrelated dimensions of experience while a cognitively simple person is one who uses constructs which are highly interrelated.

Our measure of Functionally Independent Construction or FIC (Landfield, Danforth, and Baugh, 1968) bears resemblance to Bieri's approach. However, there are certain theoretical and methodological differences which will be examined later.

Kelly's position on methodological construction, considered within the context of the Organization Corollary, suggested the interesting possibility that client-therapist organizational differences may be important indices of methodological stimulation. In other words, the therapist's capacity to provide his client with problem-solving stimulation is related, in part, to organizational differences existing between client and therapist personal construct systems.

Assuming that the FIC organization score measures one aspect of methodological construction, it was hypothesized that a client-therapist difference in FIC scoring, at the beginning of therapy, provides an important context of relationship within which the client may reconstrue or reinterpret events of importance to him. I reasoned that a client whose constructs are tightly interrelated will profit most from interaction with a therapist whose own constructions are less well organized. Conversely, I hypothesized that a client whose constructs are loosely interrelated will profit most from interaction with a therapist whose own constructions are more tightly systematized.

The significance of organizational incongruence can be illustrated. A therapist can assist his client in placing a particular experience either within a broader framework or within a more restricted framework of meaning. And this can be done without drastically changing or invalidating the experience for the client. A client's complaint about a friend's cruel behavior can be accepted by the therapist as having validity but only in the context of time, situation, and people. A client's report of an unexplainable kindness by another person can be tentatively reflected by the therapist as having larger or more profound implications.

A confused client might find it easier to sort out competing life demands and competing desires in conjunction with a more systematically organized therapist who shares with his client certain points of personal language focus. A "tightly bound" client might profit from the more relaxed, free floating approach of a less systematic therapist who also shares with his client certain points of common focus.

A therapist, assuming the importance of this organizational-methodological dimension, might deliberately and helpfully vary his role along the axis of functionally independent construction. However, it is likely that some therapists cannot easily and consistently alter their own personally preferred styles of organizational responses and concurrently maintain much authenticity of role. In the event that a psychotherapist cannot modify his organizational role without loss of integrity as a person, it is important for him to more carefully select his clients, taking into consideration the similar or contrasting organizational styles that he and his prospective client hold.

CONGRUENCY HYPOTHESES OF PREMATURE TERMINATION

Three hypotheses, discussed more thoroughly in Chapter 4, are concerned with the relationship between client-therapist congruence and premature termination in psychotherapy. Congruence, as measured by perception of the other person as meaningful within one's own personal construct dimensions, perception of the other person's constructs as meaningful, and similarity in the contents of personal constructs, is related to premature termination as defined by early termination from longer-term case assignment and dissatisfaction with the relationship.

Hypothesis I: In those client-therapist (C-T) pairs in which T and C perceive each other as more meaningful figures at the beginning of therapy, the conclusion of therapy will be nonpremature. In those C-T pairs in which T and C perceive each other as less meaningful figures, therapy will conclude prematurely. Although perception of the other person as meaningful does not guarantee a productive or successful therapy outcome, to be able to understand or encompass something of the other person's role within one's own construct system is an important aspect of initiating and maintaining a therapy relationship.

Hypothesis II: In those C-T pairs in which T and C perceive each other's construct dimensions as more meaningful at the beginning of therapy, the conclusion of therapy will be nonpremature. In those C-T pairs in which T and C perceive each other's construct dimensions as less meaningful, therapy will conclude prematurely. An ability to use the construct dimensions of the other person suggests some potential for subsuming the other person's constructs, i.e., for understanding some aspects of the other person's ways of thinking. Ability to use the other person's dimensions of thinking contributes to the maintenance of the therapy relationship.

Hypothesis III: In those C-T pairs in which there is more similarity in the content of their personal constructs at the beginning of therapy, the conclusion of therapy will be nonpremature. In those C-T pairs in which there is less similarity in the content of their personal constructs, therapy will conclude prematurely. Congruence in areas of interest, value, or concern does not guarantee that change will occur in a client. However, some sharing of interests and values seemingly may enhance the likelihood that the therapy relationship can be initiated and maintained.

CONGRUENCY HYPOTHESES OF IMPROVEMENT

Content incongruence between client and therapist was linked theoretically with an inadequate interpersonal relationship as defined by premature termination. However, we did not anticipate that greater content congruency, per se, necessarily would result in greater improvement among clients viewed as nonpremature. And to the extent that premature terminators may be viewed as less improved, a lack of congruency can be seen as an important factor in one type of least-improved client.

Two hypotheses, discussed in more detail in Chapter 5, are concerned with the relationship between client-therapist incongruence in the way their constructs are organized at the beginning of therapy, organizational convergence over therapy, and improvement in psychotherapy. A third hypothesis encompasses the convergence of the client's self-identification with the ideals of his therapist as measured separately within the construct dimensions of the client and those of his therapist.

Hypothesis IV: Greater improvement in the nonpremature terminator requires a difference in the way in which the client and his therapist organize their personal constructs. Restating this hypothesis, nonprematurely terminating clients in C-T dyads which show greater congruence in the organization of their personal constructs at the beginning of therapy will evidence less improvement. Nonprematurely terminating clients in C-T dyads which show less congruence in the organization of their personal constructs will evidence more improvement. Kelly's position that some commonality in personal construct systems is important in establishing social relationships, together with the idea that a difference in construct organization at the beginning of psychotherapy may be a critical component of *methodological stimulation,* suggested that congruence in the content of personal constructs may provide a shared context within which communication processes may develop. Conversely, an incongruence in the way personal construct dimensions are organized may facilitate the emergence of new ideas, particularly if one of the social participants is seeking assistance and guidance from the other member of the dyad.

Hypothesis V: Greater improvement in the nonpremature terminator is accompanied by a convergence with his therapist in the organization of their personal construct systems. In other words, nonprematurely terminating clients in C-T dyads which show greater convergence in the organization of their personal constructs over a three month period of therapy will evidence more improvement. Nonprematurely terminating clients in C-T dyads which show less convergence in the organization of their personal constructs over a three-month period of therapy will evidence less improvement.

Hypothesis VI: Improvement in therapy is accompanied by a shift in the present self of the client towards the ideal of the therapist as described within the client's language dimensions, i.e., *personal constructs of the client rather than those of the therapist.* That the ideals of a therapist may have some influence on his most-improved client seems reasonable, although when the hypothesis is anchored within personal construct theory, the self-therapist ideal convergence will more likely take place within the social language system of the client, particularly in shorter-term therapy of less than six months duration. In order for the client to identify with his therapist's ideals within the social language system of the therapist, a therapy period of long duration might be required.

CONGRUENCY HYPOTHESIS OF ATTRIBUTED PATHOLOGY

Content congruency was linked with the negative descriptions, e.g., hostile, anxious, rigid, confused, and uncooperative, employed by a therapist as he rated his client at four different points in therapy.

Hypothesis VII: Client-therapist congruence in the content of their personal constructs is inversely related to the therapist's negative clinical description of his client. Restating this hypothesis, lower coefficients of client-therapist congruence will be related to a greater number of negative clinical descriptions as the therapist describes his client. This hypothesis is based on the assumption that the confusion, uncertainty, and anxiety experienced by both client and therapist in a low-content congruent dyad will eventuate in a more negative view of this client. Findings in relation to this hypothesis provide several intriguing leads for future research. And, as you may have correctly guessed, specific predictions and results are related, but in an unexpected manner.

CHAPTER TWO

RESEARCH DESIGN

THIS CHAPTER COVERS THREE MAIN TOPICS: DEFINITION OF SUBJECT groups, research chronology, and a discussion of the criterion measures —initial maladjustment, improvement, and change. The latter section includes statistical information on interjudge and intrajudge consistency as well as comments by our judges on improvement and change.

CLIENTS

Clients were university students being seen in a student health service mental hygiene clinic, typically for one session each week. They were voluntary referrals, although others may have encouraged them to seek therapeutic help. None of them could be classified as acutely psychotic or obviously suicidal. At the same time, the clients considered to be in need of longer-term therapy were not simple counseling cases. And there was risk of psychotic or suicidal behaviors in some clients if their conditions worsened. A total client population of 349 students provided the base from which client samples were drawn.

In Phase I of the study, a longer-term assignment group of thirty-seven clients (*LT 37*) was subdivided into a longer-term therapy group of twenty-four clients (*LT 24*) and a prematurely terminating group of thirteen clients (*PT 13*). In Phase II, a variable-term assignment group of forty-four clients (*VT 44*) was subdivided into several overlapping groups of prematurely terminating variable-term clients (*PVT*) and nonprematurely terminating variable-term clients (*NPVT*). Phase I clients initially were selected as those likely to be longer-term cases.

Their problems seemed to be more complicated or serious, and at least two months of therapy contact was anticipated. Phase II clients represented the typical range of cases referred to the clinic and included students with mild, moderate, and serious problems.

Longer-Term 24 Clients: *LT 24* is comprised of twenty-four students (thirteen male, eleven female) who completed twelve sessions and thirteen weeks of therapy. Originally they had been assigned as longer-term and more difficult cases. *LT 24* was subdivided by one set of three experienced judges into twelve most and twelve least maladjusted (*MM, LM*) at intake, as judged from intake typescripts. A second set of judges divided them into the twelve improving most and the twelve improving least (*MI, LI*), and the eleven changing most and the thirteen changing least (*MC, LC*). All decisions about improvement and change made by the second set of judges were based on pre- and terminal research interview typescripts. *LT 24* cases also were separated into six unimproved or minimally improved clients (*U 6*) and eighteen improved clients (*I 18*). Nine months later the second set of judges re-rated most and least improvement. Additionally, at research termination, each therapist was asked to judge his own cases along a dimension of improvement. The presenting complaints of the *LT 24* clients, as described by their therapists, were varied and many of these students might have visited a private psychiatrist as an alternative to the Mental Hygiene Clinic. A brief description of these clients is given in Appendix E.

LT 24 clients, separated by individual judges into those who were most and least maladjusted, most and least improved, and most and least changed, also were quartiled by the judges. The judging procedures will be further elaborated in a later section.

Prematurely Terminating Longer-Term 13 Clients: *PT 13* includes thirteen students (five male, eight female), originally assigned as candidates for longer-term therapy but who terminated therapy prior to seven interviews. These clients also are described in Appendix E.

Variable-Term 36 and 39 Clients: Phase II includes variable-term (*VT*) clients, those seen for two or three interviews or possibly for a period of several months. Variable-term clients, as a group, were considered less maladjusted than the longer-term clients and also more representative of the total Mental Hygiene Clinic population. *VT 36* is comprised of seventeen males and nineteen females while *VT 39* is composed of seventeen males and twenty-two females. *VT 36* and *VT 39* overlap to the extent that they share thirty-one clients. In other words, *VT 36* includes the thirty-one shared clients plus an additional five clients. *VT 39* includes thirty-one shared clients plus an additional eight clients.

Why did we use two different groups? First of all, we did not plan it that way. While the principal investigator was preoccupied with the completion of certain questionnaires on the first thirty-six variable-term clients, those who could be subdivided into the eighteen most and the eighteen least improved, the research assistant was focusing on premature termination, a study which entailed the collection of additional information from our variable-term clients. Since this information could be obtained on only thirty-one of our clients, and since we needed to increase the number of clients who prematurely terminated, eight clients were added, all of whom did provide us with this specific information about premature termination. The thirty-one clients (*VT 31*) as well as *VT 39* were used in studies of premature termination.

Prematurely Terminating Variable-Term Clients: Premature termination of clients assigned as longer-term cases was defined by number of interviews, while premature termination of clients assigned as variable-term cases was defined by the nature of the client-therapist relationship at the point of termination. This distinction between the two definitions will be clarified later. At this point we wish only to acquaint the reader with the symbols used for the two types of prematurity. Long-term prematures are given the symbol *PT*. Variable-term prematures are given the symbol *PVT*.

A Review of Symbols for Client Groups: *LT 24* is comprised of clients assigned to longer-term therapy who do not prematurely terminate. These clients are seen for at least twelve interviews over a period of thirteen weeks. *PT 13* is comprised of clients assigned to longer-term therapy who prematurely terminate prior to seven interviews. *VT 36* is composed of the first thirty-six clients assigned to variable-term therapy who have completed both pre- and posttherapy interviews. However, only thirty-one of them (*VT 31*) also completed a termination assessment questionnaire. *VT 39* includes *VT 31* and an additional eight clients who completed the termination questionnaire. *PVT 13,* as distinguished from *PT 13,* is composed of clients included in the *VT 39* group who prematurely terminate. *PVT 8* or *9* refers to certain *VT 31* clients who prematurely terminate. When the letter (*N*) is placed before *PVT,* i.e., *NPVT,* we are referring to variable-term clients who do not prematurely terminate. *NPVT* and *PVT* represent the nonpremature-premature dimension as defined by the nature of termination at the point of termination, whereas *LT 24* and *PT 13* represent the nonpremature-premature dimension as defined by length of stay in therapy.

THERAPISTS

Four therapists were faculty members of the Department of Psychology. The other four therapists were advanced graduate students finishing Ph.D. requirements in clinical psychology. Six (*T 6*) of the eight therapists (*T 8*) were regular members of the Mental Hygiene Clinic staff, and the other two had been employed previously in this capacity.

These eight therapists (seven male, one female), all with the equivalent of at least one year full-time experience as psychotherapists, could be described at the time as espousing a developmental, learning approach with a de-emphasis on illness. None of the therapists focused on pathology, although all of them were alert to problem seriousness. Some of the therapists might reinterpret confusion as a necessary aspect of change. Rigidity, in certain contexts, might be reconstrued as a positive characteristic, supporting acts of responsibility and competency. Hostility, although troublesome and often an aspect of failure and self-defeating behavior, could also be viewed as an index of strength.

All therapists could agree that problems of living within oneself or with others are resolved in the context of new perspectives and alternatives, particularly related to the present and anticipated future. However, they differed as to whether new alternatives should be more internally or more externally construed. Some focused more on feelings while others focused more on behavioral solutions. None of the therapists belonged to any specific school of psychotherapy, and they could vary their approaches somewhat with different clients. The therapists, with certain qualifications, could accept Fromm-Reichmann's (1949) definition of the goals and aims of psychotherapy.

> Treatment . . . is aimed at the solution of the patient's difficulties in living and of the symptomatology for which cure he seeks . . . these goals will be accomplished by aiming psychotherapeutically at the development of growth, maturation, and inner independence of the patient, at his potential freedom from fear, anxiety, and the entanglements of greed, envy, and jealousy in his interpersonal relationships, and at his capacity for self-actualization and for forming durable relationships of intimacy with others (p. 375).

ADDITIONAL SUBJECTS

Reference will be made to additional subjects, *BA 10, C 13, C 17,* and *IJ 20,* none of whom were clients of the Mental Hygiene Clinic. *BA 10* is comprised of ten better adjusted students (four male, six female) as judged by short clinical interview. Fourteen students volunteered to participate in a short interview session. Four of the fourteen students were eliminated on the basis of obvious adjustment problems. Only one student of the remaining ten had ever considered seeking counseling for personal problems. All students were making at least a "C" average in their course work, and all seemed to be making fairly adequate interpersonal adjustments. Finally, these students felt their own adjustment was at least average, and the clinician, Dr. Walter Danforth, concurred with their judgments. A Rep Test was administered after the interview.

C 13 and *C 17* are two different groups used in test-retest consistency studies of Rep Test content. *IJ 20* refers to twenty Rep Test protocols used in the final interjudge consistency study of content post-coding.

RESEARCH CHRONOLOGY

1. The client receptionist asked each client to fill out an Intake Sheet for the purpose of eliciting actuarial information.
2. All clients coming voluntarily to the clinic were given an appointment with the research interviewer. The interviewer, Dr. Lynn Ourth, combined both service and research functions. He interviewed each client, asked him to cooperate in a research project, and then assigned him to a therapist. Students with acute problems of a psychotic, homicidal, or suicidal nature were not assigned to the research.
3. Ourth was first trained in short-term, semi-structured interviewing. One important criterion of training was the ability to carry out a meaningful interview within the limits of a forty-five minute Stenorette tape. It was important to gather sufficient information, but not to the extent that judges of the interview transcripts would feel overwhelmed. It also was necessary for the intake interviewer to avoid, as much as possible, the role of the therapist.
4. The function of the Clinic and the general nature of the research projects were outlined to the client. The Clinic's function was service and nothing should interfere with this mission. However, this year a research project, designed to increase the efficiency of the service, was being undertaken. We were seeking volunteers. Students did not

have to participate. Those volunteering would have two short, tape-recorded interviews (one before and a second one later in therapy) and might take several questionnaires during the therapy period. All data would be coded and kept confidential. Moreover, therapists would not have access to the research data while clients were in therapy. Thankfully, the research interviewer was very popular with the students and had little difficulty eliciting cooperation.

In the taped session which followed this introduction the interviewer covered four topics: (a) *The problem(s)* as the client sees them. How well does the client describe them? What relationships does he see between different aspects of his life? Does he perceive any background causes of the present problem(s), even though he may be uncertain about them? Can he report a specific episode which recently occurred which is relevant to his problem(s)? (b) *Everyday functioning.* How is he performing academically? Does he see any correlates to his academic difficulties? How does he relate to his friends and peer group? What is the nature of his dorm and dating relationships? Is he aware of the feelings of his friends? Is he sensitive to them? How does he perceive them? How does he relate to his superiors and to his family? How comfortable does he feel in relationship to his superiors and family? Can he communicate with them and in what manner? What is the nature of his dependency relationships? (c) *Self-image.* To see how well the client can pull together the several things discussed, he is asked to give a descriptive portrayal of himself. This also reflects his capacity for self-appraisal, his sources of evaluation, etc. (d) *Expectations of therapy.* At some point in the discussion we asked about his anticipations of therapy. These expectations may reflect how much the client may become involved in therapy as well as the nature of his dependency and autonomy.

5. The research interviewer structured the terminal research interview, held approximately thirteen weeks and twelve therapy sessions later, in the following manner. At the time the client initiated contact with the Clinic, how did he construe his problems? How does he now look at the problem(s) for which he originally sought help? What changes have taken place in his life since initiating contact with the Clinic, changes that are especially important to him? What contribution did therapy make to these changes? What does he anticipate in the future as the result of his therapeutic experiences? If the client did not mention the problem(s) talked about originally in the intake interview, he was asked about these presenting problems. The interviewer then directly stated these problems and asked the client to reflect upon them.

6. Greater emphasis was placed at the beginning of the academic year on assigning longer-term clients to the Phase I study. Experi-

ence indicated that a greater proportion of more disturbed students could be expected during the first semester. Case assignment to therapists was done on a rotational basis.

7. In Phase I the interviewer assigned a total of thirty-seven longer-term cases, in rotation, to eight therapists. Assignments continued until each therapist had carried three clients to the research termination criterion of twelve interviews and thirteen weeks. Twenty-four clients (*LT 24*) thus were carried to this criterion, and thirteen premature clients (*PT 13*), originally assigned as longer-term cases, terminated prior to seven interviews.

8. In Phase II the interviewer assigned a total of forty-four variable-term cases, in rotation, to the six therapists regularly employed at the clinic. The first thirty-six clients, those on whom completed pre- and posttherapy typescripts were available, were designated as *VT 36*. Thirty-one of these clients who completed a termination questionnaire, *VT 31,* as well as an additional eight clients, were designated as *VT 39*. These variable-term groups were also broken down into prematurely terminating groups (*PVT*) and nonprematurely terminating groups (*NPVT*).

9. Immediately following the first therapy session each therapist routinely rated his clients on a check list called the White Card. About a dozen items were included on this check list such as Prognosis: good, fair, poor; Seriousness of Problem: severe, moderate, mild; and Problem Areas and Behavior: immaturity, hostility, academic, sexual, withdrawnness, situational, and creative attitude. "Creative" was defined by exploratory behavior, such as searching for self-definition and life orientation, or trying out new life alternatives. When the therapist filled out the White Card, he did not know whether or not his client was assigned to the research.

10. At the beginning of therapy, Phase I clients, i.e., *LT 24* and *PT 13,* took their first Rep Test and a Ways to Live Test (Ways). This latter instrument, which has not been analyzed, is a measure of philosophical outlook. The Rep Test, a primary investigative tool, is a derivation from personal construct theory and provides information about how an individual describes and dimensionalizes his world of people. (A copy of the Rep Test is located in Appendix A.) Many clients completed the first Rep Test in one and one-half hours and the Ways within one-half hour. Since the acquaintances elicited for the first Rep Test were reused, Rep Tests taken later at regular intervals of one month could be completed within an hour. Of course, some clients took much longer than others to complete the tests. Assignment to first testing and to the first therapy session occurred within a day or two of each other.

Longer-term clients retook the Rep Test one month, two months, and three months after first testing.

11. The eight therapists, each carrying three longer-term clients to a point of research completion (twelve sessions, thirteen weeks), also took the Rep Test once a month. Client and therapist Rep Tests were juxtaposed in time as closely as possible. How well this was accomplished is shown in Table 2.1.

TABLE 2.1

Days Between Client-Therapist Rep Tests

Client Rep	1	2	3	4
Average Days Intervening	4.5	6.7	4.8	6.0

Since a therapist's clients were not assigned to him at the same time, most therapists took five Rep Tests. However, one therapist took eight Rep Tests. In some instances, a client's Rep Test 1 might be juxtaposed, in the data analysis, to his therapist's Rep Test 2.

12. Thirty-seven clients were assigned to the Phase I study. The thirteen clients who terminated between one and six interviews were considered premature terminators (*PT 13*) since they were assigned as longer-term cases. Two of the *PT 13* did not fill out the grid section of the Rep Test. Since the grid ratings were used in a measure of construct organization, the designation *PT 11* is used rather than *PT 13* whenever a structural analysis is undertaken.

13. At the end of the second week following the second therapy session and every two weeks thereafter, each therapist rated his longer-term clients on a series of scales called the *Therapist Rating Schedule* (TRS). A full description of the TRS can be found in Chapter 6.

The TRS is comprised of two sections. Section I includes more theoretically relevant items such as Verbalized Desire to Explore, Hope, Central Identity Under One's Control, Willingness to Experience Incongruity, and Use of Alternatives. Section II includes items best designated by the expression *lingo scales*. The lingo scales were designed to encompass typical comments which clinicians make about their clients or patients, such as "hard to work with," "confused," "uncooperative," "very anxious," "rigid," "hostile," "apathetic," "inconsistent," "agitated," and "defensive."

At the completion of the study, the TRS was juxtaposed in time with the client-therapist Rep Test combinations. This was accomplished by taking the median date between each client-therapist Rep Test combination and using the TRS nearest this date. How well this was accomplished is shown in Table 2.2. The first TRS followed the first Rep Test combination by an average of sixteen days. However, a much better integration of the Rep Tests and the TRS was possible at later points in therapy.

TABLE 2.2

Days Between Rating Schedules and Median Dates of Client-Therapist Rep Test Combinations

Client-Therapist Combination	1	2	3	4
Average Days Intervening	16	4	4	3

14. After twelve sessions and thirteen weeks a terminal research interview, conducted by the research intake interviewer, was held with each *LT 24* client. Interviews were again taped and typescripts made. Even though the research was terminated at this point, therapy did continue with some clients.

15. Following the completion of all *LT 24* terminal interviews, pre- and terminal typescripts were submitted to two highly experienced clinicians, Dr. George A. Kelly and Dr. Janet Lyon. Both external judges felt that they would be able to do the assigned rating tasks. A third judge, Dr. Lynn Ourth, the interviewer, resolved disagreements between the two primary judges. The three judges, asked to rate improvement and change from pre- and terminal typescripts, were given the following directions:

Instructions to Judges:

Enclosed are typescripts of one pretherapy and one terminal interview for 24 student clients seen at the University of Missouri Mental Hygiene Clinic. Each set of interviews is numbered, and the pre- and terminal typescripts are stapled together with the first interview on top.

First, read through all the typescripts. This first reading will give you a general idea about the nature of these cases.

Second, separate these twenty-four sets of typescripts into two piles of twelve, on the basis of improvement. Answer the question: Which twelve of the twenty-four clients have made the most progress?

Progress will be measured by the difference between pre- and terminal therapy interviews. Progress should be understood as improvement in the client's ability to cope with his own life, to resolve those problems which are most important for him.

Next, separate the twelve most improved clients into two piles of six and the twelve least improved clients into two piles of six, on the basis of improvement. Answer the same question as before: Which six of the twelve clients in each pile have made the most progress?

Record the typescript numbers under the headings: Most improvement (six cases), upper middle (six cases), lower middle (six cases), and least improvement (six cases).

Third, place the typescripts back in original order, one through twenty-four.

Fourth, separate the twenty-four sets of typescripts into two piles of twelve, this time on the basis of change. Answer the question: Which twelve of the twenty-four clients have changed the most?

Change will be measured by the difference between pre- and terminal therapy interviews. Change should be understood as ideational, cognitive, attitudinal, or conceptual modification in the way(s) the client is viewing himself, his relationships with others, and the meanings he attributes to life and the world about him. These conceptual changes, of course, may be inferred from reports of behavioral change.

A client whom you previously rated low on the improvement dimension could be rated high on the change dimension. Not all change taking place in clients is productive.

Next, separate the twelve most changed clients into two piles of six and the twelve least changed clients into two piles of six on the basis of change. Answer the same questions as before: Which of the 12 clients in each pile have made the most change?

Record the typescript numbers under the headings: most changed (six cases), upper middle (six cases), lower middle (six cases), and least changed (six cases).

16. Although the research interviews were originally quartiled by the judges of clients' improvement, change, and initial maladjustment, the ratings of each judge were treated dichotomously, i.e., most-least. Whether or not a client was finally judged to be most or least was determined by the agreement of two of three judges. In the cases of initial maladjustment and improvement, this method resulted in an equal split, twelve clients being categorized as most and twelve as least. However, an eleven-thirteen split occurred on the change criterion. Previous work by Landfield, Stern and Fjeld (1961) indicated that 75 per cent agreement between two judges of global improvement can be anticipated.

17. Pretherapy typescripts were judged for intake maladjustment which was not defined for the judges. The procedure used in judging the longer-term group was less than ideal since it was necessary to use one of the therapists as a primary judge (Dr. Donald Poe), while a second therapist decided four cases disagreed upon by Poe and Ourth, the second primary judge. Contamination of the criterion was minimal since only Poe judged three of his own cases.

18. Therapists were asked to quartile their own three cases assigned to the *LT 24* group on the dimension of improvement; however, these ratings were later treated dichotomously.

19. Nine months after Drs. Kelly and Lyon finished judging *LT 24* improvement and change, they were asked to rejudge the pretherapy and terminal typescripts on the dimension of improvement. Instructions were the same as those used previously.

20. Using the ratings of the judges, six clients of the *LT 24* group were designated as minimally improved or unimproved (*U 6*), and eighteen clients were considered improved (*I 18*). The *U 6* clients had the following characteristics: (a) They received the lowest average quartile scores for improvement as assessed by three judges. (b) They received one or more fourth-quartile ratings on improvement. (c) No judge rated them as either first- or second-quartile improvement cases. (d) Two of the more experienced judges rated four of the six clients as fourth-quartile cases. (e) Five of the six clients were rated among the twelve most maladjusted clients at intake. (f) The three judges rated all six among the twelve least changed clients. (g) A 75–25 per cent cutting score for improvement versus minimal improvement seemed reasonable on the basis of clinical experience and a study by Varble and Landfield (1969) in which clients judged as unimproved constituted 25 per cent of the sample.

21. Therapists rated their three clients at research completion on two dimensions: positive-negative feelings and friendship potential. The latter dimension was placed in the context of, "If you were the client's age or if the client were your age. . . ."

22. Each therapist periodically dictated case notes on his clients. This was routine clinic procedure.

23. One year after research termination, follow-up letters were sent to all *LT 24* clients. The follow-up questionnaires covered several questions asked in the terminal interview. Eleven clients returned their questionnaires, primarily those (seven clients) who had been rated as most improved by external judges. Four least improved clients who did not answer their questionnaries voluntarily returned to the clinic within two years for further assistance. Another least improved client who also did not return his questionnaire remained in therapy for another year and eventually was rated by his therapist as remarkably improved.

24. In Phase II of the project, forty-four variable-term clients took the Rep Test only once at the beginning of therapy. Personal construct descriptions from the first Rep Tests of each client-therapist dyad were placed on seven point scales from *flighty* to *steady,* mixed together, and written on separate rating sheets, one for each dyad. Approximately thirty mixed construct dimensions were placed on each rating sheet and represented the content of social language for every client-therapist pair.

Clients and therapists in each dyad were asked to rate one another on these mixed social-language dimensions at the beginning of therapy (Ourth and Landfield, 1965). In addition, therapists were asked to rate their own ideals on both client and therapist dimensions (Landfield and Nawas, 1964). Clients were asked to rate both their present and ideal selves on the same scales once a month until therapy termination (Varble and Landfield, 1969).

25. Four senior and two junior staff members participated in Phase II. The research interviewer assigned cases to these therapists on a rotational basis without regard for case difficulty. Again, no acutely psychotic or suicidal students were among the assigned clients. It was hoped that the Phase II or variable-term clients would represent the clinic population as a whole, whereas the Phase I clients would represent those carried in longer-term therapy, the more disturbed, or those with more complex problems.

26. The variable-term clients had pre- and posttherapy interviews, and typescripts of those interviews were separated into most and least improved and most and least changed, as well as most and least maladjusted at intake. The first thirty-six clients were labeled *VT 36* and only these clients were used in certain studies. This criterion judging procedure was the same as used with *LT 24* in Phase I of the project. Dr. Ourth, the research interviewer, and Dr. Loretta Cass, external rater, served as primary judges of improvement and change. Since Dr. Poe did not carry any cases in Phase II, he served with Dr. Ourth as a judge of improvement, change, and initial maladjustment.

27. Thirty-one of the *VT 36* clients, plus an additional eight clients, participated in a study of premature termination. Five clients among these first thirty-six failed to appear for a special session which followed the posttherapy interview. The nature of termination, premature or nonpremature, was determined at this last session. In this instance premature termination for the *VT 39* clients was not defined by number of interviews as in the *PT 13* group of Phase I; rather, the nature of termination was considered. Regardless of the number of interviews, the determining factor was whether or not termination was meaningful to both client and therapist.

IMPROVEMENT, CHANGE, AND MALADJUSTMENT

Measurements of improvement, change, and maladjustment may reflect the life style and personality of the investigator as well as his assumptions about the nature of man. A review of therapy-criterion measures by Zax and Klein (1960) tends to support this hypothesis if one accepts the multiplicity of measurements as validating evidence.

Some investigators accept self-reports about improvement in a literal way. Others hold the self-report in high esteem, yet reserve the right to place their own interpretations upon it. External criteria such as the ability to hold a job, achieve academically, or gain the actual support of a peer group is the primary standard of adjustment in some investigations. Self-regard and feelings may be the focus of other studies. Then there are content biases about which kinds of thoughts, feelings, and behaviors are most appropriate. Sometimes judgment about what is most appropriate is restricted to the norms of a particular social group. Experts may throw up their hands in despair and turn to other types of research. Others suggest that since there is little possibility of agreement on the nature of mental health, one's only recourse is to state with great care why a particular criterion was chosen as well as how it was applied. Zax and Klein believe that some integration of experiencing and behaving is needed. However, the work of Fiedler, Dodge, Jones, and Hutchins (1958) suggests that such an integration may be extremely difficult.

Having no firm guide lines for the development of criterion measures and accepting the inevitability of criticism, we selected highly experienced psychotherapists and asked them to judge improvement, change, and maladjustment from pretherapy and terminal typescripts.

Verbatim typescripts were based on semistructured interviews conducted by a specially trained interviewer who carefully separated the research from the ongoing therapy. Clients were told that their therapists would not have access to the research interview material. The judges were asked to focus on how well the client was coping with his life. However, no instructions were given as to which dimensions of experience and behavior should be emphasized.

Whether global judgments of improvement, change, and initial maladjustment are really useful or meaningful measures will have to be sought in the context of the entire investigation.

THE JUDGES SPEAK

Believing that the feelings of man should count as importantly as his externally judged behavior, we asked our three external judges to report on their experiences as they completed the task of judging. They comment:

> After the preliminary reading, I did both judgments twice, having great difficulty with some borderline cases. Informally computed, my reliability in the extreme groups was about .80; in all four groups, less than that. Often the judge's value judgments would be important. . . . I also found inconsistencies when variations in what was elicited in the interviews led to inferences which might not be justifiable.
>
> . . . . .
>
> Perhaps I should mention a few matters which I noted. In judging progress, I took into account the severity of the problem, as I understood it from the protocols. Thus what appeared to be a minor problem that was largely cleared up was not judged as being as much improved as a very severe problem in which the client had made substantial progress in spite of its inherent difficulties.
>
> . . . . .
>
> There were a number of instances in which it seemed reasonable to assume that the improvement was related to the easing of external circumstances. It is always difficult to assess this kind of improvement, for often the client has, as a result of his own therapeutic progress, had a hand in altering the circumstances in some subtle way. I therefore occasionally discounted such improvements, but only when I could see no way in which the client could have influenced the circumstances himself.
>
> . . . . .
>
> My judgment of change was considerably influenced by what I inferred was the underlying difficulty and by my own experience with recurrence of symptoms in such cases. For example, in what

appeared to be an established character disorder, I was reluctant to take the client's positive statements in the terminal interview altogether at face value. However, I was somewhat influenced by anecdotal reports in such cases. On the credulous side, however, I was inclined to take clients' assessments of change in themselves pretty much the way they were stated unless I had reason to suspect that such statements were merely characteristic of the disorder. Thus, if a client said that difficulties seemed to be diminishing for some unexplained reason that puzzled him, I was inclined to accept such a statement as evidence of genuine improvement, even though there was no expression of so-called insight. Many therapists would not agree with my ratings in this respect.

. . . . .

Furthermore, I accepted changes in the pattern of interaction with the interviewer as evidence of therapeutically significant change in the client. I am on shaky grounds here, since the client may merely be reflecting his greater familiarity with the interviewer, possibly only from having seen him in the hallways around the clinic. He also presumably had greater familiarity with the clinic situation, and thus found it easier to interact freely the second time. Nevertheless, I accepted such changes as important.

But I don't know what you could do about it. Every therapist has his own way of selecting and pursuing leads, even those who are followers of Rogers and who claim they limit themselves to acceptance, reflection of feeling, and clarification. Often the interviewer seemed more inclined to pursue minor leads than major ones, as if he already knew what he might be getting into and wanted to avoid it. For example, in Case———, during both interviews the client seemed close to a breakthrough in discussing relations with her father. But the interviewer seemed to avoid the issue.

. . . . .

I found myself concerned with the way the interviewer pursued some leads and did not pursue others. . . . But what should he have done? Obviously, from the standpoint of assessment, it would be better to have conducted a normal probe of something she seemed so ready to communicate by her mannerisms, if not by direct statements. But the interviewer did not pursue the matter and, in view of what I suspect might be just below the surface and the importance of having such matters elaborated within the security of a therapeutic relationship, I doubt that I would have either. So I have no solution to offer you.

. . . . .

More time was spent on the assessments than I had expected, and probably more than was actually needed. I keep having the feeling that I might make considerably different judgments if I were to see the protocols on another occasion. Yet, when I went back to reappraise protocols, I came out with judgments that were very close to my original ones.

. . . . .

Well, here are the ratings and I must say it was quite an experience! It strikes me that we *talk* about what improvement in therapy is but it's quite an eye-opener to have to sit down and make definitive judgments about it.

. . . . .

I think the greatest difficulty came in trying to separate out progress and changes. I found, after I was through, that there was much overlap with the cases that I picked for the most progress being, by and large, those I thought had made the most change. The ones who were very ill to start with seemed to be the ones who made the least progress and who changed least also. Not unexpectedly.

. . . . .

I think that in some cases the length of treatment was too short to expect much change.

. . . . .

I am not sure what this means, but that, I take it, is your problem.

ANSWERS TO SPECIFIC QUESTIONS

1. *How well do judges agree with one another on improvement?* Table 2.3 indicates that the two primary judges (1, 2) of improvement in *LT 24* agreed on eighteen cases ($p < .02$) when a dichotomous (most, least) criterion was used. Judges 1 and 3 also agreed on eighteen cases; however, Judges 2 and 3 agreed on only sixteen, or two-thirds, of the cases ($p < .20$). Table 2.3 indicates also that the two primary judges of improvement in *VT 36* agreed on thirty cases ($p < .001$). Eighty-

TABLE 2.3
Interjudge Agreement* on LT 24 and VT 36 Improvement

Judges	A	D	Chi-square Probability
	LT 24		
Judge 1 vs. 2	18	6	$p < .02$
Judge 1 vs. 3	18	6	$p < .02$
Judge 2 vs. 3	16	8	$p < .20$
	VT 36		
Judge 1 vs. 2	30	6	$p < .001$

* Cases of agreement (A), disagreement (D).

four per cent agreement among primary judges of *VT 36* was slightly better than the 75 per cent agreement among primary judges of *LT 24*. However, 75 per cent agreement on improvement is consistent with the data from a previous study (Landfield, Stern, and Fjeld, 1961) done in the same therapeutic setting. Nine months later, *LT 24* cases were re-judged. Table 2.4 indicates that all judges agreed with one another on improvement ($p < .02$).

TABLE 2.4
Interjudge Agreement on LT 24 Improvement Nine Months Later

Judges	A	D	Chi-square Probability
Judge 1 vs. 2	20	4	$p < .01$
Judge 1 vs. 3	18	6	$p < .02$
Judge 2 vs. 3	18	6	$p < .02$

2. *How well do judges agree with one another on change?* Table 2.5 indicates less interjudge agreement among judges on change than on improvement. Judges 1 and 3 agreed ($p < .02$); however, Primary Judges 1 and 2 did not agree at a significant level ($p < .20$). Table 2.5 indicates that the two primary judges of change in *VT 36* agreed at a significant level ($p < .01$).

TABLE 2.5

Interjudge Agreement on LT 24 and VT 36 Change

Judges	A	D	Chi-square Probability
	LT 24		
Judge 1 vs. 2	16	8	$p < .20$
Judge 1 vs. 3	18	6	$p < .02$
Judge 2 vs. 3	16	8	$p < .20$
	VT 36		
Judge 1 vs. 2	26	10	$p < .01$

3. *How well do judges agree with one another on maladjustment?* Table 2.6 indicates agreement between the two primary judges of intake maladjustment in *LT 24* ($p < .01$) and agreement between the two primary judges of intake maladjustment in *VT 36* ($p < .01$).

TABLE 2.6

Interjudge Agreement on LT 24 and VT 36 Maladjustment

Judges	A	D	Chi-square Probability
	LT 24		
Judge 1 vs. 2	20	4	$p < .01$
	VT 36		
Judge 1 vs. 2	26	10	$p < .01$

4. *How well do judges agree with themselves on improvement?* Table 2.7 indicates that two of the three judges of improvement in *LT 24* significantly agreed with themselves over a period of nine months. The research interviewer was the most consistent judge, agreeing with himself in twenty-two of the twenty-four cases. A third judge (primary) agreed with himself on only two-thirds of the cases ($p < .20$), but he had a higher level of agreement with the other primary judge on the second ratings ($p < .01$). In other words, the less stable primary judge

changed in the direction of the more stable primary judge over the nine-months interval.

5. When the three judgments of improvement are combined, *how well do the judges agree with themselves?* Table 2.7 indicates that consistency of the combined judgments is high. There is agreement on twenty of the twenty-four cases in *LT 24* ($p < .01$).

TABLE 2.7

Individual and Combined Judge Self-consistency: First to Second Judging of LT 24 Improvement

Judges	A	D	Chi-square Probability
Individual Judges			
Judge 1: Rating 1 vs. 2	16	8	$p < .20$
Judge 2: Rating 1 vs. 2	20	4	$p < .01$
Judge 3: Rating 1 vs. 2	22	2	$p < .001$
Combined Judges			
Judges 1, 2, 3: Rating 1 vs. 2	20	4	$p < .01$

6. *How well do the combined judges agree with the therapists who judge their own cases on improvement?* There is high agreement between therapists and judges on twenty cases of the *LT 24* group (tetrachoric $r = .86, p < .01$).

7. *What is the relationship between judgments of improvement and change?* Table 2.8 indicates a high relationship between improvement and change in both *LT 24* and *VT 36* ($p < .001$).

8. *What is the relationship between judgments of improvement and intake maladjustment?* There is a tendency for improvement to be inversely related to intake maladjustment, but this tendency does not reach significance in either group.

9. *What is the relationship between judgments of change and intake maladjustment?* There is a slight tendency for change to be inversely related to intake maladjustment, but the relationship is not significant.

What did we conclude from these analyses of improvement, change, and initial maladjustment? First, there is satisfactory interjudge agreement on improvement and initial maladjustment. And the improvement criterion seems to be consistent over time. Further, we may infer a high

TABLE 2.8

Relationships Between Initial Maladjustment, Improvement, and Change: LT 24, VT 36

Group	Improvement and Change	Improvement and Maladjustment	Change and Maladjustment
LT 24	$\chi^2 = 13.4$ $p < .001$	$\chi^2 = 2.6$ $p < .20$	$\chi^2 = 1.4$ $p < .30$
VT 36	$\chi^2 = 21$ $p < .001$	$\chi^2 = 1.3$ $p < .30$	$\chi^2 = 1.3$ $p < .30$

relationship between the points of view of external judges and therapists as to what constitutes improvement. Although agreement among the *LT 24* judges on change was less than for improvement, the research interviewer can be seen as a stabilizing influence on the judgment of change. He agreed with another *LT 24* judge ($p < .02$) and also with the other primary judge of *VT 36* ($p < .01$). In actual practice, the change criterion appeared to be meaningful, having most interesting relationships with a number of variables, including many items of the Therapist Rating Schedule (TRS).

CHAPTER THREE

PERSONAL CONSTRUCTS: MEANINGFULNESS, CONTENT, AND ORGANIZATION

THE REP TEST

Kelly (1955) proposed a Role Construct Repertory Test (Rep Test) as one method of eliciting Personal Constructs. In this chapter a modified Rep Test is described which places greater emphasis on the range corollary which states: "A construct is convenient for the anticipation of a finite range of events only" (p. 68). A copy of this modified test, which includes a Response Sheet, is located in Appendix A.

The "objects" of personal constructs usually are the people with whom the subject interacts in his everyday living. The testing procedure begins by asking the subject to record on the Response Sheet the first names of fifteen different acquaintances fitting certain role types such as mother, father, close friend, a person with whom the subject feels uncomfortable, etc. The role types are listed on the Role Specification Sheet. Role types may be varied for different experimental purposes. Although variation in roles may affect the constructs elicited, Fjeld and Landfield (1961) and Hunt (1951) found evidence for the relative stability of the Rep measure when acquaintances were systematically varied from test to retest.

The next step in the procedure outlined by Kelly is to ask the subject to compare triads of acquaintances, in specified combinations, by stating how two of the three acquaintances in each triad are similar to each other and different from the third. Verbalized constructs are comprised of the contrasting statements elicited by this instruction. This triad approach was modified by asking the subject to compare dyads of acquaintances rather than triads. Clinical experience with the triad approach suggested that a subject, when restricted to finding a similarity prior to stating a difference, occasionally is unable to respond. However, the subject may perceive all three acquaintances as similar and be able to think of someone outside the triad as being different. Feeling that data are lost in the triad approach, we had subjects consider pairs of acquaintances, asking whether they were primarily similar or primarily different and requiring contrasting descriptions. Then the subject was asked to locate another acquaintance who could be described as a contrast.

Following the establishment of a construct dimension from acquaintances, the thirteen acquaintances not differentiated in the development of this particular construct also are rated. For example, if *sense of humor* versus *sour puss* is a construct elicited from one pair of acquaintances, the subject then is asked to rate each of the other thirteen acquaintances on this construct. They are rated as *1*, best described by the first part of the contrast, i.e., *sense of humor; 2,* best described by the second part of the contrast, i.e., *sour puss; N,* neither contrast is applicable; or *?,* not able to decide.

After the subject has rated all fifteen acquaintances within the first construct dimension, he constructs more dimensions from other combinations of acquaintances and he rates his fifteen acquaintances on each of these dimensions. The final rating grid (15 × 15) is comprised of fifteen acquaintances rated within fifteen dimensions. Ideally we would have preferred using the larger grid (19 × 22) suggested by Kelly (1955); however, experience indicated that the smaller grid provides interesting data, is fairly consistent on retest, and can be completed in one and one-half hours. A completed Response Sheet is located in Chapter 7, p. 105.

The use of *N* and *?* ratings is suggested by Kelly (1955, vol. I) in the following quotation:

> The assumption which is specific to the grid form of the test is that all the figures fall within the range of convenience of all the constructs . . . . This may not be a good assumption in all cases; it may be that the client has left a void at a certain intersect simply because the construct does not seem to apply one way or the other (p. 271).

Kelly further states that "a construct's range of convenience comprises all those things to which the user would find its application useful" (p. 562). Applying this definition to the Rep Test, one may refer to the utility of a personal construct dimension for encompassing acquaintances. The number of acquaintances to which a certain construct can be usefully and clearly applied is the range of convenience or the range of application of that construct. For example, one may meaningfully and clearly apply the personal language dimension *dedicated* versus *not dedicated* to adult friends Tom and Mary but may find it difficult or meaningless to think about little sister within this context.

THE REP TEST AS A CLINICAL METHOD

Mair and Crisp (1968) state that the Rep Test fulfills the four essential requirements of a clinically useful measure, namely that it (1) is tailored to the individual's particular problems and outlooks, (2) allows for assessment and exploration of personal organization in psychological functioning, (3) focuses on unique as well as common meanings which an idea, action, or feeling may have for the person, and (4) can be utilized in measuring psychological change. They further state that the "study of how a person's view of the world is organized is, in fact, likely to be a necessary preliminary to the assessment of personal meaning" (p. 16).

The idea that personality is organized is not a unique assumption. However, the idea that one should focus on the ways in which a person's "outlooks" are organized is not shared by all theorists. Moreover, those theorists who are most phenomenologically inclined often do not provide the clinician or researcher with methods which systematically encompass the organization of personal awarenesses, feelings, and meanings. However, Kelly, more than most theorists, has suggested systematic methods with which one may assess personal meanings and the ways in which these personal meanings are organized. Kelly's Rep Test grid, which allows the clinician or researcher to compare patterns of how people are rated within different personal construct dimensions, has led to the development of other methodologies which also are useful in assessing conceptual organization. Bieri's (1955, 1961) measure of "cognitive complexity" and Hinkle's (1965) "implications grid" are derivations from personal construct theory. Although American psychologists have contributed to the work on grid methods, British psychologists, in particular Bannister and Mair (1968), have devoted considerable effort to the clinical and experimental explorations of grid procedure.

THREE CHARACTERISTICS OF PERSONAL CONSTRUCTS

Personal constructs may be characterized in many ways. We have chosen to emphasize three aspects of personal constructs: (1) *Mean-*

ingfulness to the user is inferred from rating scale polarization or the extent to which a subject uses more extreme ratings on his dimensional scales. (2) *Content areas talked about* are inferred from each construct pole description according to the rules which are recorded in the Content Scoring Manual. (3) *The degree to which construct dimensions are interrelated* is inferred from the similarities and differences found between any two row or column grid rating patterns which either define descriptive dimensions, e.g., *introvert* versus *extrovert,* or which define acquaintance dimensions, e.g., *brother* and an implicit antithesis to brother. This latter measurement of dimensional organization, which is called the FIC score, as well as the other two measures of meaningfulness and content, will be elaborated in the remainder of the chapter.

MEANINGFULNESS AS MEASURED BY THE EXTREMITY RATING

The significance of taking more extreme positions on rating scales, i.e., scale polarization, was reviewed by O'Donovan (1965). He first cited studies which emphasize the pathological nature of polarization. Then he reviewed studies which clearly imply that the taking of more extreme positions on rating scales is an index of meaningfulness. Feeling that these interpretations need not be treated as being mutually exclusive, he suggested ways of reconciling them. One type of reconciliation is based upon three hypotheses: neurotics are polarizers; schizophrenics are depolarizers; and normals are both, discriminating between that which is more and less meaningful. We will not debate whether or not the assumption of strong positions is a source of strength, vitality, and meaningfulness or is the hallmark of bigotry, neurosis, and unreality. We will accept the extremity rating as an index of meaningfulness within the context of personal construct theory.

Although Kelly defined the basic unit of meaning as a dichotomy, he did not reject the idea that bipolar constructs could be used as continua. He took the position that binary and continuous applications may be interchangeable. A continuum may be comprised of dichotomies in combination. Even as Kelly accepted a relationship between binary and continuous approaches, he emphasized the central role of the dichotomy in the decision making process.

In a lecture on alternative thinking, Kelly (1952) differentiated between a naive dichotomous orientation and a more sophisticated one. He stated:

> When we say that the world can be reduced for purposes of science to dichotomies we are not saying that the world must be

> approached with the naiveté of a child. The child's difficulty is that he is unable to multiply his dichotomies. That is to say, he is dealing with the world in terms of a one-place, binary number system composed solely of 0 and 1. He cannot yet count his world in terms of 10's and 11's and 100's and 101s, etc.

In the same lecture Kelly emphasized the idea that sometimes a continuous approach can be inefficient.

> We can say, on the one hand, that a given person is somewhat "good" and somewhat "bad"; in other words, make a so-so evaluation. This is like saying that a given person is about average or that he is mediocre. This is also a way of saying that the dichotomy is inapplicable to a given situation. It is a way of casting the world in terms of grays rather than blacks and whites. The other approach is to say that while, as a whole, we cannot evaluate the person as either black or white, there must be elements in the situation which can be evaluated as black or white. . . . The first is actually a way of avoiding the making of a precise evaluation or prediction. It is a way of ignoring alternatives. The second is a way of accepting certain specified alternatives—a way of quantifying the data within a binary system. Now which of these approaches is more meaningful, which is more scientific?

Kelly (1955) set forth the personal construct as the basic unit of understanding and then suggested a test of meaningfulness.

> If a person sets up the construct of black versus white, an object cannot, for him, be both black and white. The construct tends to force upon him either one or the other of two alternatives. If it were not so, the construct would have no meaning (pp. 65–66).

The criterion of meaningfulness which we have deduced from the above statements, as well as from the general theory, is that one rates more extremely on those dimensions which are most meaningful.

Since Kelly's personal constructs are assumed to be basic constructions of communication, they should pass Kelly's extremity test of meaningfulness. The hypothesis that *the personal construct language of the individual is more meaningful to him than is the language of others* has been tested by a number of investigators.

Mitsos (1961) gave subjects a list of twenty-one semantic differential adjective scales from which they chose the nine most meaningful to themselves in thinking about people. To guarantee reliability, Mitsos had his subjects make their choices on three separate occasions. The subjects then described seven concepts (e.g., politician, communist, foreman) across the twenty-one original Semantic Differential Scales. Mitsos found that the nine adjective scales selected as being personally most meaningful were rated more extremely than the other scales.

Cromwell & Caldwell (1962) asked subjects to rate six recent and six old acquaintances along dimensions which were composed of their own personal constructs and constructs which were elicited from other subjects. Ratings were more extreme when subjects were rating on their own personal constructs than when they were rating others' constructs. O'Donovan (1964) reports that the tendency toward more extreme rating is associated with verbal reports of greater meaningfulness, whether the object being rated is seen as positive or negative, desirable or undesirable.

A study by Landfield (1965) suggests that personal meaningfulness may be related to extremity of rating. Clients in psychotherapy were given the opportunity to rank order the importance of a mixture of personal construct dimensions derived from their own Rep Test protocols and protocols of their respective therapists. Ranking choice was based on felt usefulness in describing others. In addition to rank ordering, clients did self-ratings on their own and their therapists' dimensions. First, it was found that at the beginning of therapy the top five chosen constructs were more likely to be those of the client, the bottom five those of the therapist. Second, disregarding whether constructs belonged to client or therapist, the top five chosen constructs showed greater rating extremity than the bottom ranked constructs. Finally, the clients' present and ideal self-ratings on their own constructs were more extreme than their ratings on their therapists' constructs.

Isaacson & Landfield (1965) hypothesized that subjects will do more extreme self-ratings within their own personal construct language than within the more generalized language of the Butler-Haigh Q Sort statements. It was reasoned that Butler-Haigh language—generalizations from statements made by students undergoing psychotherapy—would be less relevant for describing the self than personal construct language which was elicited from each subject and used by him. The greater relevance and meaningfulness of personal construct language would be shown by more extreme ratings and the personal construct language would be more accepted as highly descriptive of the self as opposed to not-self.

The hypothesis that self-ratings within the more generalized Butler-Haigh language would be less extreme than ratings within the more personal language elicited by the Rep Test was supported. Not only was personal construct language more extreme but it also was skewed towards "most like me," whereas Butler-Haigh language piled up in the center of the distribution, between most like me and least like me. Furthermore, an additional finding that personal construct items, even the negative ones, are more acceptable in describing the self has important implications for psychotherapy. If the therapist wishes to help a client face certain negative characteristics within himself, it is best whenever possible to utilize the client's language of negative characteristics rather than insist that the client accept the language of the therapist as reflected in his personal and professional constructs. The openness and willingness of the therapist to utilize the client's language, even that which is negative, should enable the client to feel more open to explore those characteristics which may have brought him into therapy.

Isaacson (1966) compared personal construct dimensions with semantic differential dimensions and Manifest Anxiety Scale items put into dimensional form. Ten personal construct dimensions, ten semantic differential dimensions and ten Manifest Anxiety Scale dimensions were mixed together. Ten acquaintances then were rated on the thirty pooled dimensions on a seven-point scale. Additionally, a seven-point scale of certainty of position was rated for each extremity rating. Further, the pooled dimensions were rank ordered for personal usefulness in understanding people. Results of these analyses show that personal construct dimensions are significantly more meaningful as determined by rankings and ratings of extremity and certainty.

Bonarius (1968), using the extremity rating procedure in a series of studies, concluded that personal constructs may be most meaningful "if applied to the kind of people from whom the person has originally derived his personal constructs. These people are the individual's 'significant others' with whom he has a personal and emotional relationship" (p. 5).

CONTENT AS MEASURED BY POSTCODING MANUAL

In this section the history of Rep Test content postcoding is reviewed and parallels are drawn between categories used by others and certain categories of the present system. The specific development of our own manual is evaluated and information pertaining to test-retest consistency is considered along with the interjudge consistency of the coding task. The complete manual and directions for its use are located in Appendix B.

Other investigators have postcoded the content of personal constructs (Maher, 1957; Lemcke, 1959; Tippett, 1959; Tyler & Simmons, 1964; Rosencranz, 1966). Maher developed a category of "nondynamic construction" which included descriptions of physical appearance, health, weight, kin relationship, degree of acquaintance, legal status, age, sex, occupation, geographical, cultural, and social group membership. Maher's category is similar to what we have called "concrete content," comprised of factual descriptions, external appearance descriptions, and descriptions connoting low imagination. Tippett and Lemcke employed the categories of "extreme construction," "dependency construction," and "value construction." Such constructions are similar to our categories of "extreme qualifiers," "high social interaction," "high tenderness," "self-reference," and "high" and "low morality." Rosencranz, in a sociological study of aging, developed three content categories which he labeled "humanitarian," "work ethic," and "religion." These three categories overlap our categories of "high" and "low morality." Tyler defined categories of self-reference and physical characteristics which are similar to our "self reference" and "external appearance" classifications.

The most comprehensive assessment of personal construct content would be a highly complex process, going beyond the scope of present methodology. The most comprehensive approach might require asking each subject to operationally define each pole of his verbalized constructs. For example, how do you know a person is "steady"? What does a steady person say and do or think and feel? When is he most likely to be steady? If he were to be less steady, when would this occur? The most comprehensive approach would require an understanding of how a particular construct pole relates to its contrast. It also would require understanding how each construct and construct pole relates to other constructs within the system.

Our postcoding method was not used in conjunction with operational definitions of personal constructs and construct contrast was ignored since a construct pole was rated without considering its contrast. In retrospect, we wish more sophisticated methods had been available to us. Nevertheless, the coding of brief descriptions on the Rep Test proved to be a valuable tool in our investigation and lays the groundwork for more sophisticated approaches to understanding Rep Test content.

Development of the Manual. Our first attempt at postcoding is outlined in an article by Landfield, Stern, and Fjeld (1961). Two judges agreed on thirteen categories which included "social interaction," "forcefulness," "self-sufficiency," "intellective," "morality," "emotional arousal," "tenderness," "factual description," and "orderliness." Several of these categories were scored as dimensions. For example, the content descriptions, *lacks energy* and *energetic* were coded as "forcefulness." This particular category, as well as others, later was subdivided into "high" and "low," forming two categories.

The task of creating postcoding categories which have a semblance of interjudge consistency was more difficult than anticipated and covered a span of several years. Judges argued endlessly and it became obvious that they would hold onto certain of their own individualized constructions. For example, the category of "hostility" is a cherished professional construct, yet no way could be found to define the category, either through description or examples, in a way that would guarantee interjudge agreement. The category finally was eliminated. In contrast, various sets of judges experienced no difficulty in agreeing on the category, "emotional arousal," which is difficult to define. It was intriguing to find one judge who equated optimism with "open to experience" and another judge who equated optimism with "closed to experience." At one point we seriously considered turning the whole project upside down and studying the judges of personal constructs. The category of "diffuse generalization" has particular relevance in this context. Judges seemed to be consistent with themselves about what is or is not diffuse or vague, but could not agree with one another. Paradoxically, these problems which plagued us made good sense within personal construct theory. Postcoding, as we did it, is not a simple matter if the notion of personal constructs has validity.

Prior to the final interjudge consistency study, which will be reported later in detail, Isaacson and Landfield coded approximately four hundred construct descriptions. The task was more difficult for Isaacson since he did not have access to the alphabetized list of scored descriptions appended to the scoring manual. Scoring problems highlighted in this study led to the revision of the manual which was used in the final interjudge study done by Landfield and Rodgers. This latter study led to the selection of the thirty-two most reliable categories used in the therapy research project.

Final Interjudge Study. Approximately six hundred personal construct pole descriptions were taken from twenty Rep Tests given to volunteer college students (*IJ 20*). These descriptions were submitted to two raters who independently placed each one with one or more of thirty-nine content categories. Landfield, the first rater, was well acquainted with the postcoding task and was responsible for the scoring of all Rep Tests used in the therapy study. Rodgers, the second rater, a departmental secretary and receptionist, was given only minimal training. First, she studied the manual for four hours, as specified, and then discussed the postcoding task with Landfield for one-half hour.

The task was complex since the raters could use one or more than one of thirty-nine categories in coding each description. Taking this into account, the results reported in Table 3.1 are quite satisfactory. Only seven categories with interjudge agreements ranging from 0 to 62 per cent were eliminated, leaving thirty-two categories with a mean agreement of 80 per cent. Thirteen categories with a mean agreement of 84 per cent accounted for three-fourths of the total category scoring. Seven categories with approximately 70 per cent agreement were retained. Most of these seven categories had fared better in earlier studies and we needed more categories.

TABLE 3.1

Thirty-two Categories with Highest Interjudge Agreement

Category	% Agreement	Category	% Agreement
High Social*	89	Closed*	75
Low Social	71	Sexual	83
High Forceful*	87	High Moral	80
Low Forceful*	88	Low Moral	68
High Organization*	76	External Appearance	62
Low Organization	70	Emotional Arousal*	95
High Sufficiency	69	High Egoism*	87
Low Sufficiency	70	High Tenderness*	87
High Status*	79	Low Tenderness*	83
Low Status	78	Past Orientation	100
Factual	79	Future Orientation	82
High Intellect	94	High Involvement	70
Low Intellect	84	Low Involvement*	85
Self-Reference	86	Extreme Qualifier*	78
Low Imagination	75	High Humor	82
Multiple Description*	83	Low Humor	80

* The asterisk designates the most frequently scored categories, accounting for three-fourths of the total scoring across the thirty-two categories.

Per cent of Agreement: common use by Raters 1 and 2, divided by (unique use by Rater 1, plus unique use by Rater 2, plus common use).

Multiple Description. Rep Test instructions for eliciting personal constructs encourage a subject to focus on the one way in which a certain set of people are alike or different. However, a subject may give several descriptions instead of one. For example, "Tom is friendly and honest, but Mary is dishonest." Use of such multiple description can inflate the base for content scoring. The actual influence of multiple description is not serious. Nevertheless, content scoring used in the therapy research was recast into prorated scoring. In other words, when a subject used multiple description his category scores were reduced in proportion to the use of multiple scoring. Multiple scoring is measured by the total number of construct poles in which multiple description is used. The number of descriptions used at a pole are not counted since use of more than two descriptions occurs infrequently. This prorating procedure may be illustrated by a subject who uses multiple descriptions at six of his thirty construct poles. Since multiple description appears 20 per cent of the time, all category scores are reduced by 20 per cent. If the subject obtains a raw score of six on "emotional arousal," he is given a prorated score of five.

Test-Retest Consistency. Fjeld and Landfield (1961) described the consistency of the Rep Test over a two-week period. Consistency was analyzed in the context of four questions and four subject groups: (a) Given the same acquaintances and the same constructs used on the first test, does he rate his acquaintances in the same way? (b) Given the same acquaintances but no constructs, does he give a similar set of constructs? (c) Given neither the acquaintances nor the constructs used on the first test, does he give similar acquaintances and similar constructs? (d) Given the original list of acquaintances and asked to use acquaintances different from those of the list, does he give similar constructs despite the use of different acquaintances? The authors concluded that the degree of reliability found in each group supports the Rep Test as a reliable research tool and further suggests that people employ similar axes of meaning, even though the "objects" of these conceptual axes change.

In a second study of consistency Landfield analyzed two student groups, *C 13* and *C 17*. Two Rep Tests were administered with a two-week interval between them. In the *C 13* study the same acquaintances were used at each testing and constructs could vary. Protocols were scored for content within the newer postcoding system of thirty-one categories. "Multiple description," a reliable category, was used only for prorating scores. Pearsonian correlations were used in analyzing those categories having larger score distributions.

Information given in *Table 3.2* indicates that only fourteen of the thirty-one categories can be analyzed by a parametric statistic. Of the fourteen categories analyzed, nine have significant coefficients of consistency ($p = .05$ or better, one-tailed) in both *C 13* and *C 17*. One category, "low social," could be analyzed only in group *C 13* and did show significant consistency. Two categories, "low status" and "emotional arousal," were used consistently by *C 13* but not by *C 17*. Correlations for "low self-sufficiency" and "low involvement" were not significant.

TABLE 3.2

Rep Test Content Consistency in C 13 and C 17

Category	Correlation (*r*)	
	C 13	C 17
High Social Interaction	.77	.87
High Forcefulness	.59	.75
Low Forcefulness	.70	.58
High Status	.79	.65
Factual Description	.89	.77
High Intellective	.82	.63
Low Intellective	.80	.68
Closed to Alternatives	.68	.41
High Tenderness	.64	.82
Low Tenderness	.65	.55
Low Social Interaction	.61	—
Low Self-Sufficiency	.10*	.29*
Low Status	.59	.36*
Emotional Arousal	.89	.38*
Low Involvement	.26*	.27*

* not significant

Eight additional categories were analyzed by combining them. "Factual description" was combined with "low imagination" and "external appearance." This new category was called "concreteness." The combination of "high organization" and "high involvement" was called "high structure." The combination of "low organization" and "low involvement" was called "low structure." "High egoism" was combined with "high self-sufficiency" and was labeled "high self-sufficiency." "High" and "low morality" were combined, as were "high" and "low organization." Results of this analysis are reported in Table 3.3. Correlations are significant with the exception of *C 17* on "high structure" and "high-low organization," and all are in the predicted direction of consistency.

Test-Retest Content Consistency: Use and Non-use. In this analysis, consistency was measured by the percentage of the thirty-one categories

TABLE 3.3

Rep Test Content Consistency in C 13 and C 17 on Combined Categories

Category	Correlation (r)	
	C 13	C 17
Concrete	.83	.63
High Structure	.80	.32*
Low Structure	.66	.45
High Self-Sufficiency	.49	.74
High-Low Morality	.73	.77
High-Low Organization	.56	.14*

* not significant

used and not used at both Rep Test 1 and Rep Test 2. Degree of use was not considered. The consistency question involved three groups of subjects: *C 13,* a nonclinic group discussed in the previous section; *LT 24,* the longer-term therapy clients subdivided into most and least maladjusted (*MM 12, LM 12*); and *T 8,* the eight therapists. The test-retest interval for *C 13* was two weeks. The interval for *MM 12, LM 12,* and *T 8* was one month.

Results of this analysis give added support to the hypothesis that Rep Test content is relatively stable. The lowest median percentage of consistency is 70 per cent which is found in *MM 12* of the *LT 24* group.

Test-Retest Content Consistency: Frequency of Use. The assessment of score congruence across the thirty-one categories was executed by a Common Elements Formula (Edwards, 1946). The formula is a simple one. The total amount of overlap scoring across the postcoding categories is divided by the square root of the total score on one test multiplied by the total score on the other test. Now there is serious question about how well the common elements coefficient approximates the Pearsonian correlation. And one must assume that each of the two variables compared, i.e., the two series of Rep Test content scores, are summations of equally likely independent elements. Fortunately, our use of the common elements coefficient did not involve the assumption that the intervals between scale points are equivalent. We did assume an ordinal level of measurement, i.e., higher coefficients represent more congruence.

Turning now to Table 3.4, the Rep Tests of *MM 12, LM 12,* and *T 8* are compared on content consistency using an interval of one month between tests. Inspection of this table shows that the *MM 12* group tends to have both higher and lower consistency coefficients than *LM 12* or *T 8*. One may conclude that, early in therapy, the most maladjusted are both more and less stable in the content of their personal constructs than the least maladjusted or the therapists. This makes sense. Rigidity and instability are common descriptions of more maladjusted people.

TABLE 3.4
One Month Consistency in Content Frequency

Group	Coefficient of Congruence*		
	.50–.66	.67–.78	.79–.90
MM 12	7	1	4
LM 12	5	7	0
T 8	2	6	0

12 MM >< 12 LM $\chi^2 = 5.4$, 2 df, $p < .10$
12 MM >< T 8 $\chi^2 = 6.1$, 2 df, $p < .05$

* As determined by common elements formula.

Summarizing this material on content postcoding, the development of the Content Manual was discussed in conjunction with studies of interjudge and test-retest consistency. Rep Test content was found to be relatively stable over short time intervals and more maladjusted clients were found to be both more and less stable than their better adjusted counterparts.

ORGANIZATION AS MEASURED BY FIC SCORE

Kelly created a variety of approaches to construct elicitation and analysis. He recognized that a method useful in one context might have less relevance in another. He understood that new methods would evolve and Rep Test procedures were introduced as examples, as points of departure for the clinician or research worker interested in personal construct theory. In such an evolutionary process, there can be a separation of theory and method. Bannister and Mair (1968) suggest that such a separation has taken place within personal construct theory. The study of cognitive complexity is a case in point. A measure which originally was used in conjunction with personal construct methodology "now is virtually a self-contained research area" (p. 70).

Cognitive complexity is essentially a measure of how many cognitions are interrelated. If a person has many independent cognitions at his command, he is more complex. If he has few cognitions which are independent of one another, he is cognitively more simple. Even though our method of construct organization scoring bears a resemblance to measures of cognitive complexity (Bieri, 1955, 1961), we have used the term *functionally independent construction* (FIC) rather than complexity. FIC is defined as the total number of separate construct units employed by a subject on a particular Rep Test. For example, fifteen construct dimensions are elicited from the subject. Assuming that seven constructs are "grid" unrelated (seven points), five constructs are interrelated (one point), and the remaining three are interrelated (one point) but not to the other cluster, the total unit score for concepts is nine. A score of fifteen would represent little organization. The pattern of interrelationships within a cluster or constellation of constructs does not affect the FIC score. Construct 1 might be related to 2 and 3, yet constructs 2 and 3 might be unrelated. Constructs 1, 2, and 3 would constitute a cluster and is scored as one FIC unit if none of the three concepts is related to constructs outside the cluster.

The term functionally independent construction has three advantages over the term complexity. First of all, FIC refers more directly to personal construct theory and does not imply anything about complexity. This is an advantage since complex behavior, to some extent at least, must be organized behavior. It is assumed that comprehension of complexity must be associated with a system. Scientific theorizing may be described as an organized way of approaching infinite complexity. In this context, the presence of many separate and unrelated units of personal construction that some psychologists call complex cognition may well be related to an inability to effectively encompass complexity. To the opposite extreme, highly organized conceptualization could lead to excessively simple behavior.

A second essential feature of the FIC score is that it takes into account Kelly's range corollary which was discussed at the beginning of this chapter. Explicit in this corollary is the assumption that each construct dimension has a range of application and this range of application may vary from construct to construct. In the traditional grid form of the Rep Test, a subject, after formulating a construct, e.g., "humor" versus "lack of humor," applies his construct to other acquaintances which are not part of the initial response to the construct forming question. However, he is asked to apply just one pole of the dimension, e.g., "humor," and the investigator then assumes that acquaintances not so designated lack humor. That neither "humor" nor "lack of humor" apply to a particular acquaintance is not considered.

FIC has a third advantage, one which is related to Danforth's (1968) position that "measures of organization must be analyzable into component properties in order to describe the organization" (p. 19). The FIC score is derived from an analysis of these component properties.

Obtaining the FIC score. The essential nature of how one goes about discovering whether two descriptive constructs are interrelated was discussed in Chapter 1. The operational definition of a descriptive contrast such as *open* versus *closed* is the rating pattern one uses as he describes a sample of acquaintances within the construct. The definition of this particular construct might be as follows: "Pete is open; Sally is open; Sam is closed; Mary may be either, I can't decide which one applies most; and John—well, I never think of him in these terms." Translating this into Rep grid language, Pete is *1*, Sally is *1*, Sam is *2*, Mary is *?*, and John is *N*. In other words, the left hand contrast is given the score of *1;* the right hand contrast is *2;* inability to decide is designated by a *?;* and, whenever a whole construct is irrelevant, an *N* rating, meaning not apply, is used. Figure 3.5 shows a section of a Rep Test Response Sheet in which the four types of ratings have been used. In this illustration row patterns define descriptive dimensions. The construct *feels blue* versus *feels great* is defined by the pattern: *1, 2, 1, 2, 2, 1; hard working* versus *lazy* is defined by the pattern: *N, 2, 1, 2, 1, ?*. The relationship between these two patterns may be direct or inverse as determined by an arbitrary criterion.

If row patterns define descriptive constructs, what do column patterns define? Referring again to Figure 3.1, column patterns may be used to define people constructs. The construct "Mary" and a hypothetical contrast "not Mary" is defined by the pattern *1, 2, N*. Likewise, the construct "John" and a hypothetical contrast "not John" is defined by the pattern *2, 1, 2*. It is possible to determine whether these two column patterns are directly or inversely related.

Focusing only on the fifteen descriptive constructs found on a full test protocol, it is necessary to compare each row pattern with each of the other row patterns. Knowing the interrelationships between these row patterns will enable the clinician or researcher to determine the degree to which the descriptive constructs (c) are related. This score will be expressed as FIC (c). Likewise, the interrelationships between the column patterns will allow us to determine the degree to which people constructs (p) are interrelated. This score will be expressed as

FIGURE 3.1
Section of Rep Test Protocol

Mary	John	Henry	Max	Sally	Joan		Contrasts 1	Contrasts 2
1	2	3	4	5	6		1	2
1	2	1	2	2	1	1	FEELS BLUE	FEELS GREAT
2	1	1	2	N	1	2	NOT LIKE DANCING	LIKES DANCING
N	2	1	2	1	?	3	HARD WORKING	LAZY

Column patterns define people

Row patterns define descriptive dimensions

FIC (p). A total FIC score may be obtained by adding FIC (c) to FIC (p), yielding FIC (cp). The addition of these scores is not just a redundancy since there can be some differences between the two scores. However, the two scores are positively related ($r = .69$, $p < .01$).

The general idea of the FIC (c), FIC (p), and FIC (cp) scores is not difficult to grasp; however, the specifics of scoring for direct and inverse relationships and the final determination of the FIC scores can be a bit confusing. Figure 3.2, which includes two descriptive constructs extracted from the Response Sheet of one client, will be used to explain how a relationship between two constructs is scored for (1) a positive relationship, (2) an inverse relationship, and also for (3) the number of mutual exclusions.

The ratings in Figure 3.2 indicate that this client is unable to rate his first acquaintance on construct 7, since he has placed an *N* under his Acquaintance 1 and to the right of construct 7. He rates his second acquaintance a *1* which means that he perceives this acquaintance more *outgoing.* His fourth acquaintance is rated *?* since he cannot clearly rate this person as either *outgoing* or *lacking confidence.* Acquaintance 15 is rated *2* for *lacking confidence.*

Focusing now on the rating patterns for construct 7 and construct 15, a positive relationship between the two construct patterns is determined by counting the number of acquaintances rated either as a *1* or a 2 on both dimensions. Acquaintance 2 is rated a *1* on both constructs whereas Acquaintance 12 is rated a *2* on both constructs. Paired *1*'s and paired *2*'s both contribute to the positive score. Since eight acquaintances, i.e., 2, 3, 5, 6, 10, 12, 13, 14, have similar ratings on both constructs, the score for a positive relationship is eight.

An inverse or negative relationship between two construct patterns is determined by counting the number of acquaintances rated either a *1* or a *2* on one dimension, but a *2* or a *1* on the other dimension. Acquaintance 15 is rated a *2* for lacking confidence and a *1* for *honesty.* Since only one acquaintance has opposite ratings, i.e., *1* and *2* or *2* and *1* on the two constructs, the score for a negative relationship is one.

The number of mutual exclusions between two construct patterns is determined by counting the number of acquaintances who are rated as either *N* or *?* on both constructs. Acquaintance 7 is rated *N* on construct 7 and a *?* on construct 15. Acquaintance 11 is rated *N* on both constructs. Since two acquaintances are rated as either *N* or *?* on the two constructs, the score for mutual exclusion is two.

Treating *N* and *?* ratings as identities was justified on two bases: it does simplify scoring, and *N* and *?* ratings are similar in that neither

FIGURE 3.2
Comparison of Two Construct Rating Patterns

Descriptive Constructs	Acquaintances														
	1	2	3	4	5	6	7	8	9	10	11	12	13	14	15
C 7 Outgoing—Lacks Confidence	N	1	1	?	1	1	N	N	1	1	N	2	1	1	2
C 15 Honest—Dishonest	2	1	1	1	1	1	?	2	N	1	N	2	1	1	1

is a clear application of the construct. Even as we made this decision to combine the *N* and *?* ratings, it was recognized that an uncertainty rating and a clear cut exclusion rating do have different clinical implications.

The relationship score for the two constructs shown in Figure 3.2 is found by taking the highest positive or negative relationship score and adding it to the mutual exclusion score. In this illustration, the higher positive relationship score of eight is added to the mutual exclusion score of two. The total relationship score is ten and the relationship is positive rather than inverse. However, this score of ten does not meet our arbitrary criterion of twelve out of a possible fifteen cell relationships.

Quite obviously, if a mutual exclusion score is too high, a spurious notion may be inferred about the positive or negative relationship between two constructs. For example, a score of three positive overlaps, four negative overlaps and eight mutual exclusions yields a total score of twelve negative. This score does not adequately represent the positive or inverse relationship between the two constructs since there is not much difference between positive and negative overlaps. To counteract this difficulty, we arbitrarily elevate the criterion score whenever the number of mutual exclusions reaches a certain level. Whenever mutual exclusions are not above six, the relationship score must be at least twelve. However, if mutual exclusions are in the range of seven through nine, the criterion score is raised to thirteen. Experience with this scoring indicates that a mutual exclusion score above six is very rare. Use of the correction factor, when needed, insures at least a two to one ratio between positive and negative scores.

Having discussed how a relationship between two constructs is derived, we are ready to consider an illustration of how an FIC score is obtained for either fifteen descriptive constructs or fifteen people constructs. Turning to Figure 3.3, the relationship among fifteen constructs is diagrammed. The three clusters are scored three and the four independent constructs which are unrelated to other constructs are scored four, yielding a total FIC score of seven.

FIC Consistency. One feature of any measure is that of consistency. It is assumed that over a short span of time those measures of greater utility will show stability. However, measures should not be expected to have maximal consistency if they are to encompass change and learning. Therefore, we only hope to show that the FIC score has a statistically significant degree of consistency.

Danforth (1968) administered the Rep Test modification twice to

FIGURE 3.3
Example of Construct Relationships

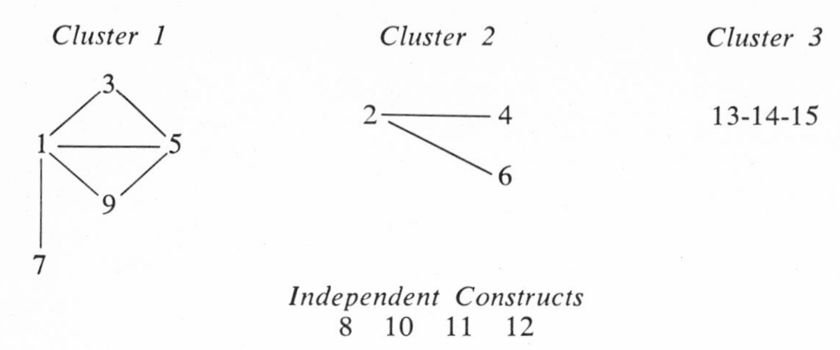

forty students, two-thirds of whom were female, over a two week period. Each time, subjects described the same fifteen acquaintances from the fifteen descriptive contrasts that were initially elicited. The FIC (c) score correlation between these two administrations was .82 ($p < .001$, one-tailed).

In a second study, Baugh (1968) administered the Rep Test modification twice to thirteen male students over a sixteen day period. The set of acquaintances described at first testing was different from the set used at second testing. The FIC (c) score correlation was .55 ($p < .02$, one-tailed).

Landfield pursued the question of consistency of both concepts (c) and people (p). The number of construction units for concepts was counted. Then the grid was rotated 90° and the number of people units was counted by noting the similarity in grid column patterns under acquaintances. Possible scoring for both concepts and people was from one to fifteen points, making a total scoring range of two to thirty points. FIC scores for concepts, for people, and for both combined were established for eight therapists and their twenty-four clients who took the Rep Test modification at monthly intervals.

The same acquaintances were described at each testing; however constructs were elicited at each administration. Consistency correlations were reported for the first, second, and third months of testing, as shown in Table 3.5. Therapist FIC (c) consistency is uniformly high. FIC (p) correlations, also high, show more variability. FIC (cp) correlations are in the range of .83 to .95. Client correlations, with one exception, are significant with lowest correlations appearing over the first month of therapy. Correlations for therapists are higher than for clients, as one would expect.

TABLE 3.5

Client and Therapist FIC Consistency Over Three Monthly Intervals

		Months		
		(1–2)	(2–3)	(3–4)
	FIC (c)	.23*	.71	.49
Clients	FIC (p)	.39	.53	.46
	FIC (cp)	.41	.48	.51
	FIC (c)	.75	.94	.93
Therapists	FIC (p)	.73	.52*	.84
	FIC (cp)	.88	.83	.95

* not significant

Computer Program for FIC. Hand scoring for FIC (c) and FIC (p) takes approximately three hours. Computer scoring, a more economical approach, also is possible. A program developed by John A. Gifford is written in Fortran IV computer language. This program, which is located in Appendix D, provides a computerized print-out of the grid matrix, showing the positive and negative relationships found between each construct and every other construct. Determination of the FIC score is a simple matter since both concept and people relationships are printed.

Summarizing this discussion of functionally independent construction, the consistency studies point to the relative stability of the FIC score over a short span of time. Consistency is apparent even when entirely different acquaintances are described on two Rep Tests, supporting the idea that organization is not merely a function of external events. Consistency is found in the longer-term psychotherapy clients and is particularly high among the therapists. It is conceivable that the use of more acquaintances and the elicitation of more constructs might elevate FIC consistency, assuming that subject motivation does not falter.

CHAPTER FOUR

CONGRUENCE AND PREMATURE TERMINATION

BEGINNING WITH THE GENERAL STATEMENT THAT *maintenance of interpersonal communication in the early phase of a therapy relationship requires some minimal degree of shared meaningfulness between a client and his therapist,* derivative hypotheses were stated in which three measures of dyadic meaningfulness were related to measures of premature termination. Premature termination indicates that members of a therapy dyad are unable to maintain interpersonal communication.

MEANINGFULNESS OF THE OTHER PERSON AND PREMATURE TERMINATION IN VARIABLE-TERM CLIENTS

Hypothesis I: In those client-therapist (C-T) *pairs in which T and C perceive each other as more meaningful figures at the beginning of therapy, the conclusion of therapy will be nonpremature. In those C-T pairs in which T and C perceive each other as less meaningful figures, therapy will conclude prematurely* (Ourth & Landfield, 1965).

Premature Termination and Dyadic Interaction. Research on premature termination in psychotherapy has focused primarily on developing client variables that will predict continuation in psychotherapy. The most useful client variables are those which Strickland and Crowne

(1963) have called "unsuitability factors," such as social class (Frank, Gliedman, Imber, Nash, & Stone, 1957), intelligence (Hiler, 1958), and insight (Katz, Lorr, & Rubenstein, 1958). These social class variables have turned out to be relatively successful predictors, particularly so when the client population is heterogeneous. However, when these client characteristics are removed, premature termination still occurs. For example, premature termination in psychotherapy with college students seems to be only slightly lower than that found in other settings. Yet nearly all of the unsuitability factors listed above are minimized in the college client group. These considerations led the authors to feel that termination should be viewed within the more fundamental context of client-therapist interaction.

The hypothesis that premature termination is related to client-therapist interaction variables assumes that client factors are indicative of premature termination only when in common with certain therapist characteristics. Membership in the middle class is just one special case of such interactive variables. If therapist and client share similar social class membership, whether it is upper, middle, or lower, social class membership would not be pertinent as a predictor of premature termination within the class. Consequently, class membership predictors are not helpful in understanding therapy or counseling in a college setting.

Four distinct types of termination evolve when looking at it from a dyadic interactive point of view:

1. *Nonpremature termination* in which the client and the therapist, while yet in therapy, can agree that they have reached one of the following modes of conclusion: (a) That the client has improved and can go on his own with no further therapy. This client might be rated as maximally improved, at least from the therapist's point of view. (b) That the client can make no further progress, at least for the time being. The client may or may not return after a period of time for further therapy. This client might be rated as moderately improved. (c) That this relationship, for various reasons, cannot be beneficial to the client, so termination is in order. The client might be rated by the therapist as either slightly improved, not improved, or not in need of therapy.

None of these three modes of conclusions is premature termination, if prematurity refers to the status of the dyad, rather than to the status of the client's problems. Employment of this dyadic approach to termination de-emphasizes the criterion of number of sessions or degree of improvement. It does emphasize the idea that therapy has progressed as far as can be reasonably expected for the particular dyad, as agreed upon by members of the dyad.

2. *The therapist terminates therapy.* The therapist believes that

one of the modes listed in 1 above is applicable, but the client does not agree. This is a case of therapist premature termination from the standpoint of the client.

3. *The client terminates therapy.* The client feels that one of the modes listed in 1 above is applicable but the therapist does not agree. This is a case of client premature termination from the standpoint of the therapist.

4. *Premature termination* in which the client and the therapist can agree that therapy discontinued before either the client or the therapist wished it to. This is, in my opinion, the clearest case of premature termination. It is defined by the inferred agreement of client and therapist, following therapy, that therapy is indeed unfinished. The client leaves therapy, does not return, and the therapist rates him as unfinished and needful of further therapy. The client, when asked to return to therapy or to discuss his therapy experience, states that therapy is unfinished but he does not want to continue working with that particular therapist. In this case emphasis is placed upon the idea that therapy has not progressed as far as can be reasonably expected for that particular dyad, as agreed upon by members of the dyad.

In the present study, only the clear-cut nonpremature and premature terminations were studied since no instances of types 2 and 3 occurred among our particular subjects. The authors selected one interactive variable that they hypothesized would predict premature termination, which could be measured following the first therapy session, and for which college students could be used. The variable that was selected is called meaningfulness as defined by the presence of extreme ratings on bipolar dimensions which have a neutral midpoint. It is assumed that clarity and definiteness of description, attributes of meaningfulness, can be inferred from the more extreme use as opposed to more central (midposition) use of rating scales. Those objects which are described in more extreme ways will be considered more meaningful to the rater than those objects which are described in a more neutral way by the rater.

Procedure. Subjects were thirty-nine variable-term clients of both sexes, seventeen males and twenty-two females, seen once a week by six therapists, one female and five males, with experience ranging from two to eighteen years. Each of the therapists saw both male and female clients. Both clients and therapists took a modified form of the Rep Test before therapy began. The construct dimensions of each C-T pair were mixed and placed on a rating sheet, comprised of seven-point scales for each of the dimensions. This produced a conventional semantic differential with the dimensions being anchored by the personal constructs of the client and his therapist. In other words, the semantic differential was unique for each C-T pair. Soon after the first session and before the second one, clients and therapists completed the following descriptions on these scales: (1) rate yourself as you see yourself now; (2) rate your ideal self; (3) rate the other person as you see him now (this means that the client rated his therapist and the therapist rated his client). Only the ratings of the other person, completed after the initial session, were utilized in this study. In other words, we focused on the client's rating of the therapist and the therapist's rating of his client.

Thirteen variable-term clients were classified as premature terminators (*PVT*s) and twenty-six were classified as nonpremature terminators (*NPVT*s). As discussed above, *PVT*s and *NPVT*s were defined in a different fashion than in other studies. Typically, length of stay has been used in determining premature termination with some number of sessions or weeks in therapy being defined as the cutoff point. Those clients that do not reach the cutoff point are considered premature terminators, and those who go beyond this point are considered remainers. In this study, dyadic agreement as to premature or nonpremature status was used as the criterion for classification of *PVT*s and *NPVT*s. Therapist's feelings concerning the end of therapy were ascertained by using a termination questionnaire which was filled out by each therapist. On the termination sheet, the therapist indicated whether he felt: (1) therapy was completed; (2) the client had left before therapy was finished; or (3) the client and the therapist had reached a point where no further therapy at that time would be profitable. The client's feelings concerning termination status also were obtained by using a termination questionnaire in a special session following the posttherapy interview. Direct questions were asked concerning whether the client thought his therapy had reached a satisfactory conclusion; whether he was not finished with therapy but wanted to leave anyhow; or whether therapy had reached the point where it no longer would be profitable to continue with that therapist. Client-therapist agreement or disagreement was checked. Using the nonpremature and premature classifications, thirteen clients were labeled premature terminators and twenty-six as nonpremature terminators. Eight premature terminators stayed in therapy four weeks or less; five premature terminators left between five and twelve weeks. Eight nonpremature terminators were in therapy four weeks or less; eighteen nonpremature terminators were in therapy from five to tweny-six weeks.

Predictions, Scoring and Analysis. Based on the hypothesis stated earlier, we made the following predictions: (1) Clients and therapists in premature dyads will have significantly smaller summed extremity ratings at the beginning of therapy than clients and therapists in nonpremature dyads. (2) Prematurely terminating clients will initially describe their therapists in significantly less extreme ways than will nonpremature clients. (3) Therapists will initially describe their prematurely terminating clients in significantly less extreme ways than they will describe their nonpremature clients.

Even though seven point scaling was used with the personal construct dimensions, the scoring was made more sensitive by dividing each scale into thirteen units; the center of each dimension was numbered zero and the scale was scored from zero to six in each direction. For each subject the deviation scores were summed for the dimensions that made up the construct semantic differential. The t test was used with the total deviation scores (rating extremity scores) to analyze the significance of differences between the premature and nonpremature groups. A one-tailed test of significance was used, and the significance level chosen was .05.

Results. The results pertinent to the three predictions are reported in Table 4.1, Rows 1, 2, and 3. Row 1 shows that the interpersonal meaningfulness of the prematurely terminating dyads is significantly lower than that of nonpremature dyads. Row 2 shows that premature terminators perceive their therapists as being significantly less meaningful. Row 3 shows that therapists perceive their premature clients as being significantly less meaningful.

Investigators such as Cromwell & Caldwell (1962) and Isaacson & Landfield (1965) have demonstrated that a rating task is more meaningful if the rater can use his own language in the task. Anticipating that the three predictions stated above will be more effectively demonstrated when the descriptions used are the subjects' own construct dimensions, the data were reanalyzed. The results of this second analysis, in which the clients and therapists rated only within the context of their own constructs, are shown in Rows 4, 5, and 6. When prediction 1 is retested, using one's own constructs, as shown in Row 4, this first prediction is more strongly supported ($p < .001$) than previously ($p < .01$). Likewise, Rows 5 and 6 show that predictions 2 and 3 are more strongly supported when only one's own constructs are used in the analysis.

Summary of Hypothesis I. Data presented in Rows 1 through 6 of Table 4.1 support the hypothesized relationship between meaningfulness of the other person as defined by the extremity rating and premature termination. This relationship is strengthened when predictions are based on combined client and therapist ratings of one another within their

TABLE 4.1

Interpersonal Meaningfulness for Premature and Nonpremature Terminators

Row	Measure	*Premature*		*Nonpremature*		t	*p*
		M	SD	M	SD		
1[1]	C/T, T/C[2]	124.53	33.12	164.30	33.23	3.59	$< .01$
2	C/T	68.13	34.30	88.46	30.89	1.91	.05
3	T/C	61.01	14.45	72.12	20.32	2.04	$< .05$
4	C/T, T/C	57.46	14.60	82.15	18.31	4.76	$< .001$
5	C/T	32.73	19.53	46.46	16.73	2.52	$< .01$
6	T/C	30.13	6.16	36.59	10.00	2.54	$< .01$
7	C/T, T/C	68.00	20.40	82.15	16.62	2.24	.05
8	C/T	36.47	19.34	43.40	17.72	1.16	ns
9	T/C	32.66	10.90	37.23	13.00	1.28	ns

1. Data in Rows 1, 2, and 3 are based upon ratings utilizing the pooled constructs of both the therapist and client. Data in Rows 4, 5, and 6 are based upon ratings using the subject's own constructs only. Data in Rows 7, 8, and 9 are based upon ratings using the partner's constructs only, e.g., client using his therapist's constructs and therapist using his client's constructs.

2. C/T refers to client's ratings of his therapist; T/C to therapist's ratings of his client. When both are listed for the same row, the extremity ratings of both have been combined, pair by pair, and summed.

own personal construct dimensions. That two of the three predictions made in the study would not have received as much support without the use of the rater's own constructs is somewhat disconcerting. How many studies utilizing the experimenter's own language preferences rather than the subject's language have failed to support hypotheses simply because rating items either do not communicate or do not communicate in relationship to subject individuality?

MEANINGFULNESS OF THE OTHER'S CONSTRUCTS AND PREMATURE TERMINATION

Hypothesis II: In those C-T pairs in which T and C perceive each other's construct dimensions as more meaningful at the beginning of therapy, the conclusion of therapy will be nonpremature. In those C-T pairs in which T and C perceive each other's construct dimensions as less meaningful, therapy will conclude prematurely (Ourth & Landfield, 1965).

The Sociality Corollary. If one's capacity to relate to another person is dependent upon his subsuming of certain points of view of the other person, then clients and therapists participating in more meaningful social interactions should be able to make some use of one another's construct dimensions. It would seem reasonable that clients and therapists in premature dyads would lack this capacity to employ the other person's constructs in some meaningful way.

Predictions. (1) Clients and therapists in premature dyads, rating one another on the other person's construct dimensions, will have significantly smaller summed extremity ratings at the beginning of therapy than clients and therapists in nonpremature dyads. (2) Prematurely terminating clients will initially describe their therapists, on the therapists' dimensions, in significantly less extreme ways than will nonpremature clients. (3) Therapists will initially describe their prematurely terminating clients, on the clients' dimensions, in significantly less extreme ways than they will describe their nonpremature clients.

Results. The results pertinent to these three predictions are reported in Table 4.1, Rows 7, 8, and 9. From Row 7 it can be seen that the first prediction is supported when C-T pooled ratings are used. When predictions are made on C or T ratings alone, results are not significant; however, the data support the direction of the predictions.

Summary Hypothesis II. Data presented in Rows 7 through 9 of Table 4.1 support the hypothesized relationship between meaningfulness of the other person's construct dimensions and premature termination when the ratings of client and therapist are pooled within each dyad. In other words, the ability to subsume the other's constructs at the beginning of therapy is less apparent in premature than in nonpremature dyads.

It may be concluded that maintaining a meaningful relationship not only requires an ability to encompass the other person within one's own constructs, but some ability to meaningfully use the constructs of the other person and to understand him within his own construct dimensions also may be important.

CONTENT CONGRUENCY AND PREMATURE TERMINATION

Hypothesis III: In those C-T pairs in which there is more similarity in the content of their personal constructs at the beginning of therapy, the conclusion of therapy will be nonpremature. In those C-T pairs in which there is less similarity in the content of their personal constructs, therapy will conclude prematurely.

Two Definitions of Premature Termination. In the previous study by Ourth and Landfield, premature termination was defined by the inadequate nature of the therapy dyad at the point of termination. This definition again will be employed in conjunction with variable-term clients. However, shortness of stay in therapy will be used with clients initially assigned as likely candidates for longer-term therapy.

Thirty-seven clients were assigned as longer-term cases but thirteen of them dropped out prior to seven interviews. Since these latter clients failed to complete the minimal three months of therapy they are considered premature terminators, as symbolized by *PT 13*. The twenty-four clients who remained in therapy are symbolized by *LT 24*. Thirty-one variable-term clients also were analyzed for this particular study, nine of whom are premature terminators, as symbolized by *PVT 9*. Twenty-two nonpremature clients are symbolized by *NPVT 22*. Employing the variable-term clients separately from longer-term clients permitted two tests of Hypothesis III.

It has been argued that short-stay clients may well be shorter-term success cases rather than premature terminators. This possibility was checked in the *PT 13* group by reviewing case dictations, in conjunction with Therapist Rating Schedules (TRS) which were filled out every two weeks. The TRSs show that after the second interview twelve of the premature clients are rated as long-term cases, supporting the judgment of the intake interviewer. One client, first rated as a short-term case, is rated as a longer-term case at the fourth week. A review of case dictations suggests that only two clients can be considered nonpremature. In both instances therapists felt that their clients might make some progress by themselves. Therapy progress could not be inferred in the other eleven cases and there is no evidence that therapists felt any of these clients should terminate.

Procedure. The first Rep Tests of the *LT 24, PT 13, NPVT 22,* and *PVT 9* clients were juxtaposed with Rep Tests taken by their therapists, a procedure which was explained in Chapter 2. Additionally, the first Rep Tests of the therapists were paired randomly with the Rep Tests taken by ten better adjusted subjects (*BA 10*). Since ten student Rep Tests were used, two of the eight therapists were represented twice, but with a different protocol.

Next, a coefficient of content congruence based on thirty-one post-coding categories with greater interjudge consistency was determined for each client-therapist dyad. A second coefficient also was obtained, one which is based on categories selected from among the thirty-one categories. These special categories are determined by first assessing which personal constructs of a particular subject are most grid related to his other constructs. The nature of grid relationships was outlined in Chapter 3. After the construct or constructs which are most interrelated have been determined, the content scoring of those constructs is recorded, and it is this content which serves as the base for measuring client-therapist congruence. This procedure may be illustrated. Assume that Client B uses *happy* versus *dishonest,* a construct found to be interrelated with six other construct dimensions. Assume further that this construct is the most interrelating construct dimension on the Rep grid. The content scoring for *happy* is "emotional arousal." *Dishonest* is scored as "low morality." Focusing only on these two categories, the Rep Tests of both the client and his therapist now may be scored and client-therapist congruency determined, but only in relation to these categories. The therapist's Rep grid also may be analyzed to determine his most interrelating construct or constructs and the contents of these therapist constructions then may serve as a base from which client-therapist congruence is determined, using the Common Elements formula described in Chapter 3. Finally, it is possible to assess congruency by employing important, i.e., most interrelating, content categories of both the client and his therapist. It is this latter approach which we used in our analysis.

The rationale for using the content of the most interrelating constructions of the client and his therapist as a basis for determining congruency is found in the Organization Corollary. This corollary encompasses the idea that constructs may be found in hierarchical arrangements, that the relationship between constructs may be expressed in terms of superordinancy and subordinancy, and further, that superordinate constructs have more deterministic and behavioral implications. To the extent that most interrelating constructs reflect superordinate construction, the content of most interrelating constructs will be more important than the content of less interrelating constructs.

Predictions. (1) Using thirty-one postcoding categories in the analysis, *LT 24* dyads will have higher coefficients of content congruency at the beginning of therapy than *PT 13* dyads. (2) Using thirty-one postcoding categories in the analysis, *NPVT 22* dyads will have higher coefficients of content congruency at the beginning of therapy than *PVT 9* dyads. (3) Using only the combined content of most interrelated construction of the client and his therapist, *LT 24* dyads will have higher coefficients than *PT 13* dyads; and (4) *NPVT 18* dyads will have higher coefficients than *PVT 8* dyads. Five *VT* clients of the thirty-one clients used in the previous (2) analysis were eliminated since they did not fill out the grid section of the Rep Test. Finally, assuming that therapists should have more in common with better adjusted students than with maladjusted clients, it was predicted that (5) *BA 10* dyads will have higher coefficients of congruence than other dyadic groups.

Results. Tables 4.2 and 4.3, Rows 1, show that at the beginning of therapy nonpremature dyads in both longer-term and variable-term assignment groups tend to be more congruent than premature dyads on thirty-one content categories. However, only the results on the variable-term group are statistically significant. Table 4.4, Rows 1 and 2, shows that at the beginning of therapy nonpremature dyads in both longer-term and variable-term assignment groups are significantly more congruent than premature dyads on the combined content of client and therapist most interrelated constructs. In other words, the significance of the relationship between content congruency and premature termination is increased by focusing on more important content categories.

Tables 4.2 and 4.3, Rows 1, 2, and 3, indicate that therapists are most congruent with better adjusted students and are more congruent with nonpremature terminators than with premature terminators. This finding, which holds for both the longer-term and variable-term assign-

TABLE 4.2

Content Congruence of Nonpremature and Premature Longer-term Assignment Dyads at the Beginning of Therapy

Row	Dyadic Groups Compared	Group with Greater Congruence	Mann-Whitney U*
1	T 8—LT 24 vs. T 8—PT 13	T 8—LT 24	U = 112, Z = 1.4 $p = .08$
2	T 8—BA 10 vs. T 8—PT 13	T 8—BA 10	U = 30, $p < .02$
3	T 8—BA 10 vs. T 8—LT 24	T 8—BA 10	U = 82, Z = 1.4 $p = .08$

* One-tailed test
LT—Nonpremature, longer-term assignment clients
PT—Premature, longer-term assignment clients
T—Therapists
BA—Better-adjusted comparison students

TABLE 4.3

Content Congruence of Nonpremature and Premature Variable-term Assignment Dyads at the Beginning of Therapy

Row	Dyadic Groups Compared	Group with Greater Congruence	Mann-Whitney U*
1	T 6—NPVT 22 vs. T 6—PVT 9	T 6—NPVT 22	U = 138, Z = 1.7 $p = .04$
2	T 8—BA 10 vs. T 6—PVT 9	T 8—BA 10	U = 28, p not sig. (U = 24—$p = .05$)
3	T 8—BA 10 vs. T 6—NPVT 22	Neither	U = 110, Z = 0.0 $p = .50$

* One-tailed test
NPVT—Nonpremature, variable-term clients
PVT—Premature, variable-term clients
T—Therapists
BA—Better adjusted comparison students

ment groups, suggests that therapists work best with those who are most "content similar" to themselves and also with those who may be less maladjusted.

Summary Hypothesis III. Data presented in Tables 4.2, 4.3 and 4.4 support the relationship between greater client-therapist congruency in the content of their personal constructs and nonpremature termination. This relationship is strongly supported in two different groups of clients when congruency is measured in relation to the content of the most interrelated constructs used by a client and his therapist. Restating this point, an emphasis on the content of central constructions used by a client and his therapist increases the significance of relationship between content congruency and nonpremature termination.

TABLE 4.4

Congruence on Combined Content of Client and Therapist Most Interrelated Constructs at the Beginning of Therapy

Row	Dyadic Groups Compared	Group with Greater Congruence	Mann-Whitney U*
1	T 8—LT 24 vs. T 8—PT 11	T 8—LT 24	$U = 205$, $Z = 2.6$ $p = .004$
2	T 6—NPVT 18 vs. T 6—PVT 8	T 6—NPVT 18	$U = 33$, $p < .02$

* One-tailed test
LT—Nonpremature, longer-term assignment clients
T—Therapists
PT—Premature, longer-term assignment clients
NPVT—Nonpremature, variable-term clients
PVT—Premature, variable-term clients

Our emphasis on the content of the most interrelated construct dimensions is based on the assumption that most interrelated construction will more likely represent superordinancy. Kelly defines a superordinate construct as "one which includes another as one of the elements in its context" (p. 564) and therefore is more functionally important. A superordinate construct is of a higher theoretical order and has more organizing and deterministic implications. There is some support for the assumption that interrelated construction is more important construction. Danforth (1968), using Landfield's Rep Test modification, found a relationship between construction perceived as more important by subjects and the greater comprehensiveness or interrelatedness of that construction. Studies by Levy (1956) and Hinkle (1965), which are less directly relevant, support a relationship between construct organization and change.

ORGANIZATIONAL CONGRUENCE AND PREMATURE TERMINATION

Although a hypothesis about client-therapist organizational congruence and premature termination was not stated, the author did explore this relationship by associating the nature of termination with the difference between the FIC (cp) scores of the client and his therapist. Since the FIC score for concepts (c) is combined with the score for people (p), the possible scoring range, based on fifteen descriptive dimensions and fifteen acquaintances, is from two to thirty points. By subtracting the FIC (cp) score of the client from that of his therapist, a measure of organizational congruence for the dyad is obtained. The higher the FIC (cp) difference, the less will be the client-therapist congruence.

Table 4.5, Rows 1 and 2, indicates that in both the longer-term assignment clients and the variable-term clients, greater FIC score difference at the beginning of therapy is found more often in premature dyads. However, this relationship is significant only in the longer-term assignment group. Nevertheless, the definite trends found in both groups suggest that not only is prematurity related to lower-content congruence,

TABLE 4.5

Structural Congruence of Premature and Nonpremature Dyads at the Beginning of Therapy

Row	Dyadic Groups Compared	Group with Greater Congruence	Mann-Whitney U*
1	T 8—LT 24 vs. T 8—PT 11	T 8—LT 24	U = 61, Z = 2.5 *p* = .01
2	T 6—NPVT 18 vs. T 6—PVT 8	T 8—NPVT 18	U = 63, *p* not sig.

* Two-tailed test
LT—Nonpremature, longer-term assignment clients
T—Therapists
PT—Premature, longer-term assignment clients
NPVT—Nonpremature, variable-term clients
PVT—Premature, variable-term clients

but prematurity also may be related to less congruence in construct organization.

Perspective. The data presented in this chapter offer strong support for the position that premature termination can be predicted when interactive variables are used. The discriminating power of our dyadic congruency measures is more significant, it is felt, because this investigation was conducted with college student clients, a far more homogeneous population than those ordinarily found in community outpatient clinics or other agencies. Such a population provides a more critical test of the predictive power of the variables selected than does the more heterogeneous population ordinarily used.

The proposition that maintenance of interpersonal communication in the early phase of a therapy relationship requires some minimal degree of shared meaningfulness between a client and his therapist is supported by our data. A relationship was found between premature termination, an index of interpersonal failure, and less meaningfulness of the other person, as well as less meaningfulness of the other person's constructs as understood by the members of the dyad. Restating these findings, a client and his therapist should make some sense to one another at the beginning of a therapy relationship and within their own personal systems of communication, i.e. personal constructs. Also, a client and his therapist should be able to subsume, to some extent, the other's personal constructs, as demonstrated by an ability to meaningfully employ the other's personal construct dimensions.

Support for the content congruency interpretation of premature and nonpremature termination is found in two different therapy groups, one which is a more seriously disturbed, longer-term group, and the other which is a less disturbed, shorter-term group. Support for the hypothesis is particularly strong when congruence is measured on the combined contents of client and therapist central or more organizing types of construction. Although no hypothesis was stated, a relationship between prematurity and lower client-therapist organizational (FIC) congruence was evident, particularly in the longer-term therapy assignment group. Apparently premature termination may be related to lower client-therapist congruence in both the content and organization of their personal construct systems.

A survey of actuarial and therapist rating data suggest that therapists may perceive their longer-term, nonpremature clients as more similar to themselves by attributing more creativity and greater maturity to them than to their premature clients. Moreover, longer-term, nonpremature clients tend to be slightly older and more advanced academically than premature clients assigned to longer-term therapy. Although these differences are apparent, they are not significant statistically. Moreover, these differences are not evident in the variable-term group. Examination of the first Rep Tests taken by clients assigned to longer-term therapy does not reveal any significant differences between premature and nonpremature clients either in the content or organization of their personal constructs. Examination of the first Rep Tests taken by variable-term clients does not reveal an organizational difference; however, nonprematures in this group are scored significantly higher in the content areas of "high status" ($p < .02$) and "low morality" ($p < .05$). Since thirty-one categories were examined, the appearance of only two significant differences cannot be taken very seriously.

Assuming that our measures of Rep Test content and organization are meaningful and encompass important aspects of personality, it seems reasonable, then, to conclude that any one of the prematurely terminating clients, if assigned to a more congruent therapist, might have emerged as a nonpremature client. This type of reasoning is not very comforting for those therapists who adhere to the idea that the outcome of therapy is only a matter of proper technique and adequate training.

CHAPTER FIVE

CONGRUENCE AND IMPROVEMENT

IMPROVEMENT IN THERAPY REFERS TO CONSTRUCTIVE CHANGE WHEREAS nonpremature termination refers to the maintenance of the therapy dyad. The relationship between these two dimensions is a complex one. Clients who terminate prematurely most likely are unimproved. However, clients who do *not* terminate prematurely may or may not be improved. The most enjoyable therapy hours may not be the most constructive ones, and something beyond client-therapist congruence may facilitate more profound change.

Continuation of the therapy dyad may increase the probability of improvement in therapy; however, variables other than minimal congruence are hypothesized to be important in explaining constructive change in longer-term, more seriously disturbed clients. It was our concern with the other variables that led to an investigation of improvement as related to organizational incongruence.

Beginning with the general statement that *maintenance of interpersonal communication in the early phase of a therapy relationship requires, in addition to some minimal degree of shared meaningfulness, a difference in the organizational structures of a client and his therapist,* two derivative hypotheses were stated. Hypothesis IV will encompass the organizational difference between a client and his therapist at the beginning of therapy and the relationship between this difference and improvement. Hypothesis V will focus on change in the organizational structures of client and therapist.

ORGANIZATIONAL INCONGRUENCE AND IMPROVEMENT IN NONPREMATURE, LONGER-TERM THERAPY DYADS

Hypothesis IV: Nonprematurely terminating clients in C-T dyads which show greater congruence in the organization of their personal constructs at the beginning of therapy will evidence less improvement. Nonprematurely terminating clients in C-T dyads which show less congruence in the organization of their personal constructs will evidence more improvement.

Methodological Construction. Constructive therapy relationships are based on the therapist's ability to subsume his client's constructs, and one important way for a therapist to subsume them is with methodological structures which contribute to some newness in the relationship and assist his client in perceiving his problems within new contexts. The methodological structure in this investigation is defined by the organizational difference between the client and his therapist. More specifically, methodological construction is defined by the difference in FIC (cp) scores within each dyad, a smaller difference score signifying greater congruence.

At this point in the discussion, the reader may become confused about the paradoxical implications of organizational congruence-incongruence. In the previous chapter it was stated that incongruence in both content and organization is associated with premature termination. In this chapter we are pointing out the facilitating effects of incongruency. To make sense of this apparent dilemma, it is important to recognize that it is a moderate amount of client-therapist organizational incongruency, found in the context of greater content congruency, that appears to facilitate improvement. More will be said about this point later in the chapter.

Improvement. Briefly reviewing the improvement criterion which was discussed in Chapter 2, twenty-four longer-term clients were divided into the twelve clients who improved most and the twelve clients who improved least by three judges working from pre- and terminal research typescripts. The twenty-four clients also were subdivided into six minimally improved and eighteen improved clients.

The question of whether any of these clients improved is answered, in part, by the observations of the judges and therapists that many of these clients seemed to change in constructive ways. Furthermore, a special study of unimprovement in the variable-term clients, in which two independent judges (Danforth and Froburg) read the pre- and post-therapy typescripts, shows that these judges could agree that twenty-seven clients or 75 per cent of thirty-six clients are at least somewhat improved. This study, as well as other research done within the same clinical setting, suggests that one may assume that at least 50 per cent of the longer-term clients made some improvement. A study of quartile ratings done on the twenty-four longer-term clients suggests that only six clients can definitely be placed in a minimally improved or unimproved group.

Procedure. Subjects were twenty-four longer-term, moderately to severely disturbed clients of both sexes, thirteen males and eleven females, seen once a week by eight therapists, each of whom carried three cases for the minimal period of twelve interviews and thirteen weeks. Rep Tests taken by the clients and their therapists were juxtaposed within each therapy dyad as explained in a previous section. The time interval between client Rep Test 1 and Rep Test 2 is approximately the same for each client.

Predictions, Scoring, and Analysis. The following prediction was derived from Hypothesis IV: Clients and therapists in most improved dyads will have larger FIC (cp) score differences at the beginning of therapy than clients and therapists in least improved dyads. Distribution differences between the most and least improved dyads were analyzed by the Mann-Whitney U statistic.

Results. Since it has been shown that premature terminators from longer-term assignment are less congruent with their therapists at the beginning of therapy in both content and organization of their personal constructs, the above prediction may seem to be in jeopardy. This is not the case. Most improved, longer-term clients are found more often in those dyads in which there is a greater difference, i.e., nine or more points, between the FIC (cp) score of the client and that of his therapist ($U = 39$, $p < .05$). As a cross check on this finding, the author predicted that the eighteen improved clients will be found more often in less congruent dyads at the beginning of therapy than the six minimally improved clients. This prediction was supported ($U = 25$, $p < .05$). The hypothesis that structural incongruence in the therapy dyad may facilitate psychotherapy again is upheld.

ORGANIZATIONAL CONVERGENCE AND IMPROVEMENT IN NONPREMATURE, LONGER-TERM THERAPY DYADS

Hypothesis V: Greater improvement in the nonpremature terminator is accompanied by a convergence with his therapist in the organization of their personal construct systems.

Convergence. If greater organizational incongruence, within the context of greater content congruence at the beginning of therapy, is a source of methodological stimulation for the client, one may expect convergence of FIC (cp) scores in those client-therapist dyads which initially are more incongruent. Rather than measuring client convergence or divergence in relation to the first juxtaposed FIC (cp) score of the therapist, the possibility of therapist change was accepted and convergence-divergence was plotted by comparing the first juxtaposed client-therapist scores with their last juxtaposed scores. Therapists did contribute to the convergence or divergence scores, but not to the extent of their clients. A review of Table 3.5, Chapter 3, indicates that month to month change in therapist FIC (cp) scoring is minimal over a three-month period. Consistency correlations for the therapist group range from .88 to .95. Correlations for the longer-term therapy group range from .41 to .51. When FIC (cp) change is plotted between Rep Test 1 and Rep Test 4, which was taken three months later, client change is significantly greater than therapist change ($\chi^2 = 5.5, p < .02$). Based on a twenty-nine–point FIC scoring spread, the median change score for therapists is 3.5, for clients, 7.0.

Procedure and Predictions. Defining convergence as a decrease in FIC (cp) difference, measured from the first juxtaposed client-therapist Rep Tests at the beginning of therapy to the last juxtaposed Rep Tests at the thirteenth week, and divergence as an increase in the difference, two predictions are made. First, the twelve most improved clients, in contrast to the twelve least improved clients, will be found more often in dyads showing convergence. Second, the eighteen improved clients, in contrast to the six minimally improved clients, will be found more often in dyads showing convergence. Fisher's Exact Probability was used as the primary statistical test and dyads neither converging nor diverging were split, one-half being designated as converging, the other half as diverging. A secondary statistical test, the Mann-Whitney U, was used to ascertain the significant of score distribution differences between most and least improved groups.

Results. There is support for both predictions. The twelve most improved clients are found more often in converging dyads ($F_p = .05$; $U = 37$, $p < .02$). The eighteen improved clients also are found more often in converging dyads ($F_p = .05$; $U = 28$, $p < .05$). Table 5.1 shows the number of clients diverging and converging; first in the most-least improved subgroups; then in the improved-minimally improved subgroups.

TABLE 5.1

Client-Therapist FIC (cp) Convergence and Divergence in Most-Least Improved and Improved-Minimally Improved, Longer-term, Nonpremature Dyads

	Divergence	Neither	Convergence
12 Most Improved	2	1	9
12 Least Improved	8	1	3
18 Improved	5	2	11
6 Minimally Improved	5	0	1

Summary Hypothesis IV and V. Employing the client-therapist FIC (cp) score difference as a methodological structure and change inferred from pre- and terminal therapy typescripts as a criterion of improvement, clients in therapy dyads with greater FIC (cp) score differences at the beginning of therapy were judged to be more improved. Additionally, convergence in FIC (cp) scores was found to be greater among the most improved clients.

A PERSONAL CONSTRUCT VIEW OF CHANGE

Kelly (1955) distinguished between several types of change. One type of change, *slot change,* was differentiated from a more profound and lasting *organizational* change. A person who changes his self-conception and/or his behavior from one pole of a personal construct to another may easily revert to the pole from which he departed. Slot change without organizational change may be unreliable and can lead to an extreme situation in which the individual shifts back and forth across one or more of his construct dimensions.

Theoretically, slot change can be more easily precipitated than a change in the hierarchical and relational arrangements of personal construct dimensions. Furthermore, slot change should occur more readily on construct dimensions which are more peripheral than central to the construct system. Some evidence for this latter hypothesis was presented by Varble and Landfield (1969). In this study, discrepancy changes between client-self and client-ideal ratings were found to be greater on construct dimensions ranked as less important.

Our theoretical position on slot change and organizational change suggested that hypotheses about organizational incongruence and convergence should be used in conjunction with the longer-term *LT 24* clients, all of whom were seen for at least twelve sessions. It also seemed reasonable to apply a hypothesis about slot change to the shorter-term *VT 36* clients, only six of whom were seen for as many as twelve sessions. Slot change conceivably would be the most appropriate type of change to expect from shorter-term clients who are not seriously maladjusted.

That *VT 36* clients are less maladjusted than *LT 24* clients at intake is supported by the way in which these clients were preselected. *LT 24* clients should represent the most seriously disturbed clients seen in therapy within a student health service complex. *VT 36* clients should represent the typical intake of the clinic, the majority of whom are less seriously disturbed. As a cross check on the assumption that, as a group, *VT 36* clients are less maladjusted than *LT 24* clients at intake, typescripts of intake interviews of five of the most improved, longer-term cases were mixed with the intake interviews of five of the most improved, variable-term cases. Dr. Donald Poe separated the ten typescripts into the most and least maladjusted. Results of this analysis tend to support the greater maladjustment of *LT 24*. Four longer-term clients were placed in the most maladjusted category. Four variable-term clients were placed in the least maladjusted category and two clients could not be differentiated.

CLIENT CONVERGENCE WITH THERAPIST IDEALS AND IMPROVEMENT IN SHORTER-TERM DYADS

In the first part of this chapter a case was made for organizational convergence in therapy dyads in which clients were longer-term and whose problems were more serious than those found in our variable-term group. In this study, we will provide evidence that improvement in less disturbed, variable-term clients, seen for an average of six to seven interviews, is linked with the convergence of the client's self-ratings with his therapist's stated ideals, but as plotted within the dimensional framework of the client rather than that of his therapist. In other words, the next hypothesis will focus on slot change.

Hypothesis VI: Improvement in therapy is accompanied by a shift in the present-self of the client towards the ideal of the therapist as described within the language dimensions, i.e., personal constructs, of the client rather than those of his therapist (Landfield & Nawas, 1964).

Procedure. Subjects were thirty-six variable-term and less disturbed clients of both sexes, seventeen males and nineteen females, seen once a week by six therapists. The construct dimensions from the first Rep Tests of each client-therapist pair were mixed and placed on a rating sheet comprised of thirteen-point scales. Once a month from initial testing each client and his therapist rank ordered the mixed client-therapist construct dimensions and were asked to do the following self-sorts on the rating sheets: (a) rate yourself as you see yourself now in the present; (b) rate your ideal; and (c) rate the other person as you see him now—client rating his therapist and therapist rating his client. Assuming that the therapists would be fairly stable in rating their ideals during the period of data collection, they completed only one ideal rating sheet. Finally, working from short pre- and posttherapy typescripts, three highly experienced external judges classified the clients into two equal groups, those improving most and those improving least.

Predictions, Scoring, and Analysis. Two predictions were made: (1) The direction of change in the present-self of the most improved clients, from the beginning to termination of therapy, would be significantly toward the ideal of the therapist as described in the client's language dimensions. (2) When the therapist's, rather than the client's, language dimensions are used as the basis for determining the direction of change in the present-self of the client, from the beginning to termination of therapy, the direction toward or away from the therapist's ideal would be unrelated to improvement-unimprovement.

Three scores are compared: the client's initial present-self (P1), the client's terminal present-self (P2), and the therapist's ideal-self (I). We started with I and scored every construct dimension anywhere from zero to thirteen depending on where the therapist rated his ideal on each dimension. The next step was to determine, through comparing P1 and P2, whether the change was in the direction of I or away from it. Our interest was in the direction of the change and not in the degree of change. The following example will illustrate the scoring method. Suppose in one protocol a therapist rated his ideal as 12 on the dimension of *warm-*

distant. Suppose also that the client rated himself as 3 on P1 and as 8 on P2 on the same dimension. The change, from 3 to 8, shows a movement toward I. Suppose, instead, that the client's P1 on *warm-distant* was 8 and he rated P2 at 3. Since the therapist's ideal was rated at 12, the change from P1 to P2 indicates a movement away from I. Whenever the therapist's I rating was equidistant between the client's P1 and P2, movement was not scored. Bypassing the therapist's I rating sometimes was scored as movement away. For example, if the client rated his P1 as 2 and P2 as 7, and the therapist rated his I as 4, movement away was scored.

When scoring was completed, each client was placed in either the category of "moving away" or "moving toward" I, depending on which category the majority of his construct dimensions fell. The four cells of the 2 × 2 table which pertain to prediction were these: most improved and change toward I on client's (or therapist's) construct dimensions; most improved and change away from I; least improved and change toward I; least improved and change away from I.

Results. The predictions that the most improved clients will move toward the ideals of their therapists (1) when the change is plotted on the client's own dimensions, but (2) not when the change is plotted on the therapist's dimensions, are supported. On client dimensions 14.5 most improved move toward therapist ideals and 3.5 move away; 5 least improved move toward therapist ideals and 13 move away ($\chi^2 = 10.1$, $p < .01$). On therapist dimensions 12.5 most improved move toward therapist ideals and 5.5 move away; 11 least improved move toward therapist ideals and 7 move away ($\chi^2 = .30$, $p < .80$). The number of movements toward and away from therapist ideals was equal in five cases on client dimensions and one case on therapist dimensions. In such instances, one-half case was placed in the hypothesis hold cell and the other half case in the not-hold cell.

Initial Congruence in Ratings. The question arises as to whether most improved, shorter-term dyads of *VT 36,* clients showing greater convergence of client-self with therapist ideal, initially are more incongruent than least improved dyads in either (a) client-therapist ideal ratings, or (b) client-self–therapist ideal ratings, plotted within the client's dimensional system. The answer to both parts of this question is in the negative. Most improved clients do not differ from least improved clients.

A similar analysis in which only nonpremature most and least improved clients are compared also indicates no significant differences at the beginning of therapy. However, when *VT* premature terminators are compared with *VT* nonpremature terminators, group differences become apparent. The prematurely terminating dyads tend to be less congruent in the sharing of ideals than nonpremature dyads ($U = 50$, $Z = 2.1$, $p < .04$, two-tailed).

Summary Hypothesis VI. The hypothesis that improvement in the shorter-term therapy clients is accompanied by a shift in the present-self toward the ideal of the therapist, as described within the personal construct dimensions of the client rather than those of his therapist, is supported by the data. When clients are asked to rate themselves within the social language framework of their therapists, identification with therapist ideals is not apparent. Within certain therapeutic contexts, improved clients might conceivably move toward the ideals of their therapists within the therapists' construct dimensions. The conditions for such an outcome might be that (1) clients and their therapists employ very similar dimensions, (2) therapy contact is of six months duration or longer, and (3) therapists actively teach the words and meanings of their own social language. Since most therapy is of shorter duration and since many therapists presumably do try to communicate with their clients in a language which the clients will best understand, it is more likely that the improved client will move toward the therapist's values which are plotted within the client's own language framework—or personal construct system.

Perspective. A client-therapist difference in personal construct organization at the beginning of therapy has been linked with improvement in more disturbed, longer-term clients who do not prematurely terminate. Clients and therapists in most improved dyads are more incongruent in their organization scores than members of least improved dyads. Clients and therapists in most improved dyads also converge more in their organization scores than members of least improved dyads. These results are interpreted within personal construct theory as supporting the influence of methodological construction, defined as the difference between the FIC (cp) organization score of a therapist and that of his client. The meaning of organizational incongruence in longer-term, improved dyads was elaborated further by hypothesizing that incongruence in organization facilitates therapy primarily in the context of greater content congruence.

The prediction that greater organizational incongruence will be found in the context of greater improvement was not employed with the less disturbed, variable-term clients who were seen for half as many sessions as the longer-term clients. The rationale for applying the organizational hypothesis only to the longer-term group is based on the distinction made between slot change and organizational change, the former change being associated more with shorter-term, supportive therapy which is most appropriate with less disturbed clients.

Stating the theoretical distinction between slot change and organizational change in operational terminology, a change in self-conception and behavior which is plotted only within personal construct dimensions, i.e., slot change, is a more likely occurrence and is more easily precipitated in therapy than is a change in the interrelationships between two construct dimensions or in the relative importance of these constructs, i.e., organizational change. It seemed reasonable that improvement in less disturbed clients would not require the more basic organizational changes that would require a longer period of therapy. The rationale for thinking that a more supportive therapy could be used successfully with the variable-term clients makes good sense when it is realized that the clients assigned to longer-term therapy, i.e., *LT 24* and *PT 13,* are significantly less congruent with their therapists in the content of their personal constructs than are the shorter-term clients with their therapists, i.e., *VT 36* ($\chi^2 = 4.7, p < .05$).

The hypothesis that the convergence of client-self with therapist ideal will take place in most improved dyads of the variable-term group, but only on the dimensions of the client, was confirmed. Even though our research design did not permit testing this slot change hypothesis in the longer-term therapy group, it is conceivable that such change also may occur in this latter group; however, such change would be more likely to occur later in therapy. The rationale for this hypothesis is that the greater content commonality found among the shorter-term dyads would facilitate a more rapid identification process which might not be possible in the longer-term, less congruent dyads.

The Rosenthal hypothesis (1955) that improved clients will internalize their therapists' values was confirmed, but only in the context of the construct dimensions or the social language of the client. Whether this finding is peculiar to therapy which focuses more on the conceptual systems and language of the client cannot be assessed. It would seem as though a therapy aimed at teaching the client the therapist's own social language would take longer than one in which more emphasis is placed on working within the language framework of the client. Certainly an average of six or seven interviews is too brief a treatment to accomplish this goal.

CHAPTER SIX

CONGRUENCE AND ATTRIBUTED PATHOLOGY

To state that observing and describing people are not merely straightforward, objective, and uncontaminated tasks is not a revelation within the field of psychology. Nevertheless, psychological scientists and particularly clinicians need to be reminded, from time to time, of the paradoxical nature of observation, sometimes reflecting some valid aspect of the observed, sometimes reflecting the nature of the observer or the interrelationship between the observer and the observed. This chapter will focus on the interrelationship between the observed client and his observing therapist as measured by congruency in the content of their personal construct systems, and the implications of this congruency-incongruency as to how the therapist describes his client at different points in therapy.

The following hypothesis was made concerning the idea that confusion, uncertainty, and anxiety experienced by both client and therapist may be related to difficulties in communication. *Hypothesis VII: Client-therapist congruence in the content of their personal constructs is inversely related to the therapist's negative clinical description of his client.* Restating this hypothesis, lower coefficients of congruence will be related to a greater number of negative clinical descriptions appearing on the Therapist Rating Schedule.

The Therapist Rating Schedule. Following the second interview and every two weeks thereafter, the eight therapists of the longer-term clients filled out the Therapist Rating Schedule (TRS) on their clients. The TRS is divided into sections I and II. The first section includes rating items which have more specific theoretical implications for personal construct theory. For example, in Section I, Items A and I focus on the client's willingness to explore and to take a multidimensional approach to events. These items, as well as several others, can be derived from statements of personal construct theory. The second section includes rating items which are less specifically related to any one theory and represent typical statements of pathology and change in pathology which any clinician might use in describing a client or patient. Anxiety, hostility, confusion, rigidity, agitation, and defensiveness are encompassed by items of Section II. Certain rating responses in this section have been marked with asterisks, which were not used in the original schedule, to designate more negative or pathological descriptions of the client. What is or is not negative description is debatable in some instances. For example, under certain conditions hostility or anxiety could be considered appropriate behavior. However, a casual sampling of opinion from colleagues supports our decisions about what clinicians might consider negative description.

THERAPIST RATING SCHEDULE

SECTION I

A. *Verbalized Desire to Explore:* The student states that he would like to try out or consider new ideas and behavior. (It is *not* necessary for the student actually to be thinking or behaving differently.) (yes) (no)

B. *Developmental Concept of Change:* The student expresses an attitude toward himself and/or others from which one may infer an understanding that personality is developmental. He realizes that one changes with age and experience, that attitudinal and behavioral change is part of the developmental process. (yes) (no)

C. *Optimal Generalization:* The student either dwells overly much on that which is specific, or on the other hand, dwells overly much on that which is general.
   1. Overly specific (yes) (no)
   2. Overly general (yes) (no)

D. *Disengagement:* The student is unable or unwilling to talk about an aspect of his past, present, or future.
   1. Disengagement from the past (yes) (no)
   2. Disengagement from the present (yes) (no)
   3. Disengagement from the future (yes) (no)

E. *Hope:* The student expresses a positive anticipation that problems can be resolved. Feels that he probably can resolve his own problems (yes) (no)

F. *Central Identity Under One's Control:* The student expresses the feeling that he has certain important or central beliefs, values, attitudes, and behavior that will not change unless he makes the decision to change himself. (yes) (no)

G. *Initiative in Therapy Situations:* The student shows initiative in attempting to resolve his problem. Initiative may be defined in terms of:
   1. Suggesting topics for discussion (yes) (no)
   2. Taking an active role in discussion (yes) (no)
   3. Feeling free to disagree with the therapist (yes) (no)
   4. Showing a desire to think things through on his own (yes) (no)

H. *Willingness to Experience Incongruity:* The student does not avoid the experiencing of incongruity, contrast, or conflict. He is willing to discuss topics of a paradoxical or conflicting nature. (yes) (no)

I. *Use of Alternatives:* The student can employ, to some degree, a multidimensional approach in discussing himself and/or others. One may infer that at least on occasion he is capable of perceiving an event in more than one way. (yes) (no)

SECTION II

A. 1. Seems improved today from last session______
   About the same today______
   *Seems worse today than last session______
   2. *This is a highly disturbed person______
   This is not a highly disturbed person______

B. 1. *Case handling more difficult today than last session______
   No change on dimension of difficulty of case handling______
   Case handling less difficult today than last session______
   2. *This person is hard to work with______
   This person is easy to work with______

C. 1. *Seems more confused today than last session______
   No change on dimension of confusion______
   Seems less confused today than last session______
   2. *This is a very confused person______
   This is not a very confused person______

D. 1. More cooperative today than last session______
No change on dimension of cooperativeness______
*Less cooperative today than last session______
2. This is a cooperative person______
*This is an uncooperative person______

E. 1. More motivated today than last session______
No change on dimension of motivation______
*Less motivated today than last session______
2. This is a highly motivated person______
*This is not a highly motivated person______

F. 1. *More anxious today than last session______
No change on dimension of anxiety______
Less anxious today than last session______
2. *This is a very anxious person______
This is not a very anxious person______

G. 1. *More rigid today than last session______
No change on dimension of rigidity______
Less rigid today than last session______
2. *This is a very rigid person______
This is not a very rigid person______

H. 1. Makes more definite statements today than last session______
No change on dimension of statement definiteness______
*Makes less definite statements today than last session______
2. A definite person______
*Not a definite person______

I. 1. *More hostile today than last session______
No change on dimension of hostility______
Less hostile today than last session______
2. *A hostile person______
Not a hostile person______

J. 1. *More apathetic today than last session______
No change on dimension of apathy______
Less apathetic today than last session______
2. *A very apathetic person______
Not a very apathetic person______

K. 1. Shows more consistency today than last session______
No change on dimension of consistency______
*Shows less consistency today than last session______
2. A consistent person______
*An inconsistent person______

L. 1. *Shows more agitation today than last session_______
No change on dimension of agitation_______
Shows less agitation today than last session_______
2. *An agitated person_______
Not an agitated person_______

M. 1. *Seems more defensive today than last session_______
No change on dimension of defensiveness_______
Seems less defensive today than last session_______
2. *A defensive person_______
Not a defensive person_______

N. 1. *A poor bet for therapy_______
A good bet for therapy_______

O. 1. *A long term case_______
A short term case_______

P. I feel more comfortable with the client today than last session_______
No change on dimension of my comfort_______
*I feel less comfortable today than last session_______

Q. I think I understand the client better today than last session_______
No change on dimension of my understanding_______
*I think I understand the client less well today than last session_______

CLIENT-THERAPIST CONGRUENCE AND THE TRS

Clinicians not only have their own more personal social language frameworks but they also employ language dimensions which can be described as professional constructs. The professional dimensions not only capture various aspects of pathology but they also are identified by their pathological poles. We talk about anxious clients who become more anxious or less anxious, hostile clients who become more or less hostile, and defensive clients who may become less defensive. We also talk about relaxed, self-actualizing, amiable, affectionate, and creative clients. However, it does seem more difficult for the clinician to easily describe his clients in more positive and constructive ways, and when he does so, he may refer to the pathological pole as he describes his client in a more hopeful manner. There is nothing mysterious about this pathological bias. If the people with whom one interacts professionally are emotionally disturbed, there would be a tendency to place greater emphasis on the pathological end of the dimension and to perceive the opposite polar description more as an absence of the former condition rather than a positive alternative. To the extent that we, as clinicians, are rooted in this type of pathological construction there may be little hope for our clients. Most professionals who serve their clients will consider positive alternatives to pathology, and in states of greater and lesser awareness fall back upon their own personal construct systems, the poles of which may not be as heavily laden with pathology.

The above introduction simply orients the reader to my doubts about the value of certain aspects of professional thinking. These doubts provide a context for a hypothesis in which incongruency is related to attributed pathology.

Procedure and Predictions. It was predicted that higher coefficients of C-T content congruency will be related to lower total negative description scores at four different testing periods. Both longer-term clients (*LT 24*) and premature clients (*PT 13*) assigned for longer-term therapy were used in testing the above prediction. Client-therapist Rep Tests, juxtaposed in time at client Rep Tests 1, 2, 3, and 4, were also juxtaposed to the TRS which was completed at the second, fourth, eighth, and twelfth weeks of therapy. At each of the four different periods of therapy, client-therapist congruency coefficients, transformed into ranks, were correlated with the total pathology scores which also were transformed into ranks. Pathology scores were based on Section II of the TRS, items A through O.

Results. Table 6.1 shows how inaccurate my prediction was. Not only is Hypothesis VII not supported but the results support the opposite position that client-therapist congruence in the content of their personal constructs is directly related to the therapist's negative clinical description of his client. At the beginning of therapy there is a low positive correlation between client-therapist congruence and negative description on the TRS in the longer-term group ($p < .10$, two-tailed). The same relationship is found in the premature group. This relationship rises precipitously at the fourth week in the longer-term group ($p < .001$), then declines somewhat at the eighth week ($p < .05$), and is nonsignificant at twelve weeks.

Dyads Used as Own Control. The following question was asked in a second analysis in which each of the longer-term dyads was used as its own control: When congruency increases or decreases in an individual dyad, does negative scoring also increase or decrease? Selecting a higher and lower coefficient from the four congruency coefficients available on each therapy dyad, it was predicted, in accordance with our previous finding, that the higher coefficient of congruency in each dyad would

TABLE 6.1

Coefficients of Client-Therapist Rep Test Content Congruency and Juxtaposed Therapist Ratings of Client Pathology

Relationships	Group	Rep 1	Rep 2	Rep 3	Rep 4
Client-therapist coefficients on 31 contents and pathology ratings	LT 24	$r_s = .35$ $p < .10$	$r_s = .69$ $p < .001$	$r_s = .46$ $p < .05$	$r_s = .18$ p — ns
	PT 13	$r_s = .51$ $p < .10$			

The Spearman rank difference correlation is used with a two-tailed test.

be associated with the higher pathology score. Since seventeen of the twenty-four dyads fit the prediction ($\chi^2 = 4.0$, $p < .05$), the direct relationship between negative description and congruency again is supported.

Summary of Findings on Hypothesis VII. Within and between dyad analyses there is an indication that greater client-therapist congruence in the content of their personal constructs is related to more negative description of the client by his therapist, particularly at the beginning of therapy.

REEXAMINATION OF HYPOTHESIS VII

That higher pathology scores should be found in the context of greater C-T incongruency was based on the idea that a lack of commonality between client and therapist will generate an uneasiness in the relationship to which the therapist will respond by using more negative descriptions of his client. In other words, a highly negative description of one's client may be, in part, a description of difficulties in communication experienced by members of the dyad. This line of reasoning appears to be inappropriate since a sharply contrasting hypothesis was supported: *Revised Hypothesis* VII. Client-therapist congruence in the content of their personal constructs is directly related to the therapist's negative clinical description of his client. This reversal in hypothesis needs to be explained. Why would a therapist who shares greater commonality with his client in the content of his personal language describe his client in more negative ways in the early phase of a therapy relationship?

If we assume that both the client and his therapist employ a complaint-pathology orientation in the beginning stages of the treatment relationship, the hypothesis that congruency is related to attributed pathology makes sense. The more congruent client, sensing the possibility for a freer communication, may reveal more of himself—his behavior, problems, and conflicts—earlier in the therapy sequence. The more congruent therapist may more readily pick up cues of pathology in those with whom he can communicate best.

It is also possible that a therapist could feel threatened by those clients who are more congruent with himself in ways possibly reminiscent of his own past role. The client may embody role characteristics which are rejected by the therapist but which remain a part of the dimensionality of the therapist's personal construct system. More extensive acquaintance with a client would allow the therapist to become aware of the many differences between himself and his client, lessening the negative effects of reminiscence. Studies by Landfield (1955) are relevant to understanding this type of therapist (or client) problem.

If psychotherapy is associated with "getting away from the complaint" and perceiving one's client in a context of strengths, resources, and potentialities for growth, and further, if psychotherapy is associated with a lessening of interpersonal threat experienced within the dyad, one would expect a decrease in the relationship between congruency and professional negativism in the later stages of therapy. In other words, the therapist who is more sensitive to the pathology and negative characteristics of his more congruent client will tend to move away from an emphasis on the negative in the context of a developing relationship with his client. This change away from the negative and toward the positive is partially supported by the following analysis: When the twenty-four clients are separated into the eleven clients assigned higher pathology scores at the beginning of therapy and the thirteen clients assigned lower scores, the initially higher negative scoring group tends to decrease more in negative scoring from TRS 1 to TRS 6 ($U = 41$, $p < .10$, two-tailed).

PERSPECTIVE

Should we relegate to the trash heap the initially stated hypothesis that greater content congruency in personal construction will be associated with less attributed pathology? It is obvious that the hypothesis is inappropriate in the context of the present study; however, the hypothesis should not be discarded. The reason for not discarding the hypothesis is related to a careful review of how subjects in the study were selected and how this selection procedure may have restricted the distribution of scores on both the congruency and attributed pathology measures.

Clients assigned to longer-term therapy represent the more maladjusted students seen within the service context of a university health center. Their problems are neither minor nor psychotic ones. Even though certain cultural differences between clients and therapists may be noted, for the most part the clients and their therapists in the present investigation share a similar socioeconomic background. Furthermore, scoring on the TRS measure of attributed pathology, although varying from zero to twenty-two points, may have been somewhat constricted since the median score at the beginning of therapy is eight points. This relatively low median score suggests that the TRS total negative score may well differentiate between a student client group and a hospitalized patient group. However, the assumption that the average psychotic patient would receive a higher negative score than the average student client does not mean that the TRS is only a measure of pathology. It is conceivable that both congruency and pathology may influence TRS scores, and when the range of pathology is limited, congruency may have the greater influence on the TRS score.

If the above discussion has validity, it may be that the revised hypothesis, in which congruency and attributed pathology are directly related, is most applicable to clinical settings where there is some homogeneity among clients and therapists in their socioeconomic backgrounds. This homogeneity presumably is reflected in their personal constructs. The hypothesis may also be applicable to clients showing homogeneity in level of pathology. Homogeneity in pathology may be found in state hospitals as well as in student clinics. Furthermore, as much constriction in client-therapist congruency may be found in the state hospital setting as would be expected in the student clinic. The only differences between the two settings would be that the congruency scores in the hospital dyads would be lower and their TRS scores would be higher. Nevertheless, we suspect that congruency and attributed pathology are inversely related in the state hospital setting and that the relationship between content congruency and attributed pathology is curvilinear when the score distribution on both variables is marked. In other words, higher pathology scores at the beginning of therapy would be associated with either very low or very high client-therapist congruence in the content of their personal constructs.

It seems most plausible that the hypothesis, as it was stated originally, is most appropriately related to research done by authors such as Hollingshead and Redlich (1958) who found that the psychotic label, a symbol of greater pathology, was applied by middle class professionals more frequently to their hospitalized, lower class patients who were different but not necessarily "sicker" than their middle class patients. If we were to take the seemingly ridiculous position that the revised congruency-pathology hypothesis can be applied even when subjects drawn from different populations are mixed in the same research group, we then would have to assume that the generic label of psychotic and the language typically used to describe psychotic behavior have few implications for understanding patient individuality, whereas the language of the TRS lends itself to more individualized use, and furthermore, can be used more readily when thinking about clients who are more content congruent with oneself. Even though this extreme application of the revised congruency-pathology hypothesis is intriguing, it seems more reasonable to believe that a more congruent therapist will perceive his client more negatively within the context of a study in which the clients and therapists share a common background, which implies at least a moderate degree of congruency in their personal construct systems. However, when client-therapist incongruency is maximized, as exemplified by the patient-professional dyad in a typical state mental hospital, the relationship between congruency and attributed pathology may be reversed and the relationship becomes inverse rather than direct.

The explanation for the direct, as opposed to inverse, linkage between client-therapist congruency and attributed pathology cannot be determined from our data. However, two hypotheses have been stated. A problem orientation held by both client and therapist, in the context of greater content congruency or familiarity, may contribute to higher pathology scores. A second explanation focuses on a type of interpersonal threat in which greater congruency is associated with distortions of one's perception of the other person. Whatever the most appropriate explanation may be, the psychotherapist should be cautious about anchoring himself to his first impressions.

BEYOND CONGRUENCY

In the preceding chapters we emphasized the idea that the personal construct systems of both the subject and the scientist should be considered. Evidence was presented which supports the greater meaningfulness of one's own personal constructs. Furthermore, a relationship between dyadic incongruency and premature termination in psychotherapy was found in two different groups. If we accept this relationship between incongruency and premature termination, are we necessarily caught with the negative implications of this incongruency? In other words, must we assume that an initial incongruence with our clients will incapacitate us as psychotherapists? The answer to this question is yes. However, it may be possible that a therapist can quickly expand his understandings of his client's personal construct system. The following clinical chapters were written to facilitate this process of communication.

CHAPTER SEVEN

CLINICAL APPRAISAL AND OTHER EXPLORATIONS

PREVIOUS CHAPTERS HAVE ENCOMPASSED THE MORE FORMAL theoretical and statistical aspects of our study. This approach has been abstractive in a way that obscures the more individual natures of our clients. However, we are essentially interested in the person as well as the full array of data available about him. This clinical chapter has been written to give my readers and myself some feeling of closure on the person—the basic unit of the investigation. To facilitate this closure, Rep Test protocols, in part or in whole, of five clients are considered together with certain background information. The first two clients, one of whom is a premature terminator, were selected because their protocols illustrate the peculiar nature of construing. Although some of their construct dimensions may not seem logical, these constructs may be psychologically meaningful. The last three clients, all longer-term therapy cases, were chosen because their protocols were among the most interesting ones in this particular group. Although these clients understood that they were participating in a research project, care has been taken to mask their identities.

As the personal construct psychologist reviews the construct dimensions of a client, he assumes that important observable behaviors of the client may well be encompassed by these verbalized construct dimensions. He assumes also that potentialities for behavior are encompassed by these dimensions. Rather than viewing the client as a collection of behaviors which the psychologist then orders within his own system, an attempt is made to understand the client as a system builder. What constructions does the client employ and how are they organized? What do such constructions and organizations of constructions imply?

Now quite obviously some verbalizable constructs may not appear on one Rep Test, and certain important constructs cannot be put into words easily. Furthermore, detailed information is lacking about the operational definitions of these constructs. Nevertheless, one begins by hypothesizing with the information at hand, with the knowledge that many ridiculous implications may be read into the client's protocol. The personal construct psychologist will employ the material from any Rep Test procedure as a catalyst for understanding something about the thinking, feeling, and behaving of his client, and as interpretable within the client's theoretical system. This task is difficult because even the personal construct psychologist must encompass the other person's system within his own system. It is inconceivable that one person could understand another person only within the other person's system. But to believe that the other person does have a system which is organized in some fashion and which has particular implications for that person is a type of personal construction that allows for and encourages the construing of another's system. Just as the assumption of a degree of freedom for one's own behavior may allow one to be a bit more creative, the belief that the other person behaves within his theoretical system may help one to perceive and understand a bit of that system. At least such a supposition is an exciting one, and it just might be a good one.

IMPLICATIONS OF CONTRAST

Sometimes the ways in which ordinary people contrast social events are most peculiar, and taken seriously, suggest intriguing hypotheses about how people think which ordinarily might be overlooked. For example, the contrasts *musical* as opposed to *tyrantish, mean* as opposed to *studious, loving* as opposed to *dumb, kind* as opposed to *impatient,* and *free* as opposed to *busy* all have interesting implications for thinking and behavior. Taken literally, an acquaintance who lacks interest in music might be treated with some suspicion by the person using the contrast *musical versus tyrantish.* Furthermore, a sudden dimming of this person's own interest in music might presage behavior correlated with the role of tyrant. The contrast *free* versus *busy,* not found in a dictionary of antonyms, suggests that an absence of externally observed hard work may imply something other than laziness, lack of involvement, depression, or physical sickness.

CLIENT JOE

Figure 7.1 shows a Rep Test protocol given by a client who terminated therapy after only two weeks and two interviews. The therapist could not explain the sudden termination and the client, whom we will refer to as Joe, told the research interviewer that he could no longer talk with his therapist.

Focusing on the content of his contrasting descriptions, *attitude* and *math* (constructs 10 and 15), convey little meaning to the external observer. And the contrasts to these descriptions, *carefree* and *tramp,* fail to clarify the nature of these contrasts. One may wonder if these statements are contrasts. If they are contrasts, are they pitched at different levels of abstraction or do they represent a most private language system? That such contrasts may well be antithetical is given support by Resnick and Landfield (1961).

The skilled clinician may find many things of interest in this protocol and particularly so if he assumes, along with personal construct psychologists, that these dimensions of meaning which are applied to others may be turned back upon Joe. When Joe is *not perfect* (construct 5), does he feel irresponsible? Does he behave more effectively (construct 8) when he is *not afraid?* Is he trying to close out the frustrating outer world (construct 9) when he does *not care?* When Joe is *not trying hard on the athletic field* (construct 12), does he feel *selfish?*

Joe's Rep Test responses suggest great variation in the communication value of his construct descriptions, and when FIC (c) and FIC (p) scores are analyzed, no relationships whatsoever appear among either his fifteen descriptive constructs (row patterns) or his fifteen people constructs (column patterns). This total lack of grid organization is a rare occurrence and suggests conceptual confusion. His frequent use of the nonapplication rating *N* suggests a definitive type of constriction in the use of his personal constructs.

Summarizing the Rep Test analysis, it may be hypothesized that Joe is confused, narrowly fixed in his approach to life, and may have difficulties in communicating with other people. The following excerpts from Joe's intake and terminal research interviews tend to support the hypothesis of confusion, constriction, and difficulties in communication.

JOE'S INTAKE INTERVIEW

I: Tell me very briefly what it is that brought you here to make an appointment.

FIGURE 7.1

NAMES

1	2	3	4	5	6	7	8	9	10	11	12	13	14	15		1	2
(1)	1	2	N	N	N	(2)	N	N	N	2	2	N	1	N	1	KIND	STUPID
1	(1)	1	1	2	N	N	1	N	N	2	2	(1)	1	N	2	DEPENDABLE	IGNORANT
1	N	(1)	1	N	N	N	N	N	N	(2)	N	N	1	N	3	PERSONALITY	BUM
2	2	2	2	2	2	(1)	N	N	2	(1)	2	2	2	2	4	UNAWARE	FRIENDLY
N	1	1	N	2	2	2	(1)	1	1	2	(2)	1	N	N	5	PERFECTIONIST	IRRESPONSIBLE
N	N	2	(1)	1	(1)	1	N	N	N	N	2	N	2	1	6	WILD	FUNNY
N	2	2	N	N	2	N	N	(1)	N	N	2	2	2	(1)	7	ASTUTE	SPORTSMAN
(1)	2	N	1	1	(1)	N	N	N	N	N	1	2	N	N	8	AFRAID	CONFIDENT
N	2	N	N	(1)	N	N	N	N	N	1	1	2	N	(1)	9	DON'T CARE	AWARE
N	(1)	N	N	2	2	2	(1)	N	N	N	2	N	N	N	10	ATTITUDE	CAREFREE
N	2	2	(1)	1	2	N	2	2	(2)	N	1	2	2	2	11	GET ALONG	ABILITY
N	N	(1)	N	2	1	N	1	N	N	N	N	1	(1)	2	12	ATHLETIC	SELFISH
2	N	1	1	(1)	1	1	N	2	N	N	1	(2)	N	1	13	MIXED UP	CHUBBY
2	2	2	2	2	1	N	1	(1)	1	N	(2)	N	N	N	14	TAKE CHARGE	FOLLOWER
N	1	N	N	2	1	N	N	N	(1)	N	2	1	(1)	N	15	MATH	TRAMP

J: I don't know. It seems like *I'm* pressure, built up over a period of time. It's come to a point, you know, points where . . . I don't think this was the most serious time.

I: Um hum. I see. What, what is the, the experience you have when you refer to pressure?

J: (Pause) Uh. . . . .s it's not tangible; it's just a. Something's push-pushing me. E-mea . . . it's not, eh, it's not an outward forced like any, you know, like any particular person, but it's just a, something, you know, keeps on shoving ya. An it just turns into mistakes.

I: How do you experience this push though? In other words, what does it feel like?

J: (Pause) Like you're just, uh . . . (now slurring) in a, you know, in a, in a depression period, you know what I mean like everything, nothin' seems to set like you want it to be. It jus goes . . . uh, I don't know how to explain it. It just goes against . . . what you think it should be.

I: Does it frighten you some when it comes back?

J: Not so much frightened as aggravated.

I: Aggravated. I see.

J: Mostly with myself, not with others, not with anybody else.

I: Why do you feel that? Why does it aggravate you?

J: Yes, sir.

I: Um hum.

J: I only know, know exactly why but . . . I guess it's just a feeling of dissatisfaction . . . with yourself I mean, if you're it's just that I so, I might not react fast enough in a game or somethin' 'n' that just does somethin' to me and I can't forget it. I mean I, like I played most sports and then every (words are choppy) time you know, I'll stop just to daydream and just, I just think of the things, that, I didn't react the right way to. And everything. I mean I can't bring up any, anything that was good. It's just that the bad points keep on playing over and over in my mind.

. . . .

J: I have, I have, I, it's not that I can't do anythi—. It's just that I have . . . no confidence in myself for things that I do. I mean I have, I have, nn, it's just a lack of trust in myself.

. . . .

J: Well, I mean, uh, people, people couldn't see what I did, you know, what I mean, it sorta, it wasn't as, uh, public as if you'd play sports or something. You know, um, I couldn't, it was more personal than it was public.

I: You mean . . .
J: I mean the grades.

. . . .

I: You went on through the season. How did you wind up? Did you wind up being a pretty good player?
J: Um, according to myself?
I: According to yourself.
J: I think I ended up pretty lousy.
I: I see, how about according to them?
J: Oh, I was about, uh, I guess I was about seventh high league scorer.

. . . .

J: Uh, I, I guess it's just the feeling of giving up. I mean, I know I, I coulda done a lot better caused I loafed during the practices, you know, an my attitude toward the whole, whole game, I just didn't care any more. I mean, I just wanted to be, I just wanted to be, I guess *normal*. I never felt that I was.

. . . .

I: Well, means you must not have too many friends up here then.
J: No sir, I have . . . nn . . . quite a few.
I: You have quite a few? But how close are you—to them?
J: I'm, I'm not close to anyone.
I: O K. One other kind of question. What's your relationship with girls?
J: Do you me—uh, do you mean a lot of 'um?
I: Dating.
J: Do I date a lot?
I: Um hum.
J: Not exceptionally. I imagine just about average.

. . . .

JOE'S TERMINAL INTERVIEW

I: You were beginning to say about . . .
J: Um, it just don't matter to me. I mean, so what if I don't—But, uh, I don't think it'll affect me one w—. I don't know if it will or won't. I guess I just don't care.

. . . .

I: (Pause) How did it come about, that you shifted your feeling of one of rather intense concern, like you say the feeling that you were going batty, to one now of not caring?

J: Uh, there's no particular point where it just went like that, uh, I just don't know. I mean . . . I just don't know how to explain it, uh . . . I guess I just thought I . . . something was wrong and it wasn't . . . something like that, because it doesn't seem to bother me.

I: What about your experience here at the clinic? Mmm, how did you feel about it?

J: Rather hard to adjust.

. . . .

I: You mean you just feel like he somehow didn't particularly care about you? Or did this feeling start before you started seeing him?

J: Well, uh, not that so much that, uh, I just couldn't talk to him; uh, I never could talk to anybody in my life, but a, I just couldn't say what I wanted to say. Somehow I just, I couldn't get myself in the mood to put across what I was thinking.

. . . .

J: Uh, well, this might spec—this is one reason I came, but I, I got a little dog a home. I can sit there an I can talk ta the thing, and I think the thing is hearing me. I mean, it's just . . . she understands a lot better, and she just can't talk back. That's the reason it's easy . . . but, uh . . . I feel a lot more . . . I feel a lot more at home with my dog, than I would with a human being.

I: Do you think that if you would have started with another therapist, that you might have been able to establish this feeling?

J: Can't say. I mean, uh, I have no idea. I don't think nobody could say that. No one could even come close ta thinking what would happen . . . It didn't, 'n I guess you just can't idealize like . . . .

. . . .

I: Is there anything else you think, Joe, about this whole business that might be, uh, might be significant?

J: It's kind of general . . . uh . . .

I: Um hum.

J: (Pause) I can't put my finger on anything in particular, specific. . . .

CLIENT HENRY

Henry, a married graduate student, is the father of several children. He reports that his home life is happy. He also feels he is making satisfactory progress in his academic work. Yet he is in trouble. He has been apprehended for exhibiting himself. At the beginning of therapy Henry was asked to record the names of fifteen acquaintances, which included mother, father, or other family members, teachers, employers, and peer group. Using the traditional form of the Rep Test, he then was asked about combinations of three acquaintances, a different combination each time. "Tell me one way in which two of these three are similar which makes them different from the third." Among the contrasting ways in which Henry responded to this instruction, four sets of contrasts have special significance: *Live life* versus *unhappy, serious* versus *no good, alive* and *full of energy* versus *old-fashioned—ideals,* and *no faith in me* versus *ideals.*

One approach to the content of these four sets of contrasts is to consider what these ideas suggest about the nature of this man's preoccupations. For example, what does the description *no faith in me,* used as a description of others, suggest about this man's own interests, values, and concerns? At another level of analysis, that of organization, inferences are made about whether the four sets of contrasts are interrelated. Using a grid analysis method a strange set of relationships was found. *Live life, alive* and *full of energy, no good,* and *no faith in me* are interrelated. *Unhappy, old-fashioned ideals, serious,* and *ideals* are interrelated. In other words, people who are *alive* and *energetic* are *no good* and *have no faith in Henry. Unhappy* people are *serious, idealistic* and *old-fashioned,* and by inference, may have *some faith in Henry.* If we treat these descriptions of others as important ways of understanding what may be applied to Henry himself, certain interesting questions can be raised about the nature of Henry's problem. His exhibitionism may represent being alive and energetic.

THREE LONGER-TERM CLIENTS

The strategy for the clinical investigation of the last three clients, all from the longer-term therapy group, entails first an analysis of the original as well as the final Rep Tests that were taken by each client. Next, therapist dictations, TRS ratings, and the pretherapy and terminal typescripts are considered. Finally, the Rep Tests are reexamined, this time, in relation to the additional information.

CLIENT GEORGE

George describes his problem as a chronic nervousness which he tries to relieve by drinking. He admits to a drinking problem but is ambivalent about whether or not he is an alcoholic. He also reports a serious auto accident while drinking and states that he talked with a psychiatrist about it, but only briefly. External judges rate him as most maladjusted at intake.

CONSTRUCTS USED AT REP TEST 1

1. Humble versus ambitious, hard worker
2. Success (business-minded) versus opposite of
3. Easygoing versus ambitious, hard worker
4. Ambitious, hard worker versus lazy
5. Outspoken versus quiet, easygoing
6. Nervous versus relaxed
7. Easy to get along with versus hard to get along with
8. Self-conscious versus easygoing
9. Considerate, social-minded versus unintentionally inconsiderate
10. Nervous versus relaxed
11. Humble versus considerate
12. Indifferent versus faithful, friendly
13. Friendly versus self-centered
14. Friendly versus self-centered
15. Fun to be around versus uncomfortable to be around

Scanning the above construct dimensions, three kinds of constructions emerge: those relating to success and ambition, social interaction, and states of psychological distress. Experience with the Rep Test suggests that repeated contents very likely have particular importance for the individual. We find that George has used three constructs of psychological distress, e.g., nervousness. Constructs of ambition are expected on the Rep Tests of college students. However, four dimensions represent a high focus on ambition.

When the content of this protocol is analyzed within the Content Scoring Manual, certain contents are emphasized to a higher degree than is observed in a better adjusted group comprised of twelve males and eighteen females or in the longer-term therapy group. George is high on content connoting "high social interaction," "low forcefulness," "high status," and "emotional arousal." Curiously, he does not use a construct connoting intelligence or its contrast. Most college students use at least one dimension of this type. (Norms for the better adjusted group are shown in Appendix C.)

Several hypotheses or questions about George now can be formulated. Is his idea of success more practical than intellectual? Is it difficult for him to verbalize the dimension of intelligence because he is afraid to think about himself in relation to it? The clinician may stress the latter hypothesis, yet the intellectual dimension could be totally irrelevant. George may simply not value the intellectual area, preferring instead the practical success of business.

Another hypothesis about George is based on the possibility that high use of a content may correlate with the individual's general behavior. Since he scores high on content which connotes "high status," "low forcefulness," and "high social interaction," is it possible that he has high ambitions but is too social and passive to implement his ideal of hard working success?

A grid analysis emphasizes the content of most interrelating constructions. George employs a construct which is linked with three other social dimensions, i.e., *easy to get along with* versus *hard to get along with*. This social cluster is unrelated to a second cluster of three dimensions which link *ambition, hard work,* and *business-mindedness.* A third cluster of constructs, unrelated to the first two clusters, encompasses the psychological distress dimensions. George's construct of *nervous* versus *relaxed* appears twice in this cluster.

This grid analysis of most interrelated constructs supports the less precise scanning method and in addition, shows that the three clusters of ambition, social interaction, and psychological distress are not highly interrelated, raising an interesting question about how to interpret his nervousness. Is his anxiety related to his inability to be a success or to be more effectively social, or is it possible that the anxiety is related to experiences and feelings that are not directly related to ambition and social effectiveness? The independence of the three clusters, as inferred from the grid, suggests that we should not discount the latter hypothesis. Neither should we discount the success-minded–anxiety conflict since his least successful acquaintance is described as "not success-minded, relaxed, and not self-conscious."

An inspection of the ways in which each of George's fifteen acquaintances are rated shows that he has one cluster of similarly rated people. This cluster which is comprised of father, closest friend of the same sex, and most successful acquaintance, also a male, suggests the importance of the male role, father, and the concept of success. All three acquaintances are rated as "success–business-minded, ambitious–hard workers, nervous, and self-conscious." This analysis of presumably more important people, in contrast to the previously discussed cluster analysis, gives support to the success-minded–anxiety hypothesis.

The FIC score, which may reflect the integration of one's social constructs, is also obtained from the grid analysis of construct interrelationships. George's FIC (cp) score of twenty-one is at the median for students making serious suicidal attempts (Landfield, 1969) and is above the medians for the longer-term therapy group, a better adjusted control group, and therapists. Median scores of these groups are shown in Table 7.1. Even though his FIC score is high, he rarely utilizes the *?* rating, using it twice. Mean use of the *?* rating among serious suicidal attempters is thirty-three. George also does not use concrete description, a content employed by students who make serious suicidal attempts. This particular analysis then suggests that George tends to be confused but is not suicidal. Since he does not use a construct which connotes confusion and uncertainty, he will not talk about confusion, although his therapist may describe him in this way.

TABLE 7.1
FIC (cp) Median Scores of SA 5, LT 24, BA 10 and T 7

	SA 5	LT 24	BA 10	T 7
Males	21	17	10	14
Females	21	18	14	—

SA—suicidal
LT—longer-term therapy
BA—better adjusted control
T—therapists

Summarizing the first Rep Test, George appears to be a more passive, dependent type of person whose ideal is a hard working, business success. He is highly anxious and tends to be confused. His anxiety may reflect a success-passivity dilemma as well as a loosening of conceptual structure. There is no evidence that he is actively suicidal, and his construct language is not psychotically bizarre. Finally, the hypothesis that his anxiety is related to experiences not revealed in the Rep Test cannot be discounted.

CONSTRUCTS USED AT REP TEST 4

1. Slow versus energetic
2. Ambitious versus does not care
3. Considerate versus trying to get ahead
4. Hard workers versus lazy
5. Relaxed versus nervous
6. Self-conscious versus easygoing
7. Cares versus does not care

8. Considerate versus loud
9. Social Climbers versus sincere
10. Religious versus does not care
11. Friendly versus to himself
12. Easygoing versus nervous
13. Conceited versus realistic
14. Considerate versus inconsiderate
15. Popular versus unpopular

Scanning the constructs elicited at Rep Test 4, three constructs of psychological distress are again found, e.g., *relaxed* versus *nervous,* as well as five constructs suggesting a continuing preoccupation with the dimension of success. The most striking change from Rep 1 to Rep 4 is the appearance of *does not care,* used as a contrast to *ambitious, cares,* and *religious.* The extensive use of not caring suggests that George is unable to find constructive alternatives for ambition, religion, and social effectiveness. To the extent that he finds implementation of his own competitive, religious, and social values difficult he may withdraw completely from these areas of concern without benefit of constructive alternatives.

A content analysis shows much the same pattern as before. However, there is an increase in "low forcefulness" and "high tenderness" contents as well as a decrease in "high status."

A grid analysis finds *cares* versus *does not care* replacing *easy* versus *hard to get along with* as a most interrelating construct. The central construction of caring is related to ambition, religion, and popularity. *Does not care* implies a lack of popularity and not caring about ambition or religion. The unrelatedness of the psychological distress dimensions to other types of constructs found on the protocol tends to reinforce our original question about whether or not George's anxiety is linked to constructions absent on the Rep Test.

The persistence of the three anxiety dimensions and their unrelatedness to other construct dimensions raises serious questions about the effectiveness of psychotherapy with this client.

ADDITIONAL INFORMATION

George is judged most maladjusted at intake and least improved as well as least changed over the three months of therapy. His therapist rates him on the TRS (six schedules) as "not exploratory, lacking initiative in therapy sessions, not multidimensional about events, confused, anxious, inconsistent, a poor therapy case, but not rigid." He obtains one of the top three scores among the longer-term therapy clients on the confusion and anxiety measures and the highest score on the inconsistency scale.

Dictations by the therapist indicate that George feels rejected by his father although his father gives him whatever he wants. George feels unable to live up to what his father expects of him. He very much needs approval from others, yet he is uncertain about his relationships with them. George speaks of his drinking buddies as "pretty loose" fellows who do not really care. Dictations suggest also that the therapist has only fragmentary understandings of his client's problem.

In the pretherapy interview George stresses his need to relax, his anticipation of difficulties, his fear of being judged by others, and his inability to understand his father. His anticipation of the future is not hopeful—"I dream about things, and I don't ever think I will be the way I really should be."

The theme of the terminal research interview is captured in the following quotation:

> Well, I don't know, uh. . . see. (Pause) Well, I, I didn't think of myself as, uh, as uh, being uh. (Pause) I thought, I thought, I was, uh, worse than I am, than I really was, I should say. I felt like, uh, like I was, uh, really out, you know, and, an' uh . . . that what was the matter with me, uh, just isn't every day, you know. I mean, a lot of people probably have the same problem and never think anything about it. Un, I don't know, I . . . couldn't.

RECAPITULATION

Both the FIC score on the Rep Test and information external to the test suggest that George's world tends to be fragmented and diffuse, although he does not talk about being confused. The construct of anxiety is emphasized on both Rep Tests and is supported by external evidence. Specific correlates of this anxiety cannot be directly inferred from the Rep Tests or from interview data. External judges rate George as "least improved and least changed" as well as "most maladjusted at intake."

CLIENT PAM

Pam talks about confusions in her relationships, especially with parents. She also suffers from guilt over past homosexual behavior. External judges rate her as most maladjusted at intake.

CONSTRUCTS USED AT REP TEST 1

1. Not straightforward versus straightforward
2. Mature versus somewhat immature
3. Self-centered versus self-sacrificing
4. Interested versus disinterested
5. Lost versus plan for life
6. Reserved versus extrovert
7. No construct given
8. Not straightforward versus straightforward
9. Immature versus mature
10. Sensitive versus insensitive
11. Honest versus lies freely
12. Lacks self-assurance versus has self-assurance
13. Confused versus has direction
14. No construct given
15. Friendly versus unfriendly

The clinician might ask the following question if he scanned the constructs from Rep Test 1: If this person were to experience serious conflicts, how might they be defined? For example, what kinds of experiences do the constructs of *lost* versus *plan for life* and *confused* versus *has direction* suggest? What kinds of experiences do the constructs of *not straightforward* versus *straightforward* and *honest* versus *lies freely* suggest? The use of such constructions does point to areas of possible conflict and concern, and repeated use of particular constructs is usually a sign that they are important. In particular, multiple use of constructions which encompass anxiety or confusion usually are found among students experiencing more serious emotional problems.

A content analysis indicates that Pam focuses on "low self-sufficiency." In this respect she is high in relation to both the better-adjusted and longer-term therapy groups. She does not focus at all on the "forcefulness" dimension, and she is low on "social interaction," "emotional arousal," "high tenderness," and "multiple description." Typically, females score higher on these last four content categories.

Summarizing the first inferences from the Rep Test analysis, Pam is seriously questioning whether or not she can cope with life, although she does not have conflicts along the activity-passivity dimension. She tends to be more masculine in her responses, and problems in sex identification certainly should be considered.

A grid analysis shows the construct *mature* versus *somewhat immature* as the construct which is most interrelated with other constructs. It is a central construction which is linked with such other constructs as *has self-assurance* versus *lacks self-assurance.* The two constructs of straightforwardness are unrelated to the maturity construction. *Honest* versus *lies freely* is an independent construction not even remotely interlinked with being straightforward.

An analysis of how Pam describes her acquaintances reveals that the happiest person she knows is most interrelated to other persons described on the grid. Happy person implies father who is mature and straightforward. Mother is neither, which suggests that mother may not be an important identification figure at the present time. Father is all things good, except that he is reserved. Boyfriend is described as immature and he lies freely.

The FIC (cp) score of eighteen is on the high side in the direction of disorganization, but it is not at the suicidal level. Pam does use twenty-nine *?* ratings, indicating feelings of uncertainty which can be constructive if the disorganization scoring does not increase. She seems much better organized around people than concepts. A prorating procedure is used to obtain her FIC score by assuming the use of fifteen constructs rather than her actual thirteen. The fact that Pam uses only thirteen constructs can have implications for behavioral constriction. It is interesting that the boy that she would most like to know better appears in both construct sorts which do not elicit any description. The boy Pam would like to know better is paired with the unhappiest and most unsuccessful people. The many question marks used in relation to the person she would most like to know better suggests that Pam may have known this person only for a short time.

Summarizing the analysis of the first Rep Test, Pam tends to be confused and will talk about her feelings of disorganization. It is unclear whether her confusions relate to sex role identification problems. She appears more masculine in the content of her constructs and father is a stronger ideal figure than is mother. Father and happy person have much in common, whereas mother is rated as immature and not straightforward. High content scoring on both "high" and "low self-sufficiency," with very high emphasis on "low self-sufficiency," suggests that she may have intense conflicts in this area. Although Pam does not have concerns along the active-passive dimension, she may perceive herself as lacking in self-sufficiency.

CONSTRUCTS USED AT REP TEST 4

1. Self-conscious versus self-assured
2. Intelligence versus low intelligence

3. Energetic versus lazy
4. Sincere versus insincere
5. Confused versus has self-direction
6. Sincere versus insincere
7. Honest versus liar
8. Self-conscious versus self-assured
9. Confused versus has self-determination
10. Has self-direction versus lost
11. Sincere versus insincere
12. Lots of fun versus too serious, too meek
13. Intellectually lazy versus intellectually energetic
14. Floundering versus has plan for life
15. Intellectual interests versus few intellectual interests

Constructs used at Rep Test 4 are somewhat different from those used at Rep Test 1. Four constructs of organization-disorganization are evident in the present protocol, which is an increase from Rep 1. This increase points to a heightened concern with life planning and may not be unhealthy since she uses a new terminology as she speaks about the contrast to confusion. *Has direction in life* now becomes *has self-determination.* This new terminology suggests the emergence of a more internal, self-sufficient point of view. Life direction no longer is just chance. It is that which one actively determines. Pam still is too preoccupied with confusion but in a new way which is more hopeful.

Another change from Rep Test 1 is the appearance of three intellectual dimensions, and the pole of one of these constructs is *intellectually energetic*. Shifting to a grid analysis, we find that *intellectually lazy* versus *intellectually energetic* is not only a new dimension of the Rep Test, but it also interrelates with eight other constructs. It is a centrally organizing concept, replacing *mature* versus *immature* from Rep Test 1 as the central construction. Not only is this intellectual dimension more interrelating and organizing than the maturity dimension, but it also has implications for action since it is correlated with *self-determination.*

Pam, in the context of being even more concerned about feeling lost and being without life plans, has become better organized in her construct system. The FIC (cp) score, originally eighteen points, now is only eight points. This change toward greater organization seems to be related to constructs of intellectual energy mobilization and self-determination. I would predict a decrease in Pam's use of organizational constructs as she gains confidence in coping with her problems.

One of the most interesting construct changes is the emergence of the construct *self-conscious* versus *self-assured* as a replacement for the older construction of *not straightforward* versus *straightforward.* It appears that lacking straightforwardness has been reinterpreted to mean self-consciousness. Not to be straightforward means that the person is not self-assured. This change in construction has interesting implications. Considering it from the standpoint of content scoring, lacking straightforwardness, scored as "low morality," becomes *self-conscious*, scored as "low egoism," "low self-sufficiency," and "emotional arousal." Problems sometimes can be resolved by placing them within larger contexts of meaning, as by placing straightforward within the broader explanatory context of self-assurance. Mother's lack of straightforwardness becomes something more than just a behavior. To understand mother as lacking in self-assurance has broader implications for understanding mother than to say she is not straightforward.

The ways in which Pam organizes her acquaintances also change. Sister now becomes the key role figure, replacing father. Sister is related to eight other acquaintances, including mother, father, brother, and happy person. Father remains a good fellow, and mother is described negatively only in so far as she is self-conscious.

The analysis by the Content Scoring Manual reveals that Pam scores higher on the dimension of "forcefulness," approaching the mean scores of other student groups. She also scores higher on the "organization" and "intellective" dimensions and shows a striking increase in "emotional arousal" and "high commitment" contents.

In summary then, Pam has mobilized her energies and is making determined efforts to resolve her problems through using her own resources in creating plans and directions for her life. Presumably she is placing greater emphasis on academic pursuits. She also is identifying more effectively with her mother. She does not appear as confused as she did on the original Rep Test.

ADDITIONAL INFORMATION

Pam is judged most maladjusted at intake and most improved as well as most changed over the three months of therapy. The therapist describes her on the TRS as confused, hostile, and quite anxious. Her ratings on confusion and hostility are at the median for the longer-term therapy group. Pam ranks among the top seven of the *LT 24* group on anxiety. Her scores on other dimensions of the TRS indicate that she is exploratory, multidimensional, and takes initiative in therapy sessions. She is considered highly motivated and on no occasion does the therapist consider her a poor therapy case.

Pam, in the case notes, is characterized as being withdrawn, feeling intense guilt over past homosexual behavior, failing academically, and feeling strongly ambivalent about mother. The therapist further describes her as one who bargains for respect and admiration. Pam feels that there is nothing in and of herself worthy of love. It is only what she can produce that has importance in the eyes of other people and can bring her reassurance.

In the pretherapy interview Pam traces her problems back to a restrictive, overprotective mother. Interpersonal problems are linked to her relationship with mother. She reports being cut off from her peer group during the high school period. In the pre-high school period, she describes herself as a tomboy. She relates opportunities for leadership and responsibility which provided social contacts but not friendships. She suffers from certain rather acute somatic complaints but is beginning to realize that they could be bids for attention. The construct of *self-consciousness,* which appears on the last Rep Test, is applied to herself within two contexts: first, her feelings of uneasiness with boys; secondly her feelings of guilt and shame over past homosexual behavior. In this latter context Pam states, "A lot of girls looked up to me like some kind of saint, and I just felt like a farce."

In the terminal research interview, Pam states that she has "come a long way" since entering therapy. Her somatic complaints are decreasing, academic problems are being resolved and she finds her parents showing less opposition to her ideas. She has ceased to worry about the homosexual problem, no longer perceiving herself in this context. She construes her primary conflict in the following way.

> My main problem is a lack of ability to face people forcefully. There are times when you just can't smile and be nice. You have to, to stand up for your rights, and it's something I've never been able to do.

RECAPITULATION

The high FIC (cp) score and an excessive use of *?* ratings on the grid pointed to conceptual and behavioral disorganization. Correlated with a reduction in these measures of confusion and disorganization is the external judgment that Pam is most improved and most changed. In a final dictation on Pam the therapist states, "All in all, she seems to be handling this particular stress situation in a little more mature way, with less disorganization than characterized her earlier reactions."

Rep Test scoring suggested conflicts over self-sufficiency even though there was no reason to believe that she was of a passive temperament. Both research and therapy observations strongly support this view. The therapist saw her as immature but not passive. Research interviews indicate that Pam is an active person who quite likely is perceived by others as socially oriented but who feels interpersonally isolated, unable to stand up for her rights, and at the mercy of outside demands. Changes in the Rep Test point to a developing internal orientation which should contribute to both more freedom and satisfaction in her relationships. A vacation trip home and also to her sister's home, occurring later in therapy, turned out well, better than anticipated; however, stresses and strains began to develop at the end of her visit. At this time Pam shared new vocational plans with her family, plans which she felt they would oppose. Although she was able to obtain their support, she would have implemented her plan without their blessing.

One year after the completion of therapy Pam returned the following questionnaire: *How do you now understand the problem(s) for which you originally sought help at the clinic?*

> I first sought help at the suggestion of my physician . . . I was having a great deal of trouble with asthma. I realized long before that it was primarily psychosomatic in nature; however, it was not until I began therapy that I realized I could do something about it . . . I began therapy during that semester, and by second semester I had managed to control it to the point of being hospitalized only once . . . . I now see my asthma as a means to punish myself for negative feelings, since I was not allowed to express such feelings in any way in my home. I also know now that I have unconsciously used it as a retreat from relationships with people when I was unable to handle a situation. My asthma was made worse by severe guilt feelings arising from past homosexual relationships, and as a college student, I have great difficulty controlling the sex urge with most fellows I date.

What changes have taken place in the way(s) you understand yourself since the beginning of your experiences at the clinic?

> Before I sought help I pictured myself as being clumsy . . . I felt insecure in all of my relationships. I saw myself as being emotionally unstable and morally weak. I doubted my intelligence and felt that I was doomed to a life of failure and unhappiness. I was able to see only my weaknesses, though I still have the tendency to stress weakness. I feel more secure in my relationships with others. Whereas I used to see myself as being emotionally unstable, I now see myself as a tower of emotional strength, because I am

able to recognize problems for what they are and to do something about them as they arise and before they grow out of proportion in my own mind. I no longer feel that I shall fail in life, but look forward anxiously to the success I know will come. . . . Before I received therapy, I had built up an illusion that I didn't get mad and that if I did, I didn't stay that way for long. Now I realize that I get just as mad as the next fellow, but because of my inability to express negative feelings, I am inclined to hold it inside until it manifests itself in daydreams, asthma, or periods of deep depression. Since I have realized this fact, I have been able to show my feelings a little more openly. I have learned to adjust my own action to suit the people and the situations without feeling that I am being two-faced, because I am beginning to accept more facets of myself rather than trying to become what I am not.

What changes have taken place in the way(s) you understand the more important people in your life since the beginning of your experience at the clinic?

I am learning to relax and enjoy my parents for the first time in my life. I still find it impossible to discuss my innermost problems with them. . . . I am learning to firmly but gently show them that I am ready and capable of accepting responsibilities for which they have, to date, felt that they should carry. I am, in other words, learning to relate to them on a more mature level. Also I am learning which people are important in my life . . . .

Looking ahead to the future (within the next five years), what changes in your life do you anticipate? What is the importance of these changes to you?

In the next five years I will enter and graduate from . . . . This, I am sure, will have a profound effect on my personality. Presently, I am completing work for a degree in a field in which I have very little interest. I am doing this primarily for the sake of my parents who are a little skeptical as to whether or not I will stick it out.

A THERAPIST REP TEST

Permission has been granted by Pam's therapist to present one of the therapist's own Rep Tests and to discuss the implications of this protocol for understanding the therapist's role. Rather than asking about the therapist's association with a particular school of thought, we will ask instead what kind of person would dimensionalize his experience with people in these ways and what are the implications of such constructions for understanding how he might relate to, as well as influence, his client? This Rep Test has a special significance since it has been contributed by a therapist whom associates describe as highly competent and who appears in a dyad which gives only marginal support to the content incongruency interpretation of premature termination.

CONSTRUCTS USED AT REP 1 BY PAM'S THERAPIST

1. Sincere versus superficial
2. Disorganized versus efficient
3. Self-preoccupied versus interest in others
4. Never themselves versus at ease with self
5. Dull, uninteresting versus shares many interests
6. Stimulating ideas versus repetitive, boring
7. Involved with life versus mentally stagnant
8. Unassuming confidence versus arrogant
9. Originality, initiative versus complaining dependency
10. Procrastinating, inefficient versus efficient
11. Emotionally warm, responsive versus cold, unresponsive
12. Indecisive, vascillating versus forceful, decisive
13. Enthusiasm for many things versus no enthusiasm for new ideas
14. Wisdom versus stupidity
15. Aware of significant subtleties versus aware of gross aspects

Even though the idealized contrasts are apparent, the therapist was asked to identify the best characteristics: *sincere, efficient, interest in others, at ease with self, shares many interests, stimulating ideas, involved with life, unassuming but confident, original, takes initiative, emotionally warm, decisive, enthusiastic for many things, wise,* and *aware of significant subtleties.*

Negative characteristics are: *superficial, disorganized, self-preoccupied, never themselves, uninteresting, repetitive, mentally stagnant, arrogant, complaining dependency, procrastinating, cold, unresponsive, vascillating, lacks enthusiasm for new ideas, stupid,* and *aware of gross aspects.*

Assuming that this therapist tries to live up to his own stated ideals, he presumably would be a warm, vigorous, stimulating, and wise person who would be particularly effective with bright, confused, searching young people. However, a perpetually whining, clinging dependent, or a highly demanding egocentric might be treated with some impatience if he did not shape up and take greater responsibility for his own life and for other people. The therapist, reacting to this interpretation, states, "A client and I sometimes experience a crisis in our relationship early in therapy. I do tend to reject certain clients, and this can be both an advantage and a disadvantage. I am aware of it as a potential problem."

Turning now to the relationship between this therapist and his client, how did they feel about one another at the conclusion of therapy? As part of the follow-up procedure, each of them was asked to rate their relationship on two scales, one of feeling, the other of friendship. In response to the question, *Would you want to have this person as a close friend if he were to become your age or if you were to become his age?* the client responded with "definitely yes." The therapist, on the other hand, responded with "probably no." In response to: *My personal feelings toward this person are . . . ,* the client responded with "very positive." However, the therapist responded with "more positive than negative." The therapist later explained his position by saying that his client's status and competitive drives were too strong to be able to think of her as a close personal friend.

This discrepancy in client-therapist friendship and feeling ratings can be related to a discrepancy between two client-therapist content congruency scores at the beginning of therapy. A coefficient of .84 on the content of the client's most interrelating construct is contrasted with a coefficient of .62 on the content of the therapist's most interrelating construct. Restating this difference by comparing each coefficient with those found in the other twenty-three client-therapist dyads of *LT 24,* a congruency rank of three on client content is contrasted with a congruency rank of eighteen on the central content of the therapist. This difference suggests that Pam might have experienced greater sharing of important content than the therapist. Even though the therapist may not have experienced much congruity with his client, the ideals of the therapist, plotted within his own personal construct dimensions, suggest an openness for understanding that which is new and different. In other words, the therapist uses constructs which suggest an ability to subsume the constructions of others.

Although this dyad gives only marginal support to the incongruity-prematurity hypothesis, it strongly supports the organizational difference interpretation of improvement. Client and therapist at Rep Test 1 have FIC (cp) scores of eighteen and six, indicating that the therapist is more highly organized than his client. Pam's score of eighteen decreases markedly to an FIC (cp) of eight while the therapist receives a score of seven, showing great stability. Client-therapist organizational convergence then is accounted for primarily by Pam moving toward her therapist.

Next a comparison is made between the central or most interrelating constructs of Pam and her therapist. At the beginning of therapy, the construct *maturity* versus *immaturity* is central for Pam. However at Rep Test 4 a new construct, *intellectually lazy* versus *intellectually energetic,* is most central. The therapist uses *never themselves* versus *at ease with self* at the beginning of therapy and *fortitude* versus *weak* at Rep Test 4. The therapist perceives a relationship between these two dimensions and consequently does not accept the possibility that change has occurred in his central construct. Reflecting on the change that has taken place in Pam's central construction in relationship to his own central construction, the therapist commented, "Maybe this change to a construct which implies actively doing something is related to my statement to her that one gains freedom through commitment."

Turning now to Table 7.2, Pam and her therapist are compared on selected categories of Rep Test content at Rep Test 1 and Rep Test 4. Attending first to the great difference in "high forcefulness" scores at Rep Test 1 found in column 2a, the therapist scores ten whereas Pam scores only one. Pam's score on "forcefulness" has increased three points at Rep Test 4 and in the direction of the therapist's score which remains high. Pam's score on the organization dimension, shown in columns 3a and 3b, doubles at Rep Test 4. There is a marked increase in Pam's "high" and "low intellective" content shown in columns 7a and 7b. However, the therapist scores only minimally in these two categories. The therapist's high "closed to alternatives" score shown in column 10d is counterbalanced by a high "open to alternatives" score, which is not shown because of problems with interjudge rating consistency in this category. To the extent that the author's own scoring of "open to alternatives" may be accepted, all therapists have scored importantly in this area. The difference between the "morality" scores of Pam and her therapist, shown in Columns 12a and 12b, is marked and may be explained by Pam's excessive use of such terminology and by the fact that the therapist, a highly responsible person, does not employ a language of conventional morality. Finally, the client shows increased concerns with the dimension of "commitment," as seen in columns 19a and 19b.

Briefly summarizing the nature of the therapy relationship, the therapist seems to have stimulated Pam with methodological construction. First he provides Pam with a contrasting personal construct organization. His more structured approach to social events provides the context within which Pam discusses her less well organized world of social experience. Then he provides Pam with a context of values such as *openness* and *independence* which may promote problem-solving behavior. Finally the constructs of the therapist not only suggest the potentiality for subsuming or understanding that which is different, i.e., the constructs of his client, but also the ideals of *commitment, warmth,*

TABLE 7.2

Content Comparison of Client and Therapist Rep Tests Juxtaposed at the Beginning and End of Therapy

	Content Scoring												
Group	2a	2b	3a	3b	7a	7b	10d	12a	12b	14	18b	19a	19b
Rep 1													
T 1	10	3	2	2	1	2	6	1	0	1	0	3	1
C 12	1	1	2	2	0	0	2	4	3	0	2	2	1
Rep 4													
T 1	8	2	3	1	1	0	5	0	0	1	1	5	1
C 12	4	2	4	4	4	2	1	4	4	2	4	6	3

Content Scoring: 2a-High Forceful; 2b-Low Forceful; 3a-High Organization; 3b-Low Organization; 5a-High Status; 5b-Low Status; 7a-High Intellective; 7b-Low Intellective; 10d-Closed to Alternatives (Open to Alternatives was not scored because of low inter-judge reliability); 12a-High Morality; 12b-Low Morality; 14-Emotional Arousal; 18b-Future Orientation; 19a-High Commitment; 19b-Low Commitment.

and *involvement* which may have significantly influenced his client. The follow-up questionnaire certainly gives some support to the latter hypothesis.

CLIENT DOUG

Doug states that he feels "as though I'm sitting back and waiting for the world to blow up." A test failure provides the precipitating context which brings him to therapy. External judges rate him as least maladjusted at intake. Doug's academic qualifications are quite impressive, placing him among the most gifted college students.

CONSTRUCTS USED AT REP TEST 1

1. Religious versus obscene
2. Confident versus childish
3. Quietly, admittedly hypocritical versus bluffs aggressively
4. Takes offense at little or nothing versus endures almost anything
5. Limited interest, narrow-minded versus broad interests
6. Naive versus experienced
7. Seems lonely and concerned versus satisfied
8. Conservative, moral, religious versus liberal, immoral, irreligious
9. Frank, honest about self versus says nothing about self
10. Well versed in field of specialization versus uncertain and not opinionated
11. Faith in own convictions versus little confidence in anything
12. Talkative versus taciturn
13. Dubious of capability versus confident
14. Well read, frank versus narrow, verbose without saying anything
15. Faith in self versus uncertain about self

Constructs used by Doug seem complex. He makes frequent use of multiple description and his constructs encompass a variety of ideas. However, he does repeat a type of construction which has implications for self-confidence, i.e., constructs 2, 11, 13, and 15. It may be inferred from these constructs that not to be confident is to feel childish, uncertain, and doubtful about one's capabilities. Another type of repeated construction pertains to religion. *Religious* seems to imply morality and conservatism. In contrast, *irreligious* implies obscenity, immorality and liberality. If a person wishes to be a liberal, he may have to be open to that which is immoral and obscene.

The construct *lonely and concerned* versus *satisfied* raises a question about whether or not Doug construes himself as lonely and concerned. Is it possible that Doug is a very lonely fellow who feels apart from others in his concerns about the many paradoxes of life, paradoxes which may be of greater concern for him than for others. And, in the context of the constructs cited in the preceding paragraph, it is possible that Doug is both attracted to and repelled by what he construes as liberalism.

A content analysis indicates a low score on "high social interaction" and extremely high scores on "high self-sufficiency" and "multiple description." He also tends to be high on the categories of "high commitment," "morality," and "closed to experience" (this latter category having implications for dogmatic thinking). Summarizing this material, it is hypothesized that Doug is a self-reliant, highly complex person who is greatly concerned about ethical matters and tends to be dogmatic.

The grid analysis suggests that he is disorganized in his social conceptions and behavior. His extremely high FIC (cp) score of twenty-six and high *N* and *?* ratings, totaling sixty-eight, place him at the suicidal level. However, he does not make use of concrete descriptions which also characterize the suicidal student. There is very little relationship among his concepts, and only three of his acquaintances are interrelated: girlfriend, a female he would like to know better, and the unhappiest person he knows.

Summarizing the first Rep Test, Doug appears to be very confused and shows some suicidal potential. He tends to be a self-reliant, complex type of person who currently is experiencing great loneliness and feels apart from others in his concerns over the enigmas of life. He is probably having considerable difficulty reconciling his constructions of liberal and conservative viewpoints, and he may be questioning his capabilities.

CONSTRUCTS USED AT REP TEST 4

1. Quiet, religious versus noisy, profane
2. Skilled, confident versus uncertain
3. Bluffers versus frank
4. Loud blusterer versus retiring
5. Specialist versus diversified
6. Casual, meet easily versus not meet people well
7. Immoral in theory and practice versus immoral only in theory
8. Strict morals versus lax, little restraint
9. Critically self-conscious versus unreflective
10. Specialized versus diversified

11. Sincere versus apparently superficial
12. Confused about religion versus overly sure about religion
13. Bright versus plodding
14. Cheerful versus sad
15. Talkative versus taciturn

Concerns about morals and religion still are prominent at Rep Test 4. However a slight change in terminology is evident in construct 12: *confused about religion* versus *overly sure about religion.* Certainly this particular dimension supports the hypothesis stated at Rep Test 1 that Doug is experiencing religious and moral conflicts. Constructs 1 and 4, as well as 9 and 15, suggest a continuing and increasing concern with a dimension of *loudness* versus *quietness.* Construction focusing directly on social interaction has increased, e.g., *casual, meet easily* versus *not meet people well.*

Content analysis supports the increase in areas of "social interaction." There also is an increase in both "high" and "low forcefulness" and "low organization" contents. There is no reduction in concerns over morality. In fact, there is an increase in this dimensional content from Rep 1. And, as we noted previously, "morality" scoring at Rep 1 is very high. Finally, there is a large reduction in scoring on multiple description, a complex approach to the Rep Test which is more characteristic of females.

Grid analysis shows little change in the FIC (cp) score. The extremely high score of twenty-five suggests that Doug remains as confused now as he was at the beginning of therapy. An increase in total *N* and *?* ratings from sixty-eight to seventy-eight may be interpreted as an increasing constriction in the application of constructs.

The excessively high FIC (cp) score, the increase in conceptual constriction, and the excessive and increasing use of morality constructions do not support the inference that this client has significantly improved over three months of therapy.

ADDITIONAL INFORMATION

Doug is judged least maladjusted at intake and least improved as well as least changed over the three months of therapy. The therapist describes him on the TRS as "not exploratory, uncooperative, apathetic and rigid." However, the therapist's rating of Doug's anxiety places him among the seven least anxious clients in the *LT 24* group. Even more interesting, on no occasion does the therapist rate him as confused. Nevertheless, after the third session, the therapist states in his case notes, "He is an exceedingly complex fellow who will want to tie the threads of his life together in rather unique ways."

At therapy termination the clinician commented that he had been of little assistance to Doug, and furthermore, Doug may well have been confused in a most profound way. In retrospect the therapist observed that Doug's behavior at each interview was highly organized, but there was no continuity between sessions. Doug focused on a different topic each time.

Case dictations indicate that Doug has shifted graduate programs three times. Furthermore he has experienced extreme changes in his religious thinking, feels he is misunderstood by his parents, describes himself as a practical joker, and has ideas about putting man and his thinking into science but does not focus on psychology. Moreover, he feels shy with girls, identifies with acquaintances who make out with girls even as he rejects their disrespect for women, fears that he may be unable to consummate sexual relationships, wants to find a girl his intellectual equal, and is fascinated with rebelliousness, bizarreness, and instability.

The pretherapy interview supports the observations of the therapist that Doug is a highly complex fellow. This interview indicates that he comes from a very strict religious background and perceives himself in a state of flux, not only in the religious area but in other areas as well. At the conclusion of this interview Doug was asked, "What do you make of all this?" He replied, "The whole thing just depresses me. I don't do anything with it."

A reading of the terminal research typescript reveals a diffuse young man who is unable to state clearly any gains from therapy. He appears confused, and the following excerpts from this interview capture the essence of his statements:

> It doesn't bother me so much that I'm not going out. It's just that I'm not going out—even as much as last semester . . . . I could work on the separate sections of the problem rather than having the whole . . . . It was, uh, straightening—getting a thing into more or less orderly arrangement.

This highly talented but confused young man departed from the University shortly after terminating psychotherapy. There is no evidence that psychotherapy was of any benefit to him.

RECAPITULATION

Would therapy have progressed in a different direction if the therapist had clearly understood the confusion of this student early in therapy, a confusion inferable from the Rep Test? He might have been more alert to the lack of continuity between sessions and less inclined to follow his client from one conceptual island to another.

I believe that this boy's problems, although involving contents of feelings, behaviors, and insights, should have been approached from the standpoint of conceptual organization. The therapist did have an appreciation of his client's need to integrate threads of his life, but he probably spent too much time trying to help him attain certain specific behavioral goals and failed to appreciate the criticalness of helping his client to first work out a more internally consistent life plan.

SUMMARY

The usefulness of the Rep Test as a clinical tool was explored by examining test protocols of five clients and linking hypotheses developed from the test material with other information about these clients. The analysis of three longer-term therapy clients entailed an examination of first and fourth Rep Tests as well as external information gleaned from pre- and terminal research interviews, therapist case notes, and rating scales. Provocative clinical relationships were found between FIC (cp) organization scores and personality disorganization, content focus and actual behavior, and multiple use of construct dimensions and central areas of conflict.

The empirical demonstration that a particular test is correlated with information external to that test is only one aspect of its usefulness. Equally important is the relationship between a test and its broader realms of theory and speculation which give the test heuristic value. Innumerable tests and procedures are available to the clinician. However few clinical tools are as intimately linked with or derivable from explicit theory as the Rep Test.

I WONDER WHAT WILL HAPPEN IF . . . .

The reader, now that he has been exposed to a variety of clinical and research interpretations, may ask for more information. This wish to know more does not really differentiate the reader from myself. Knowing the danger of becoming mired in outdated methods and compulsive statistical adventures, I did, nevertheless, intercorrelate all items of the Therapist Rating Scales (TRS). Additionally, I analysed the relationship between each TRS item and the criterion measures of initial maladjustment, improvement, and change. Certain specific contents of personal constructs also were related to the criterion measures. However, the most interesting use of these data was recently illustrated when a student said, "Dr. Landfield, for my class paper I want to hypothesize that father and mother will be construed most differently from one another by those experiencing greater personal problems." I responded, "That sounds interesting and I just happen to have some data . . . ." The result was that Mr. Teichman (1970), employing personal construct information from ten subjects of the longer-term therapy group and ten subjects as a better-adjusted control, found strong support for his hypothesis.

CORRELATES OF PERSONAL CONSTRUCT CONTENT

A presentation of the myriad of relationships which were found in our data is beyond the scope of this volume; however we will comment briefly on a selected few content postcoding categories, examining the relationships between content usage and improvement or change in the longer-term therapy group. Additionally, sex bias will be explored within a group comprised of forty-eight male and fifty-two female students. As a point of focus we have chosen the single categories, (10a) "Multiple description," (21) "extreme qualifiers," and (4a) "high self-sufficiency," and the combined categories, (10d plus 16a) "high dogmatism," (2a, 14, 21) "high intensity," (3a, 19a) "high structure," (1a, 17a) "high social orientation," and (6, 9b, 13) "high concreteness." Content norms for thirty better-adjusted students are found in Appendix C.

"Multiple descriptions" are exemplified by such descriptions as "He is friendly but dogmatic," or "She is flighty and very bright." Since the Rep Test instructions tend to discourage such multiple descriptions by emphasizing the "one way" in which people are alike or different, most subjects receive a low score in this category. Nevertheless, when using cutting scores of zero and one, females tend to use multiple descriptions more frequently than males ($\chi^2 = 4.1$, $p < .05$). One explanation for this male-female difference may be that females are more adept at construing other people and also tend to perceive them in more holistic ways.

"Extreme qualifiers" are exemplified by such modifiers as very, always, and never. Once again, females use such modifiers more frequently than males ($\chi^2 = 4.8$, $p < .05$). This finding is given indirect support by Berg and Collier (1953) in their study of extreme response sets and suggests the greater social focus of our female subjects.

"High dogmatism," which encompasses "high egoism" and "closed to alternatives," is used more frequently by females ($\chi^2 = 6.0$, $p < .02$). However, when the longer-term therapy group is examined, both males and females who are judged as most improved over therapy tend to obtain lower scores than those judged as least improved. The twelve most improved clients obtain significantly lower scores on the first Rep Test than the twelve least improved clients ($U = 35$, $p < .05$, two-tailed). Furthermore, the relationship between "high egoism" and "closed to alternatives," as computed by the Pearsonian coefficient, is .70, $p < .01$ for the longer-term therapy group and .58, $p < .01$ for a better adjusted group of thirty students. These findings suggest the possibility that (a) women may be more certain about the nature of social events, and (b) this measure may have highlighted either the greater dogmatism or the greater concern about it in least improved clients.

"High intensity," comprised of the categories of "high forcefulness," "emotional arousal," and "extreme qualifiers," is used more frequently by females ($\chi^2 = 4.7$, $p < .05$). There also is a tendency for least improved and least changed females to score higher on the first Rep Test than most improved and most changed females ($F_p = .10$, two-tailed).

"High structure," which encompasses "high organization" and "high involvement," shows no sex bias; however least improved clients score higher than most improved clients on the first Rep Test ($F_p = .10$, two-tailed).

"High self-sufficiency," a single category, is used more frequently by females ($\chi^2 = 11.1$, $p < .001$). When the *LT 24* group is broken down into male and female subgroups, most changed males increase in their focus on "high self-sufficiency" ($F_p = .01$, two-tailed), whereas most changed females tend either to decrease or at least do not increase in using such content.

"High social orientation," comprised of "high social" and "high tenderness" contents, shows no sex bias; however Rep Test scoring changes more, positive or negative, in the least improved clients from Rep Test 1 to Rep Test 4 ($U = 34$, $p < .05$, two-tailed). This finding suggests that the least improved may be rather unstable in their social orientation. One might speak about the least improved as having greater social ambivalence.

"High concreteness," which encompasses "factual description," "low imagination," and "external appearance," is used increasingly more by least changed clients ($U = 25$, $p < .02$, two-tailed). In other words, clients judged to be least changed over the therapy period show increased constriction or impoverishment of the ways in which they view their fellow men.

CORRELATES OF THE THERAPIST RATING SCALE

The range of scoring on TRS items was increased by adding separate ratings on an item, e.g., "anxiety," across the six rating periods which covered twelve weeks of therapy. It will be noted that many items included in Section II of the TRS which is described in Chapter Six consist of two parts, e.g., more versus less anxious today; is versus is not an anxious person. Each of these two parts was assigned a score of one and the total possible scoring for the item across six rating periods was twelve points. Employing Pearsonian or Biserial correlations whenever possible, each item of the TRS was correlated with every other item, then each item was correlated with the dichotomous criteria of initial maladjustment, improvement, and change.

Summarizing the main findings, "maladjustment," as judged initially, is directly correlated with "confusion" and "inconsistency" ($r_b = .60$, $p < .01$ and $r_b = .56$, $p < .05$). However, "maladjustment" is related in a curvilinear fashion to "indefiniteness." Either too much or too little "indefiniteness" is related to the criterion measure ($\chi^2 = 18.0$, $p < .01$). Although these three items primarily are related to "maladjustment," each item also is related to "unimprovement" ($U = 6$ versus $I = 18$). However, these items are not significantly related to the dichotomous criterion, i.e., twelve most-twelve least improved. Only one other TRS item, "no hope," is related to the "maladjustment" criterion ($r_b = .46$, $p < .05$).

When the items "not exploratory" and "not multidimensional" about an event are combined, significant relationships are found between these combined items and both improvement and change ($p = .05$ or better). Even though change was more difficult to rate and interjudge consistency was lower for change than for improvement, it is the primary correlate of the TRS items. Specifically, least change is related ($p = .05$ or better) to (I A) not exploratory, (D) disengagement, (G) no interview initiative, (H) unwilling to experience incongruity, (I) not multidimensional about an event, (J) apathetic, (M) defensive, and (N) poor therapy case. The absence of strong relationships between "anxiety" or "hostility" and our criterion measures may mean that it is only when these characteristics are maximized that they are linked with pathology or unchangeability. This seems like a reasonable hypothesis. It seems equally reasonable that the therapists may have used these two concepts in idiosyncratic ways. And it is just possible that what we talk about most glibly may be that about which we communicate least well.

CHAPTER EIGHT

THE PYRAMID PROCEDURE

THE DOING OF A LARGER SCALE RESEARCH PROJECT NOT ONLY HAS THE advantage of yielding many types of information, but it also has the further advantage of deeply involving the investigator in his subject matter. This involvement encouraged me to search for newer methods for eliciting personal constructs.

In this chapter a new methodology is described which is compatible with personal construct theory and has both diagnostic as well as therapeutic uses. This new method, first called the Triangle Test and later renamed the Pyramid Procedure, is an outgrowth of the formal research and discussions I held with a colleague, Dr. Gary Isaacson. Dr. Isaacson and I were searching for a new personal construct method which could be used as an integral part of therapy. The traditional Rep Test can be used as a vehicle of discussion; however, the way in which concepts are elicited in the traditional form, e.g., subjects being asked to write in small spaces, tends to encourage the formalization of construction. Wishing to avoid this formalization without sacrificing the structure of contrast, and hoping to encourage the free expression of emotional constructs, the Pyramid Procedure was developed. The first trial balloon of this method, referred to as cheap psychoanalysis, generated some headaches among staff and graduate students who completed the procedure. But the Pyramid Procedure, in its present form, will be described, and its use in an actual therapy case will be discussed.

INSTRUCTIONS

The starting point of this procedure is the client's description of an acquaintance. The clinician first asks his client to think of an acquaintance with whom he feels most comfortable and whose company he most enjoys. The clinician does not ask for the name of the acquaintance, but he may ask whether it is a male or female. The client then is asked to give a brief description of his acquaintance, focusing on this person's most important quality or characteristic.

The clinician may modify these instructions. For example, he might begin by asking for an admired or respected acquaintance rather than one with whom the client feels most comfortable. Then again, he could ask for an acquaintance who "hangs loose" or is "not up tight." Modifications in the concept question might involve asking the client to focus on his acquaintance's most important values, his most noticeable behavior, or his usual reactions to situations as well as his feelings about the client.

It is important for the client to understand that he needs focus on only one important characteristic rather than describe his acquaintance fully. Furthermore, the client should be encouraged to say whatever comes into his mind and not to be concerned if he gives repetitive responses later in the procedure. When the client feels he should react more rapidly or finds it difficult to think of the most appropriate words or expressions, he is reassured by being told that the task is a new experience and most people have this difficulty (which is true).

Following the elicitation of a first construct pole, e.g., "He is an open guy," the clinician asks, "What kind of a person is not an open guy?"

Assuming that the client replies, "A closed one," the clinician then returns to the first construct pole and asks, "What kind of a person is an open guy?"

The client replies, "What do you mean what kind?"

The clinician says, "What more can you tell me about an open guy?"

"Well," the client replies, "he is willing to listen to you."

If the client replies, "What do you mean by what more can I say about an open guy?" the clinician asks the client to say something about how an open guy may feel, think, or act.

Let us assume that the client verbalizes *open* and *closed guy,* a construct at the top of the pyramid. He tells us also that an open guy is willing to listen to you. Then the clinician asks, "What kind of guy doesn't listen to you?"

The client replies, "Somebody not interested in you."

Next, the clinician returns to the second pole of the first construct and asks, "What kind of a guy is a closed guy?"

The client may or may not repeat an earlier construction at this point. He might say, "A closed guy is somebody people don't like."

The clinician would then ask, "What kind of a guy is not liked?"

If the client replies, "Somebody who doesn't like me," the clinician asks, "What kind of a guy doesn't like you?"

Reviewing the procedure as illustrated below, the clinician elicits a construct which is exemplified by *open guy*. The contrast *closed guy* then is elicited. The clinician records this construct at the top of the pyramid as shown below. Next, *listens to you* is associated with *open guy*, and *somebody not interested in you* is contrasted with *listens to you*. Returning to the pole *closed guy, people don't like* is associated with it. Finally, *doesn't like me* is contrasted with *people don't like*.

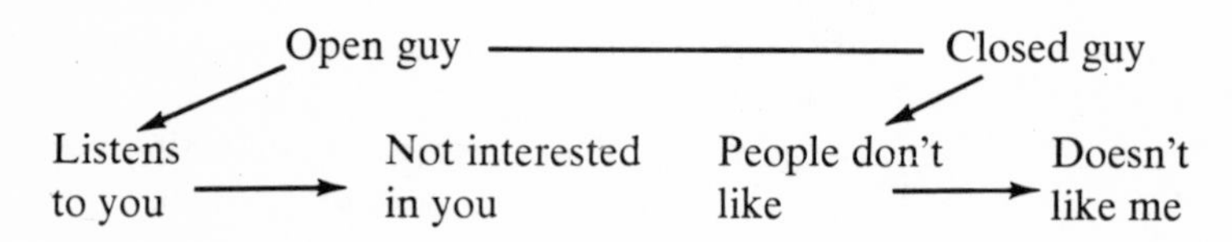

The above illustration shows only two levels of the pyramid. There is a third and final level which is elicited from the information recorded at the second level. For example, the clinician asks, "What kind of person listens to you?" and a contrast is elicited from the client's response. The clinician then asks about the client's response, "not interested in you." When a pyramid is completed, as shown in Diagram 8.1, eight sets of contrasts are recorded at the third level.

Following the development of the first pyramid, the clinician may wish to ask further questions about the meanings of his client's responses. This inquiry is done by focusing on one response at a time, e.g., *listen to you,* and asking one or more of the following questions: "How would you know if a person were listening to you?" "How would you know if a person were not listening to you?" "What would a person say, do, think, or feel if he were listening to you?" "What would a person say, do, think, or feel if he were not listening to you?" "When would a person listen to you?" "When would a person not listen to you?" This inquiry is optional and should be used in a selective manner, asking only about certain concepts and being sensitive to the client's tolerance for the operational task.

Since one pyramid can be completed within a half-hour, the clinician may wish to begin a second one; however, the development of more than two pyramids in one session is not recommended. The starting point for additional pyramids is left to the judgment of the clinician. The acquaintance for the second pyramid could be in contrast to the first one, i.e., a person with whom you feel most uncomfortable and whose company you enjoy least. Father and mother might be the starting points for the third and fourth pyramids. Girl friend, boy friend, a person whom you would like to know better, brother, sister, close friend of the same sex, etc., could be used for other pyramids.

There may be occasions when the clinician prefers supplying the first construct pole. It may be important to begin with a description elicited by the traditional Rep Test. Then again, one might begin with a symptom or complaint. I have experimented with the concept of life, but in some cases the term life may be too abstract for the client. Moreover, it may be too threatening for use on a first pyramid since it may elicit dimensions of happiness-depression.

A VEHICLE OF THERAPY

The author assumes that the effective therapist learns to communicate in the language of his client and that this is true of effective psychoanalysts, Rogerians, or behavior modifiers. The personal construct therapist also wishes to learn about his client's social language system and is free, within the limits of his own system, of course, to employ constructs useful to other theorists as these constructs fit the client. Some clients tend to function within psychoanalytic dimensions while other clients may employ sharply defined constructions which suggest an openness to a highly disciplined and "no nonsense" approach to their problems. Then there are those clients who function within dimensions of experience and awareness which suggest strong predilections for philosophical and existential thinking. Even though the personal construct therapist may not be able to work equally well with all of these clients, he at least may become aware of his client's language system early in the therapy sequence and may be able to decide to work with him further or re-refer him appropriately to a therapist who employs a more congruent language system.

Acceptance of the above logic suggests the importance of a systematic evaluation of the client's language framework early in therapy. If: (1) a clinician feels the need for such an early assessment, but one which fits within the context of the therapy interview; (2) he also feels that his client should struggle more independently with his problems, both in and out of the therapy office; (3) he wants his client to become more aware of his own language framework and how he uses it; (4) he wishes to minimize as much as possible the extraneous intrusions of therapist personal language and bias; and if (5) he wants his client to feel that he is working within a more systematic framework of treatment, then the therapist may want to explore the use of the Pyramid Procedure as a vehicle of therapy.

In the next section, use of the Pyramid Procedure is illustrated with a therapy client whom we will refer to as Mary. Mary was referred for psychotherapy by a physician who felt that there might be a relationship between her chronic nausea and psychological stress. Mary was seen in therapy for several months prior to the introduction of the Pyramid Procedure. Introduction of this procedure as a primary vehicle of treatment came at a point when both Mary and her therapist were discouraged about her lack of progress. Mary's complaints about nausea had not decreased, and the therapist felt that she had not talked about any significant emotional problems, except those which resulted from her sickness, e.g., increased academic pressures. At this point of discouragement the therapist asked Mary if she would be willing to participate in an experimental procedure in which she would describe people and ideas, a procedure which would require a certain amount of work outside of therapy. There was no guarantee for the success of such an exploratory approach. The therapist frankly stated that he did not know whether it would help and furthermore, he was inexperienced in the use of the procedure. Mary responded by saying that she would like to try the new approach and admitted that she was contemplating therapy termination. The decision then was made to try the method for an eight-week period. If Mary felt that the experience was not helping her by the end of this period, she would then terminate.

PYRAMID RESPONSES: SESSION ONE

First Pyramid

Initial instructions: Think of a person with whom you feel most comfortable and whose company you enjoy. Do not tell me who it is, but let me know if it is male or female. Give an important characteristic of this person.

Response: Mary thought about a male acquaintance whom she described as *gentle*.

Second Pyramid

Initial instructions: Think of a person with whom you feel most uncomfortable and whose company you least enjoy.

Response: Mary thought about a female acquaintance whom she described as *completely self-centered with no quality of friendship*.

Third Pyramid

Initial instructions: Think about your mother.

Response: Mary described her mother as *sympathetic*.

Fourth Pyramid

Initial Instructions: Think about your brother nearest your age.

Response: Mary described her brother as *selfish*.

DIAGRAM 8.1
First Pyramid: Session One

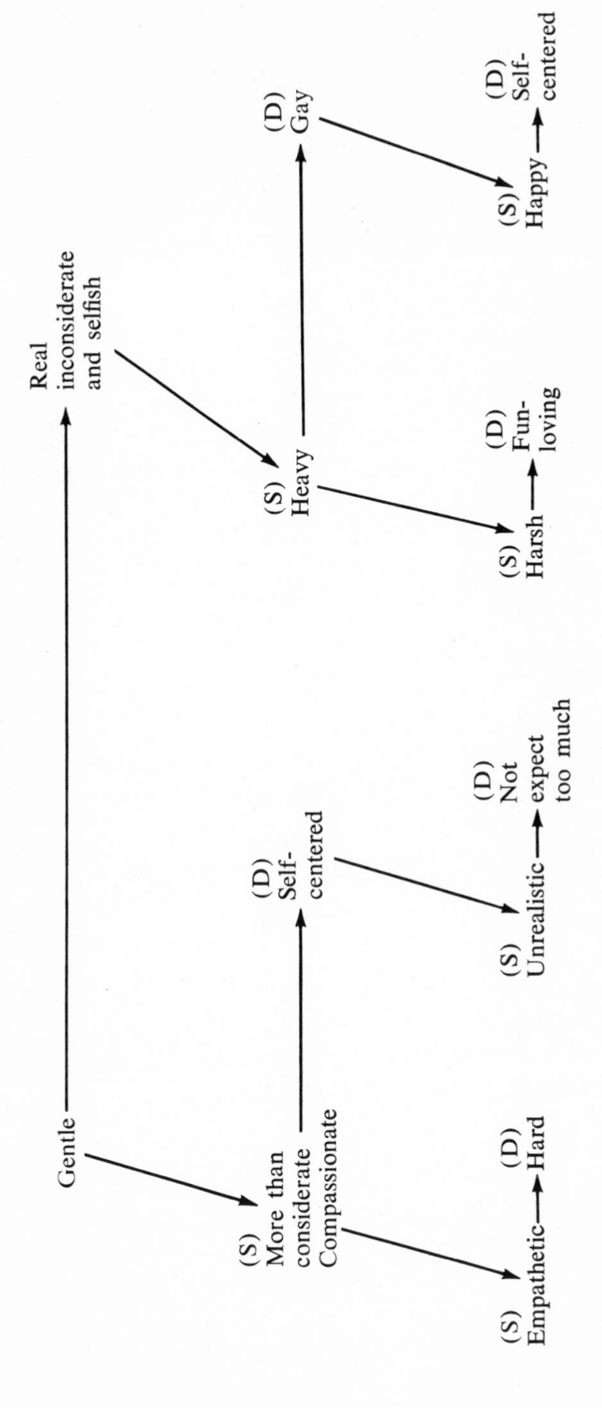

(S) = Similar
(D) = Different

DIAGRAM 8.2
Second Pyramid: Session One

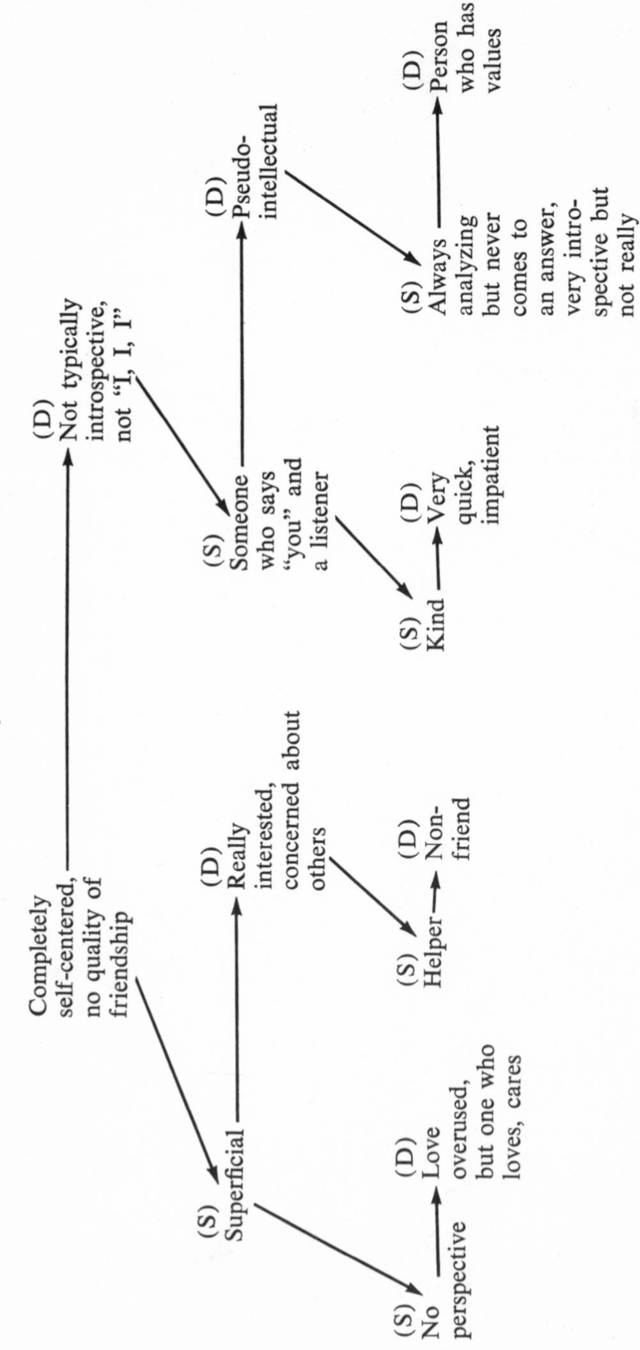

(S) = Similar
(D) = Different

DIAGRAM 8.3
Third Pyramid: Session One

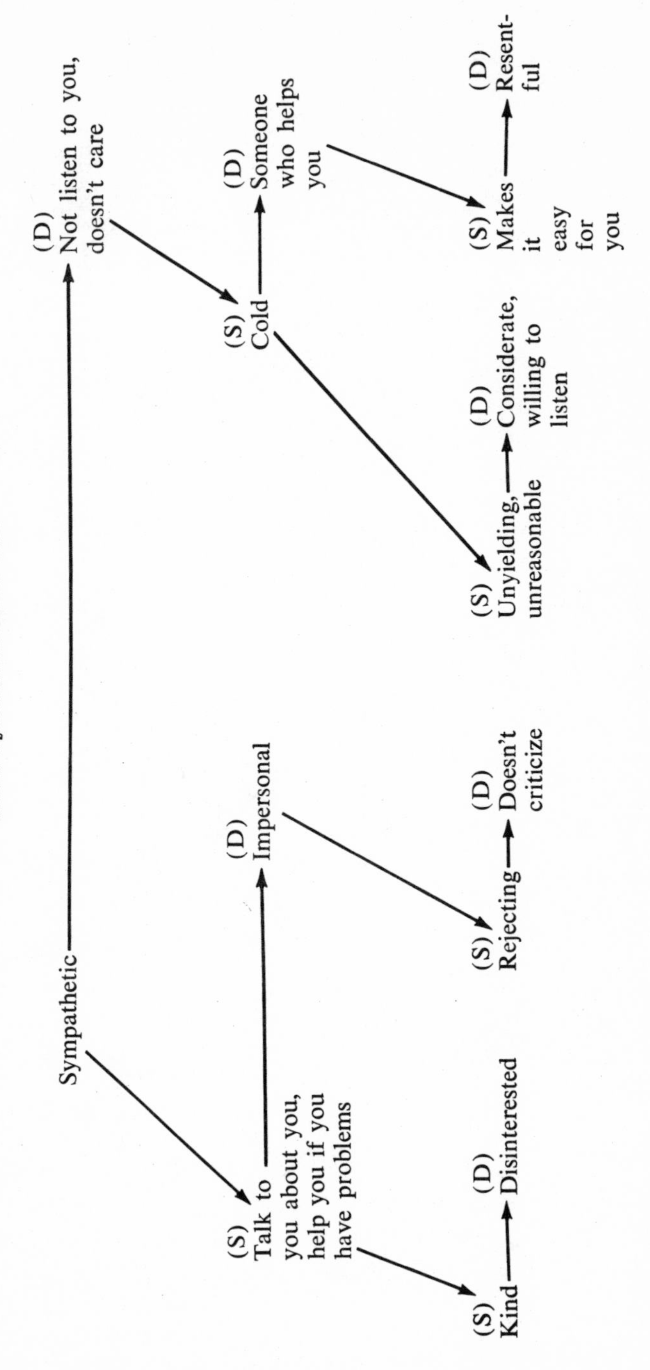

(S) = Similar
(D) = Different

DIAGRAM 8.4
Fourth Pyramid: Session One

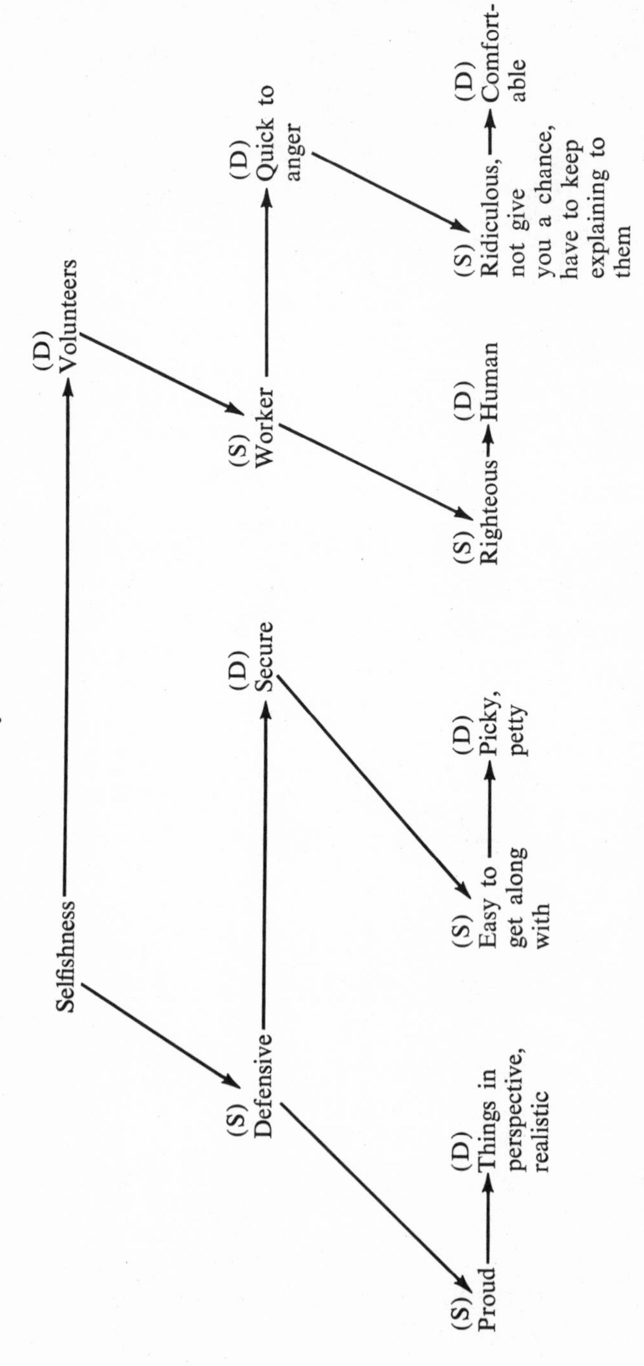

(S) = Similar
(D) = Different

Instructions Given at Close of Session One: Copies of the four pyramids were given to Mary and she was asked to read the material and think about it for fifteen minutes prior to the next session. If something came to mind as she read the material, she was to report it.

PYRAMID RESPONSES: SESSION TWO

Comment: Mary felt that she had a one-track mind and that she seemed obsessed with the idea of self-centeredness.

First Pyramid
Initial Instructions: What is it that you like most about yourself?
Response: Mary described her own most likeable characteristic as *wanting to communicate well, being able to listen as well as to talk.*

Second Pyramid
Initial Instructions: What is it that you like least about yourself?
Response: Mary described her own most negative characteristic as *not knowing what to do in a certain situation.*
Instructions Given at Close of Session Two: Copies of the two pyramids were given to Mary and she was asked to re-read the material from session one along with the new material from session two.

PYRAMID RESPONSES: SESSION THREE

Comment: Mary felt there was a lack of variation in what she had done. Selfishness was emphasized too much and there should be more sides to it. It was nice to know how she felt, but there must be more to it. She was not really bored; that was too strong. However, she felt a mixture of things that were extremely difficult to talk about.

First Pyramid
Initial Instructions: Think about a male near your own age, someone that you have not described.
Response: Mary described this acquaintance as one who *jokes a lot.*

Second Pyramid
Initial Instructions: Think about a male near your own age, someone not described previously that you feel positive about.
Response: Mary described this acquaintance as one who *does not want to be left alone.*
Instructions Given at Close of Session Three: In preparation for the fourth session, Mary was asked to copy each construct pole on a three-by-five card. Additionally, she was asked to type out her feelings at the

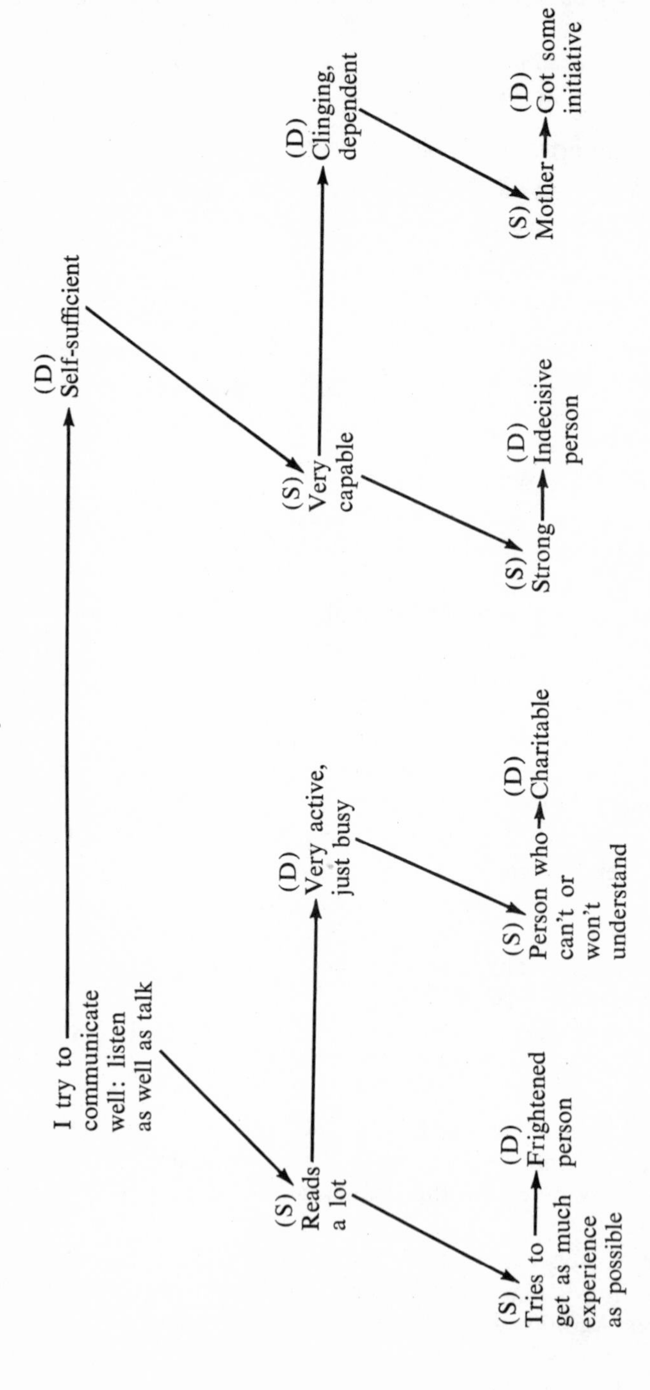

DIAGRAM 8.5
First Pyramid: Session Two

DIAGRAM 8.6
Second Pyramid: Session Two

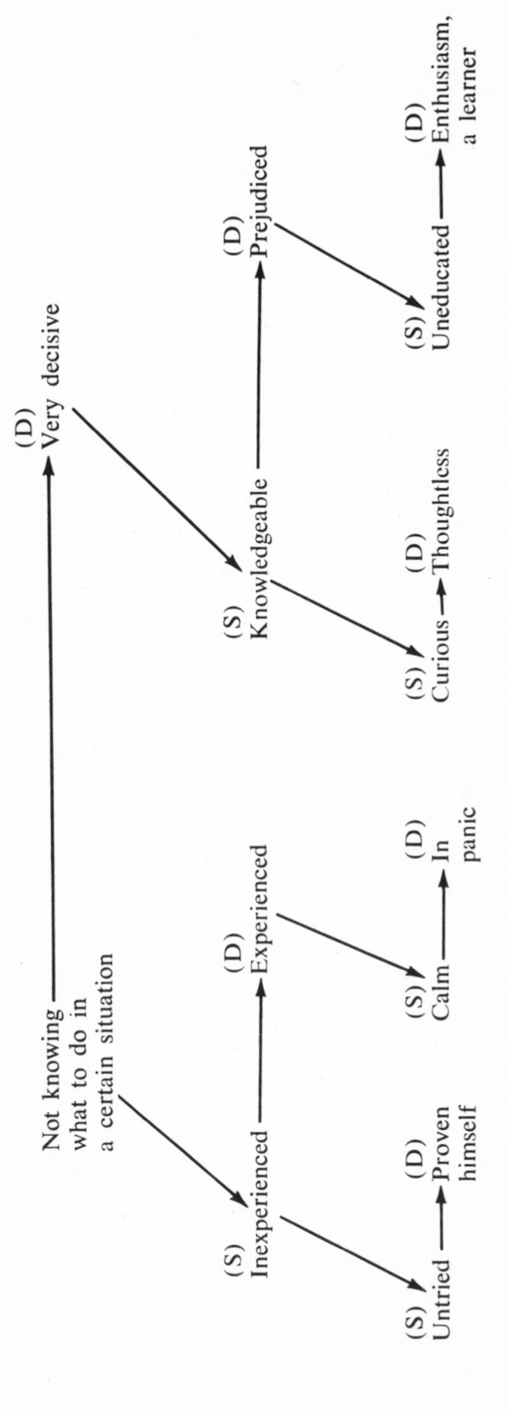

(S) = Similar
(D) = Different

DIAGRAM 8.7

First Pyramid: Session Three

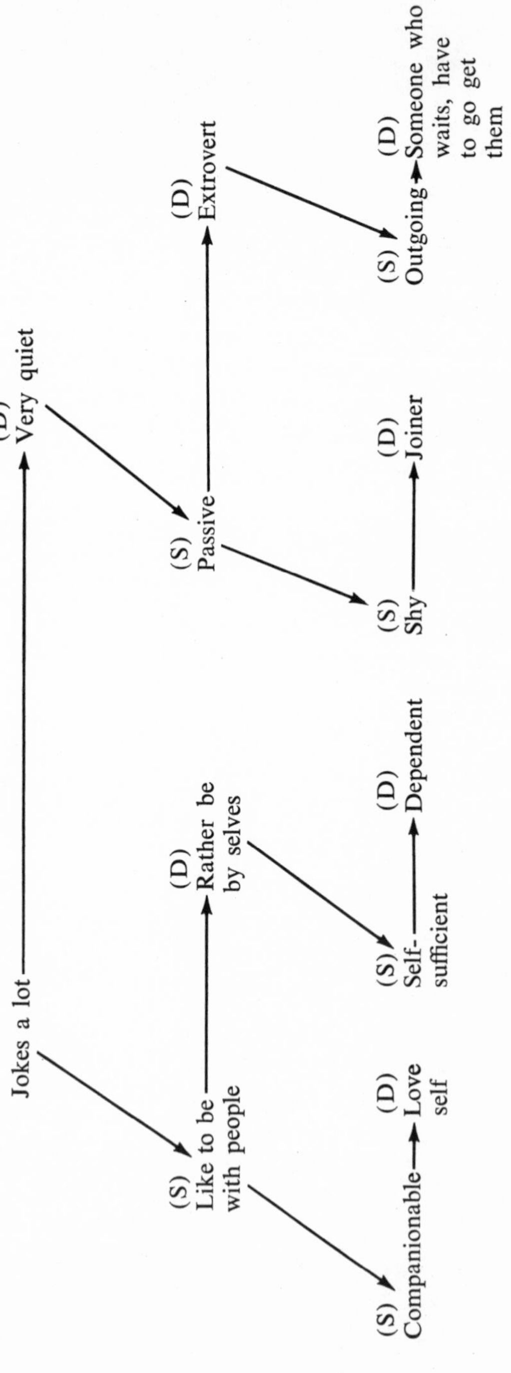

(S) = Similar
(D) = Different

DIAGRAM 8.8
Second Pyramid: Session Three

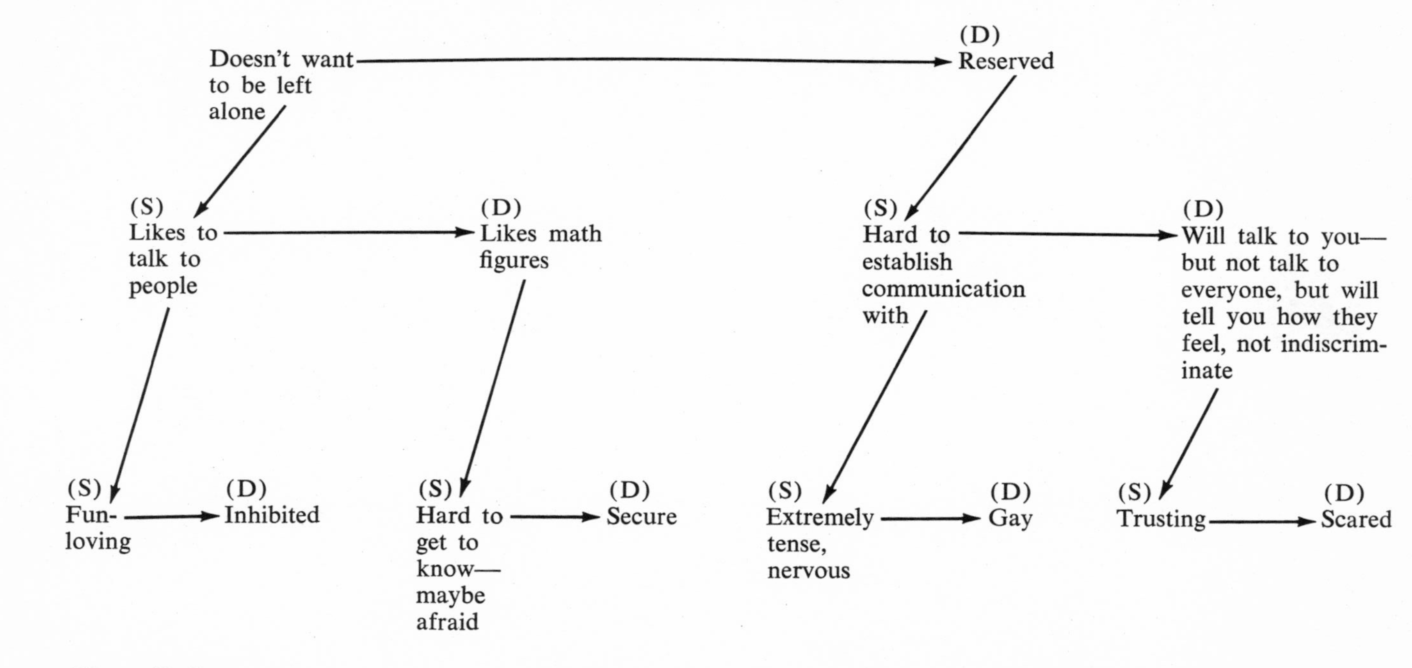

(S) = Similar
(D) = Different

conclusion of the task, express whatever feelings came to mind, and ignore spelling and sentence structure. Execution of the second task was limited to fifteen minutes. Her first response to this latter instruction was to grin and state that she guessed she was kind of rigid at times but would try to put something on paper.

SESSION FOUR

Mary's first typewritten document:

> Everybody likes to feel that he is nice. Easy to get along with, but I feel like maybe I try to be even better than good if thats possible. That these are the things I feel should be said and never let the real things that I think ever even reach the conscious. Shades of Ladies Home Journal! Some things did come out though, like being scared ob of being dependent anx identifying this with motherhood. Well I guess in a sense that is a dependency. I cant remember what all I felt the first time I tried to put it into words. I know I felt very confused, kind of like a hypocrite and yet at the same time I was pleased that I cared since well. I like people and I want them to be happy and also to like me. I do not like being hurt oh darn I just feel that I overemphasize. Its artificial. but at the same time I don't feel i could do it and sonofagun i cant I remember thinking after I finished writing up those cards Say, I'm a pretty nice person but then almost right away I thot Yeah this is for publication. I dont like admitting I"

DISCUSSION AND FURTHER INSTRUCTIONS

Mary and her therapist discussed the first typewritten document only briefly. The nature of this discussion was reflected in the theme—life is paradoxical. That a person could think of herself as independent, yet behave dependently, struck Mary as being highly important as well as disconcerting.

Following this brief discussion, Mary was asked to sort her concepts, using the three-by-five cards which she had previously filled out from her eight pyramids. First, she extracted the sixteen cards on which she had recorded the constructs used at the top of her eight pyramids. Then she categorized the remaining descriptions under the sixteen primary headings. This material was recorded, and directions for its use were given at the seventh session.

SESSIONS FIVE, SIX, AND SEVEN

The next three sessions focused on whatever Mary wished to discuss. The therapist suggested that it might be good to get away from the formal procedure for a few sessions. The therapist's purpose was to allow for the consolidation of new lines of thought and inquiry emerging within the context of the pyramid experiences.

New lines of thought and inquiry did emerge. Mary, for the first time, began openly to debate her right to plan her own life. She also began to share the depth of her fears of relating heterosexually. Finally, she shared the devastating guilt of her dishonesty. She was not the "nice" person, the "generous" person, or the "experienced" person that she pretended. These ideas, expressed to the therapist for the first time, did have behavioral implications. She decided that she should do more active planning of her life rather than just drift along conceding to the expectancies of other people. She was uncertain about how she might change her feelings and relationships with the opposite sex, but she was sure it was important to talk about the way she felt. As for the dishonesty, she decided that she could not hide any longer. Sooner or later her lies would catch up with her and she would have to face the consequences.

Further Pyramid Instructions

1. Throw out any of your descriptions which are exact repeats or which you no longer wish to use. Put them in a special pile.
2. As you do the task, if other descriptions or ways of understanding people occur to you that you have not used which you would like to use, write each one on another three-by-five card and letter these cards A, B, C, etc. You may add these descriptions at any time during this process.
3. Pick out the eight most positive ways of understanding others. Record the numbers.
4. Pick out the eight most negative ways of understanding others. Record the numbers.
5. Spread out the sixteen cards faceup before you.
6. File the remaining cards under each of the sixteen cards. Placement of these cards can be done on any basis meaningful to you. Record the number of each of the sixteen cards and then the numbers of the cards which belong under each of the sixteen cards.
7. Record the numbers of any cards which are difficult to place.

RESPONSES TO RE-SORTING TASK

Mary discarded seventy-five descriptions because they were either repeats or she no longer wished to use them. She added three new descriptions, all negative: *detached, feeling inferior,* and *feelings of indignity.* She found it difficult to sort: *prejudiced, proud, resentful,* and *impersonal.* Twenty-four descriptions were retained which she placed under her selected eight positive and eight negative characteristics. Table 8.1

shows how she sorted the twenty-four descriptions within the sixteen primary categories.

TABLE 8.1

Descriptions Sorted Under Positive and Negative Headings

Positive Descriptions	Negative Descriptions
1. *Got some initiative*	1. *Rejecting*
trusting	in panic
2. *Self-sufficient*	shy
not a frightened person	person who has values
3. *Reserved*	2. *Inconsiderate, selfish*
experienced	clinging dependent
4. *Helper*	extremely tense, nervous
companionable	very quick, impatient
5. *Enthusiasm, a learner*	3. *Superficial*
reads a lot	very active, just busy
I try to communicate	4. *Prejudiced*
well; listen as well	uneducated
as talk	5. *Person who can't or won't*
6. *Gentle*	*understand*
strong	passive
comfortable	inexperienced
7. *Secure*	6. *Impersonal*
gay	detached*
calm	7. *Proud*
8. *Empathetic*	feeling inferior*
not expect too much	8. *Resentful*
	feeling of indignity*

* new descriptions

Mary also was asked to type out her feelings at the conclusion of the re-sorting task. The following document was written in a free-associative way, according to the instructions used at session three.

Mary's Second Typewritten Document:

> Involvement and self-sufficiency. A person can be involved with somebody and still be self sufficient. I guess its a matter of degree. and interest. Maybe it has something to do with being a perfectionist, too. You know, if a person can't fulfill the requirements set for him or her then have nothing to do with them. Then there would be a kind of mixture of arrogance and insecurity or fear of other people. No feeling, I guess, is pure. Getting mixed up with somebody else's affairs means you have no control over what

happens. A person should have something in reserve. It seems to me sometimes that a person who is detached can be more involved. A family is a hostage to fortune. If you have children or someone you care deeply about it is impossible to be objective. Whereas, if a person is free and unfettered by any reciprocal demands he can be ofmore service. It's not fair to be a burden on anybody else in the name of love. I don't understand. Yet, at the same time people treat you as you treat yourself. If you're self-sufficient then they don't waste time worrying about you. It seems to me just from observation that a person who is not a perfectionist and who is dependent gets along better in this world and is more content too. When it should be the other way around, logically. There's pride in achievement too I did this and nobody but nobody helped but that's not wholly true and there's reassurance in capability and selfishness and maybe egomania . . . this is mine and no one else's. Sharing takes time and more effort, I think. and maybe loss of identity. I wish I knew what I was talking about."

DISCUSSION

I was struck with the sharp contrast between Mary's uninvolvement in the previous therapy and the heightened interest and responsiveness to the Pyramid procedures. Mary also felt the difference and admitted that she had never thought very deeply about her problems. The Pyramid Procedure seemed to set the stage for a more productive therapy interaction. For the first time Mary began to confront problems beyond a somatic complaint level. Although Mary's somatic complaints were not eliminated, they decreased in frequency and intensity, and she was able to continue with her university studies.

One year following the termination of her treatment Mary returned for a final interview with her therapist. She had no complaints at this time. She simply wanted to share with the therapist the good news that she finally was graduating, was looking forward to obtaining a position on the West Coast, and had given up the use of nerve pills. "You remember how I used to live on those pills. Well, I haven't had a pill for six months." She then laughed and expressed the thought that she had really changed. "I sure had some ridiculous ideas, didn't I?"

SIGNIFICANCE OF THE PYRAMID PROCEDURE

Psychotherapists may question the usefulness of a formal, psychiatric nomenclature diagnosis or even the more dynamic personality evaluation, both of which may be overly abstract and have few direct implications for how one talks with a client. Nevertheless, therapists usually do have diagnostic concerns about whether or not their clients will do irrevocable harm to themselves or to others. And even the most extremely committed nondirective therapist must wonder if he is validly reflecting his client's feelings and meanings and wishes, if only for the moment, for additional supporting evidence for the appropriateness of his own responses.

Frequently the diagnostic choice is to employ formal diagnostic tools which may lead the therapist to stereotype his client or to just "play it by ear." Many therapists may choose the latter course of action simply because the language of test response is such a far cry from the actual language of therapy. The Pyramid Procedure, however, provides a reconciliation of the therapist's need for structure and his equally strong desire to be relevant. It is a reconciliation of the therapist's interest in theory and the urge to learn about the client's language system. Finally, it is one answer to the therapist's quest for procedures which are both diagnostic and therapeutic.

CHAPTER NINE

REFLECTIONS

THE WRITER OF SCIENCE FICTION MAY TELL A STORY ABOUT AN OBJECT of investigation, possibly an animal or a computer robot, which turns upon his master scientist and enslaves him. Science fiction is good fun, a bit nightmarish, and not to be confused with the reality of science. The physical scientist certainly conceives of the possibility of unleashing some lethal process which he has not anticipated. However, he does not expect, as a usual course of events, to be confronted by some laboratory creation which plays tricks on him, holds back some of the truth, and contemplates what to do about him. The idea that he might be the subject of his creation's experiment would seem absurd to him. This idea also is an absurdity for those psychologists who view themselves as manipulators, whose subjects of experimentation would never dare or even be in the position to perceive and manipulate the manipulators. These psychologists, of course, would understand such events happening to other psychologists, those who do not conduct highly controlled experiments in which very specific variables are manipulated under highly specified conditions. Whether or not it is an absurd idea that subjects in controlled experiments may "do their own things" and confound experimental results or respond to internal and external cues which do not interest the investigator, we are certain that the psychotherapist, in the role of researcher or practitioner, should be concerned about the congruency of client-therapist personal construct systems, an important variable which the therapist may find difficult to manipulate and control.

Working from the dual assumptions that man is theoretical and that certain aspects of his theories are measurable, we sought out the implications of client-therapist congruency in the content and structure of their personal construct systems. We found that the lower degrees of congruency in content and structure are related to premature termination in psychotherapy. This hypothesis is supported in two groups of clients, a longer-term therapy group and a shorter-term group. However, improvement in the longer-term clients, those who do not prematurely terminate, is associated with some degree of contrast in the structure of client-therapist personal construct systems.

The finding that content congruency has particular relevence to premature termination suggests that the communication process is facilitated by some commonality of social interest, values, and language. However, the finding that improvement in longer-term therapy clients is associated with some incongruency in client-therapist conceptual structures suggests the importance of complimentary roles in which shared content allows for communication and certain organizational differences maximize the constructiveness of the relationship. These results strongly suggest that a psychotherapist should not only become aware of his client's personal construct system, but he also should try to understand his client's system in relation to his own personal construct system. Furthermore, a therapist should consider re-referring a client to a more congruent therapist.

The hypothesis that some incongruency in the organization of client-therapist personal construct systems may facilitate improvement in longer-term psychotherapy may be related to Professor Kelly's position that the therapist should surround his clients and patients with methodological constructions rather than with endless arrays of literalisms and specific prescriptions. It is how one approaches his problems which really counts. It is the framework of understanding that one brings to his problems which is most significant, and specific bits of behavior are but the implications of this framework of understanding. A therapist should address himself to the task of working with certain aspects of his client's theoretical nature rather than limit himself to a specific behavior of unknown significance for the system. To ignore the possibility that a behavior may be tied into a larger theoretical system may be as professionally undesirable as to insist that one must intrude upon all matters pertaining to one's client.

Pathways of reflection are intriguing. Beginning with science fiction, I proceeded to a discussion of controlled experiments, a topic which is not unrelated to imaginative processes; then I considered a theoretical construction called client-therapist congruence in personal construct systems, a variable which a scientist-therapist might find difficult to manipulate and control. The discussion of congruency allowed me to point out that the therapist should be concerned about his client's framework of understanding and differentiated two approaches to human psychology—the study of man's theoretical behavior and the study of behavioral bits. Since we now have differentiated the construct approach from a popular alternative, it is appropriate to illustrate what personal construct theory may have in common with certain other positions, specifically, an externally oriented behaviorism and an internally oriented, traditional psychoanalytic theory.

PERSONAL CONSTRUCT PSYCHOLOGY AS METATHEORY

The psychology of personal constructs has been described as a metatheory. It is a theory about theories and it is a theory about personal approaches to life. In this volume we have applied the idea of personal constructs to clients and therapists. Can we also apply this kind of thinking to the formal theories held by therapists? Can the theory encompass other scientific theories? Are the imaginations of other scientists discounted? How might a personal construct psychologist view the achievements of Freudians and behaviorists?

If one is willing to forego certain assumptions made by other theorists about the universal natures of men, the methods, tools, and even insights of many other theorists may be useful to the personal construct psychologist. For example, some people may well have personal construct systems bearing psychoanalytic implications. Certainly Freud may be seen as a fantastically astute and sensitive personal construct psychologist whose patients presumably did have personal construct systems resembling, at some level and to some degree, the more formal constructions of psychoanalysis. Reinforcement psychologists can be seen as reflecting certain underlying personal constructions which may be influenced by external manipulations. However, a personal construct psychologist would state that to the extent that the learning theorist's methods work he is "tuned in" to the personal-validational system of the other person. To the extent that he is not "tuned in" to the validational system of the other person, his methods will not succeed.

Psychoanalysis may not work with people who lack constructions of experience which can be caught within the network of analytic constructions. Behavior therapy, pointed toward change in a specific behavior, may not be successful with people whose behavior is intimately linked with many aspects of the construction system. Behavior therapy also may not work with people who lack dependency construction.

The implications of this line of reasoning are clear. The personal construct psychologist is free to employ some of the tools and the insights of other theoretical models. At the same time, the personal construct psychologist must adhere to his own universal assumption—that man is essentially a theorizer and experimenter. Even as he may find the insights of other scientists useful, these insights will be used in such a way and reinterpreted in such a way that man, the theorizer, will not be subordinated to the universals or literalisms of other theoretical models.

To illustrate this latter point, a personal construct therapist may employ a free-associative technique as a way of encouraging his client to bring new personal construct elements into his discussion. The therapist may also assist his client in the exploration of new ways of viewing his problem, a pursuit which might eventuate in a client's heightened awareness of relationships which have psychoanalytic implications. However, the therapist would not insist that his client's new awareness fit precisely within such a framework. He would be open to the idea that whatever he says or does in relation to his client may well be irrelevant, and that the defensiveness of his client may be, in actuality, his own inability to understand his client's emotional and behavioral system.

A personal construct therapist may employ more specific role and behavioral procedures. Kelly introduced a particular method which he unfortunately titled *Fixed Role Therapy*. In this procedure social roles are written, and the client "tries them on for size." The approach is not fixed. To the contrary, the client has a choice as to whether he participates in the procedure and which role he plays on an experimental basis. The roles also are written in such a manner that the client can implement the role prescriptions in his own style, even in ways that the therapist does not envision. Furthermore, care is taken that the essence of any role prepared for the client does not violate directly a cherished central value or core construct. Kelly (1955) describes the procedure in detail and Bonarius (1970) discusses his use of the approach in a paper given the intriguing title, "Fixed Role Therapy: A Double Paradox." Karst and Trexler (1970) report the usefulness of fixed role therapy with subjects who complain of public speaking anxiety.

INDICES OF CLIENT-THERAPIST CONGRUENCY

Client-therapist congruency, as we have noted, was measured by the commonality in content and structure of personal construct systems. Several additional measures of congruency also were used. Congruency was viewed as the meaningfulness of the other person, the meaningfulness of the other person's personal constructs, and identification with the ideals of the other person.

Defining the meaningfulness of the other person by rating scale polarization, as one member of the therapy dyad rated the other person on his own personal construct dimensions, nonpremature termination was found to be related to greater polarization. Although one's own social descriptive language, i.e., personal constructs, appeared to be more useful than the other person's language, nonpremature termination showed some relationship to an ability to meaningfully employ the other person's language dimensions. In other words, to some extent it is important to be able to enter the conceptual world of the other member of the therapy dyad as well as to make sense of the other person within one's own personal construct dimensions. Finally, improvement in therapy was associated with a shift in the present-self of the client toward the ideal of the therapist. However, this shift occurred within the dimensional language of the client and not within that of the therapist. One implication of this finding is that to the extent that a therapist may plot his personal ideal in a meaningful way within the framework of his client, his client may improve. This type of result, which is based on a somewhat homogeneous client-therapist sample, further validates the frustrations of therapists who have the courage to work with patients from a different socioeconomic class.

Returning again to a consideration of content congruency, one of the most interesting hypotheses about client-therapist congruency was unexpectedly reversed. Greater congruency at the beginning stages of longer-term therapy was associated with a more negative therapist description of his client. One implication of this finding is that a psychotherapist must be very cautious in drawing conclusions about his client during the early phase of therapy interaction. A client might be revealing more negative aspects of himself at the beginning of therapy as a function of greater congruency in the content of client-therapist social language. Then again, the therapist might be reacting to a threat induced by commonality.

METHODS OF INQUIRY

Four major approaches to personal construct data were employed: content scoring, organizational scoring, rating scale polarization, and the use of self-rating scales defined in the client's own language.

Work with the content of personal constructs shows that it is possible to postcode them and that the postcoding categories can be related meaningfully to other personality variables. Clinical evidence in particular points to a relationship between content focus inferred from one's personal constructs and actual behavior.

An organization score called the FIC, a measure of functionally independent construction, is differentiated from what some investigators refer to as cognitive complexity. Correlates of a high FIC score, such as ratings of confusion, suggest the importance of the organization measure. Although the data is limited, there appears to be some relationship between high FIC scores and serious suicidal attempts, particularly when the high FIC scores are found in the context of conceptual constriction in the application and content of one's constructs (Landfield, 1969). Inspection of Rep Tests (Landfield, 1967) obtained from a comparison group of five alcoholics hospitalized at a rapid treatment center in St. Louis shows that three of these patients obtain extremely low FIC scores, suggesting high organization to the point of simplicity. One patient obtained an extremely high FIC score and also showed conceptual constriction in the content and application of his constructs. This particular patient is described as a binge-type alcoholic whereas the other four are described as chronics. The association of binge drinking with Rep Test scoring correlated with suicidal potential tends to support the contention of clinicians that some alcoholics are acutely suicidal. Although the FIC scores of the alcoholics are found at both extremes of the organization dimension, the content of all five Rep protocols reflect an overwhelming emphasis on constructions of responsibility and morality.

Rating scale polarization or extremity use of rating scales is well documented as a measure of meaningfulness, particularly when the "objects" described are important to the person and ratings are done within the person's own language system. Our studies suggest that subject ratings done within the language framework of the psychologist may yield different results from ratings done by the subject within the dimensions of his own personal construct system. Such findings do not imply that an investigator should avoid stimulus materials couched in his own language or in a broader based cultural or common language. We only are saying that he should be aware of the possibility that an individual may function within a social language and communication framework which is somewhat different from that provided by the investigator. Quite to the contrary, it might be profitable to discover just how well an individual can function within a common language framework.

The assumption that people do function within different frameworks of meaning, even as they may share common ground, leads to a disconcerting line of inquiry. How frequently do our descriptions of another person, e.g., confused, represent the actual state of that person's thinking, and how often do they represent our own limited ability to understand the social and emotional language within which the other person is functioning? How frequently do our descriptions of another person, e.g., as defensive, point to our own lack of appreciation of the ways in which that person thinks? How often do we assume that our own language is so important that it should communicate adequately if the other person is sufficiently bright? And, most disconcerting of all, how many "objective," "scientific" studies tell more about how we function as investigators—the nature of our values and ways in which we prefer to learn—than what our subjects value most and how they prefer to learn and understand?

IN RETROSPECT

I wish that the two phases of this investigation could have been combined. Although it did not seem feasible at the time, both the variable- and longer-term therapy groups should have done the same research tasks. Moreover, client self-ratings and ratings of his therapist might have been done within both older and more newly verbalized personal construct dimensions. As newly verbalized constructions were added to the construct repertoire, and as constructs were reorganized within the system, changes in polarization on older verbalized dimensions might have been found to correlate with changes in the hierarchical positions of these dimensions.

I also wish that an inquiry had been used which would have provided more information about how clients operationally define their constructs. The idea of training a client to postcode the content of his own constructs did occur to us but was rejected as unwieldy, though nevertheless intriguing. Finally, I wish that the Pyramid Procedure had been used as part of the construct elicitation procedure. But wishes are not horses and scientific beggars do not ride.

A FINAL THEORETICAL STATEMENT

Kelly observed that psychologists sometimes ignore their own behavior as scientists. A similar observation was made by Oliver and Landfield (1962). The reflexivity of psychology lies in the fact that the psychologist is the object of his own study. This precipitates paradoxes of self-reference in connection with universal propositions. Even when his subject matter may consist of fragmentary aspects of mental life, ultimately the psychologist's observations have to fit into an understanding of the whole man, including the less tractable aspects of himself such as the qualities enabling him to be a researcher, his values, and all the facts of his consciousness. The way to surmount reflexive difficulties is to be aware of them and how they differentiate psychology from the other sciences, then to draw the consequences.

Bannister (1966), in an address to American psychologists, commented:

> . . . At a joke level psychologists may argue that a particular psychoanalyst is writing a particular paper in order to sublimate his sex instinct, or we may toy with the notion that a book by some learning theorist is evidence that the said learning theorist was suffering from a build-up of reactive inhibition. But in our more solemn moments we seem to prefer the paradoxical view that psychologists are explainers, predictors, and experimenters, whereas the organism, God bless him, is a very different kettle of fish . . . . I am not arguing here that psychological theories of what man is should be directly modeled upon and simply reflect lay common sense psychological theories of what man is. The conception of a desk held by an atomic physicist is by no means similar to the common sense conception of what a desk is. However, it is perhaps significant that the atomic physicist's notion of what a desk is, is a good deal more exciting, complex, and rich than the common sense notion. A hydrographer's conceptualization of water is likewise a good deal more elaborate and soaring than that held by you or me. It may be that psychology is the only science which has been able to produce concepts of its subject which are clearly more mean, more miserable, and more limited than lay concepts.
>
> As a simple and immediate test of the value of a psychological theory, I would suggest that you examine it and if it implies that you are much less than you know yourself to be, then such a framework should be discarded.
>
> In spite of the sense of urgency which I detect in American psychology, I would argue that we can and should take time for a great deal of such discarding and concomitantly a great deal of new invention.

It is my belief that psychological research based on a personal construct approach may provide this badly needed new invention.

APPENDIX A

The Rep Test

INSTRUCTION SHEET

This questionnaire is comprised of three sheets: (1) the Response Sheet, (2) the Role Specification Sheet, and (3) the Instruction Sheet. Read all directions before beginning. If the directions are not completely clear ask for more information.

Start with the *Role Specification Sheet.* Beginning with your mother's name, write the first names of the people described. Write their names on the *Response Sheet* in the numbered blanks in the upper left-hand corner. If you know two people with the same name, use a last initial as well. If you cannot remember a person's first name write his last name, or something about him which will clearly bring to your mind the person's identity.

Take your *Response Sheet.* Note that two cells in Row 1 have circles in them. This means that you are first to consider the two people whose names appear on diagonals 1 and 7. Think about these two people. Are the two people alike in some *one way?* Or are the two people different in some one way? If the two people are alike, is one of your listed acquaintances different from the two who are alike?

If you first see that the two people are alike in some one way, write under Column 1, Row 1, the one way in which these two people are alike. Then, if you can think of a person on your list who can be contrasted with the two people who are alike, write under Column 2 the way in which this person is different from the two who are alike. Place the number of the different acquaintance after the contrasting description. Now place an *S* in each of the two circles in Row 1, *S* meaning that the two people are similar in some way.

RESPONSE SHEET

Example:	Sal	Pete	Bill	Phil	Jill	Column 1	Column 2
	1	2	3	7	8		
Row 1	Ⓢ			Ⓢ		honest	nonreligious-3

If you first see that the two people are alike in some one way but cannot find a person on your list who can be contrasted with these two similar people, fill in Column 1 but leave Column 2 blank.

RESPONSE SHEET

Example:	Sal 1	Pete 2	Bill 3	Phil 7	Jill 8	Column 1	Column 2
Row 1	Ⓢ			Ⓢ		formal	______

If you first see that the two people are different in some way, write under Column 1 the description of the person in the left circle and under Column 2 the different description of the person in the right circle. Now place *D* in each of the two circles in Row 1. *D* means that the two people are different in some way.

RESPONSE SHEET

Example:	Sal 1	Pete 2	Bill 3	Phil 7	Jill 8	Column 1	Column 2
Row 1	Ⓓ			Ⓓ		formal	doesn't care

If you cannot see a similarity or a difference between the two people designated in Row 1, leave blanks. After you have finished with Row 1 consider the two people to be compared in Row 2. Follow the instructions given above.

After you have completed each of the fifteen comparisons start with Row 1. This time consider each of the other thirteen persons whom you have not rated with *S* or *D*. Note your descriptions under Column 1, Row 1. Put a *1* under the name of each person in Row 1 who has the characteristic described under Column 1, Row 1. Put a *2* under the name of each person in Row 1 who has the characteristic described under Column 2, Row 1. Put an *N* under the name of each person to whom neither the rating in Column 1 or Column 2 applies. Put a *?* under the name of a person when you cannot decide whether to rate the person as *1* or *2*. Of course, if there is no characteristic under Column 2, no *2* rating can be done in this row.

After finishing your ratings in Row 1, proceed to Row 2 etc.

Examples:

RESPONSE SHEET

	Sal 1	Pete 2	Bill 3	Phil 7	Jill 8	Column 1	Column 2
Row 1	Ⓢ	1	2	Ⓢ	?	formal	humorous-2
Row 2	Ⓢ	1	N	Ⓢ	1	honest	______
Row 3	Ⓓ	1	2	Ⓓ	N	humorous	serious

ROLE SPECIFICATION SHEET

Do the best you can to find people who fit the descriptions below. If you have to depart too far from the type designated in order to fill every diagonal, star those names which do not fit very well.

1. Write the first name of your mother or the person who has played the part of your mother on the first diagonal line on the Response Sheet (after number 1).
2. Write the first name of your father or the person who has played the part of your father on the second diagonal.
3. Write the name of your brother nearest your own age, or the person who has played the part of such a brother.
4. Write the name of your sister nearest your own age, or the person who has played the part of such a sister.
5. Your wife (or husband) or closest present girl-(boy-) friend. Do not repeat the name of anyone listed above.
6. Your closest present friend of the same sex as yourself. Do not repeat names.
7. A person with whom you have worked or associated who, for some unexplainable reason, appeared to dislike you. Do not repeat names.
8. The person with whom you usually feel most uncomfortable. Do not repeat names.
9. The person you have met whom you would most like to know better.
10. The teacher whose point of view you have found most acceptable. Do not repeat names.
11. The teacher whose point of view you have found most objectionable. Do not repeat names.
12. The most unsuccessful person you know personally. Do not repeat names.
13. The most successful person you know personally. Do not repeat names.
14. The happiest person you know personally. Do not repeat names.
15. The unhappiest person you know personally. Do not repeat names.

RESPONSE SHEET

Names	1	2	3	4	5	6	7	8	9	10	11	12	13	14	15		Column 1	Column 2
Row 1	O						O									1		
Row 2		O											O			2		
Row 3			O								O					3		
Row 4							O				O					4		
Row 5								O				O				5		
Row 6				O		O										6		
Row 7									O						O	7		
Row 8	O					O										8		
Row 9					O										O	9		
Row 10		O						O								10		
Row 11				O						O						11		
Row 12			O											O		12		
Row 13					O								O			13		
Row 14									O			O				14		
Row 15										O				O		15		

APPENDIX B

Rep Test Scoring Manual

INTRODUCTION

Categorizing the content of personal constructs is a difficult task. Although it was reported that the second judge in the final interjudge consistency study reviewed the manual for only four hours before rating twenty Rep Tests, she was already acquainted with the general nature of the Rep Test, found it interesting, and did not debate whether we had used the best categories or had defined them properly. Her willingness to "try" our constructs, i.e., our rating categories, undoubtedly made the task easier.

Ideally, one should memorize the rating categories, read the manual several times, then score each description in the alphabetized list of 1500 scored descriptions which is appended to the manual. Whenever the rater finds a discrepancy between his scoring and that found in the appended list, he should carefully recheck category definitions and examples, particularly those examples which are labeled *not fit*. Not fit examples are descriptions of people which one might mistakenly place in a category. Since it is possible to place a description within more than one category, there may be problems of underscoring and overscoring. For example, the description, *complete extrovert,* may be postcoded as (1a) high social, (2a) high forcefulness, and (21) extreme qualifier. However, *friendly* is simply scored as (1a) high social. Overscoring may mean that one needs to ask whether or not a description necessarily points to a particular category. If the description does not necessarily fit and if our examples in the manual and the appended list do not suggest that you should score it, don't score it. Underscoring may mean that one needs to attend more closely to the alphabetized list or perhaps one should be more compulsive about considering each description in relation to each category.

The scored alphabetized list does aid immeasurably in stabilizing the rating task. Nevertheless, the rater must be prepared to experience some conflict as he tries to reconcile his own constructs with those provided for him.

DIRECTIONS

The content categories which are to be used in postcoding the polar descriptions of the Rep Test are listed in the next section, then are defined and illustrated in the section following that. A list of fully scored descriptions is appended to this manual and should be referred to as each description is scored.

Each rating category is identified by name, definition, and examples. Examples are of two kinds: those descriptions which *fit* a category and those descriptions which *do not fit* a category. *Not fit* examples are presented because they represent kinds of descriptions which at first inspection might mistakenly be placed in a particular category.

Referring now to the Rep Test Response Sheet found in Appendix A, note that the person describes his constructions on the right hand side of this sheet under Columns 1 and 2. Note that there are fifteen responses under Column 1 and fifteen responses under Column 2, totaling thirty descriptions of people. Take each one of these thirty responses and place it under as many postcoding categories as are appropriate. Score each of the thirty responses separately. However, in some instances it may be necessary to note the contrasting response, e.g., *honest* versus *the opposite*. In this illustration one assumes that *the opposite* means dishonest.

If a multiple description is used, e.g., "Fred is biased but friendly," score the two descriptive elements separately. In this example, *biased* would be scored (10d) closed, *friendly* would be scored (1a) high social. If two elements in the same response are scored in the same way the response is scored only once in that category. Since multiple description may inflate content scores, a prorating procedure is used to reduce scores to a common base. This prorating procedure is discussed in Chapter 3.

Adhere closely to the rating definitions and the examples given for each category. Be sure to check synonyms as well as the exact description in the alphabetized list. Keep in mind that it may be impossible to score some responses within the categories. When in doubt, do not score. Do not assume that you remember the scoring of a commonly used description. Check each description against all categories.

DEFINITIONS AND EXAMPLES OF RATING CATEGORIES

Examples under the category *Fit* refer to the type of description that would usually apply to the category under consideration. Examples under *Not Fit* refer to types of description which might or might not be indices of that category, or could not fit the category at all.

1. SOCIAL INTERACTION

   Any statement in which face-to-face, ongoing, continuing interaction or lack of face-to-face, ongoing, continuing interaction with others is (clearly) indicated.

Social interaction refers to statements suggesting face-to-face, ongoing interaction or lack of face-to-face interaction. Exclude subjective type descriptions, e.g., wants to be a leader, feels talkative.

a. *Active:* Statements in which ongoing or continuing interaction with others is clearly indicated.

RATING CATEGORIES*

1. Social Interaction
   a. Active
   b. Inactive
2. Forcefulness
   a. High
   b. Low
3. Organization
   a. High
   b. Low
4. Self-sufficiency
   a. High
   b. Low
5. Status
   a. High
   b. Low
6. Factual Description
7. Intellective
   a. High
   b. Low
8. Self-reference
9. Imagination
   b. Low
10. Alternatives
    a. Multiple Description
    d. Closed to Alternatives
11. Sexual
12. Morality
    a. High
    b. Low
13. External Appearance
14. Emotional Arousal
16. Egoism
    a. High
17. Tenderness
    a. High
    b. Low
18. Time Orientation
    a. Past
    b. Future
19. Involvement
    a. High
    b. Low
21. Extreme Qualifiers
22. Humor
    a. High
    b. Low

* Seven categories were deleted because of low interjudge reliability: 9a-High Imagination; 10b-Inferable Alternatives; 10c-Open to Alternatives; 15-Diffuse Generalization; 16b-Low Egoism; 18c-Present Time; 20-Comparatives.

Fit: aggressive, brotherly, engaged, extrovert, a follower, friendly, lot of fun, good guy, great guy, sense of humor, a leader, married, motherly, has personality, polite, popular, social, talkative, understanding.

Not Fit: humorous, likes to lead others, loyal, wants a relationship, stubborn.

Active, Not Fit examples: Humorous is not considered social interaction since a person could appear humorous on the basis of some superficial characteristic. *Loyal* is not considered an example of active social interaction since one can be loyal to ideas as well as to people. Moreover, loyalty to a person may not mean face-to-face social interaction with him. *Likes to lead others* is a subjective description. One could be *stubborn* apart from face-to-face relationships with people.

b. *Inactive:* Statements in which lack of interaction with others is clearly indicated.

Fit: aloof, asocial, homebody, introvert, unsocial, withdrawn.

Not Fit: cold, indifferent, quiet.

Inactive, Not Fit examples: Quietness does not necessarily mean that a person has few face-to-face contacts. A person can be *indifferent* or neutral and still be social. However, *aloof* means to distance oneself and more strongly suggests low social interaction.

c. *Unclassified:* Interpersonal statements which do not clearly indicate which of the two meanings (a or b) is implied. Unclassified descriptions include inadequate types of interaction which *might* curtail ongoing relationships with others.

Fit: antisocial, cold, cruel, poor mixer, passive, lacks social poise, rude, unfriendly, uninteresting, unpopular.

Not Fit: good guy, likes to lead others, loyal, quiet, stubborn, untrustworthy.

Unclassified, Not Fit examples: Good guy usually implies ongoing, face-to-face contact. *Untrustworthy,* even though suggesting the possibility of face-to-face social interaction, does not emphasize the dimension of social interaction.

2. FORCEFULNESS

Any statement denoting energy, overt expressiveness, persistence, intensity, or the opposite.

a. *High:*

Fit: aggressive, ambition, avoids people, bigoted, creative, critical, devil-may-care, dogmatic, extrovert, sense of humor, impulsive, independent, intolerant, a leader, mind of own, notice everything, obstinate, prejudiced, not put things off, quick-tempered, serious, set ideas, striving, stubborn, talkative, hard worker, zest for life.

Not Fit: biased, condescending, humorous, feeling superior, uncreative.

High, Not Fit examples: The subjective *feeling of superiority* need not be an indication of forcefulness. *Humorous* may not refer to high activity by the observed or the observer. *Condescension* is a rather weak kind of expressiveness. *Biased* does not necessarily imply forcefulness.

b. *Low:*

Fit: calm, easygoing, a follower, indifferent, easily influenced, lax, lazy, lethargic, passive, quiet, relaxed.

Not Fit: achievement unimportant, dependent, humble, ideas fluctuate, feeling inferior, introvert, can't make up mind, not antagonistic, put things off, vacillating.

Low, Not Fit examples: Achievement unimportant does not necessarily mean that the person is not forceful. The individual may be very forceful in asserting the idea that achievement is not important or he may be expressive in ways not achievement oriented. *Putting things off* could represent a high degree of rebelliousness. *Dependency* may be either aggressive or passive. *Humbleness* under certain circumstances may be a strong expression of value. *Introversion,* though indicating some kind of social withdrawal, does not negate the possibility of personal forcefulness. *Not antagonistic,* though indicating absence of anger, does not necessarily mean that a person lacks forcefulness. *Feeling inferior* could involve considerable expressiveness and persistence. *Being unable to make up one's mind,* in some cases, may be a very active and energetic process.

3. ORGANIZATION

Any statement denoting either the state of or process of structuring, planning and organizing, or the opposite. The statement should indicate that a person either has or lacks a general trait of structuring, organizing, and planning ability, or can be described as organized, structured, disorganized, or unstructured.

a. *High:*

Fit: careful, committed, competent, compulsive, consistent, constructive, conventional, efficient, formal, good judgment, neat, organized, perfectionist, planning, prudent.

Not Fit: bigoted, broadminded, conservative, democratic, dependable, loyal, optimistic, passive, pessimistic, put things off, realistic, theoretical.

High, Not Fit examples: a *bigoted* person could be highly organized or less well organized. *Realistic* says little about structuring, organizing, and planning.

b. *Low:*

Fit: chaotic, cluttered mind, confused, disorganized, flighty, ideas fluctuate, impulsive, lax, messy, muddled, perplexed, reckless, uncertain of self, unpredictable.

Not Fit: abnormal, destructive, disturbed, irresponsible, maladjusted, may be this way, poor judgment, quick-tempered, sometimes friendly, temperamental, undependable.

Low, Not Fit examples: sometimes friendly does not necessarily imply unpredictability—the attitudes and behavior may be predictable. *May be this way* suggests openness more than lack of organization. *Quick temper* may be organized or disorganized. *Irresponsible* may only mean that the person does not take part in responsible activities. A person may be *maladjusted* and organized.

4. SELF-SUFFICIENCY

Any statement denoting independence, initiative, confidence, and ability to solve one's own problems or the opposite.

a. *High:*

Fit: competent, exploratory, feels self-sufficient, go-getter, independent, a leader, maturity, mind of own, not put things off, pursues ideas, realistic, thinks for self.

Not Fit: aggressive, bigoted, dogmatic, extrovert, feeling superior, get ideas, sophisticated, striving.

High, Not Fit examples: Feeling superior sometimes might be associated with a lack of self-sufficiency. Even though *striving* may be related to self-sufficiency, it can be related to a great fear of dependency. *Sophisticated* may or may not involve self-sufficiency. There are many forms of *aggressiveness. Extroversion* can be related to self-sufficiency, but not necessarily. *Bigoted, set ideas,* and *dogmatic* may or may not be related to independence.

b. *Low:*

Fit: dependent, feeling inferior, a follower, immaturity, incompetent, easily influenced, lacks self confidence, lost, passive, suggestible.

Low, Fit examples: Whereas *feeling superior* may or may not be related to high self-sufficiency, it seems reasonable that *inferior feelings* are likely to be related to low self-sufficiency.

Not Fit: puts things off.

5. STATUS

Any statement wherein references are made to either status striving or to high prestige status symbols, or to a lack of status striving or to low prestige status symbols.

a. *High:*

Fit: ambition, educated, executive type, formal, glory seeker, has good job, has money, high position, industrious, intellectual, professional, professor, refined, respected, sophisticated, striving, studious, successful in own eyes, tries to impress people, upper middle class, upward-and-onward type, wealthy.

Not Fit: educated fool, instructor, intelligent, jack-of-all-trades, teacher.

High, Not Fit examples: Teacher is neither a high nor low status term. It seems to be primarily an occupational description.

b. *Low:*

Fit: bum, drunkard, lazy, low class, shiftless, unambitious, uneducated.

Not Fit: stupid.

Low, Not Fit examples: a person who is *stupid* is not necessarily in a low status position.

6. FACTUAL DESCRIPTION

A characteristic so described that most observers could agree that it is factual. A fact would be a characteristic not open to question.

Fit: always lived in same town, brother, college educated, engaged, father, female, in business, live in Chicago, male, married, mother, older, pharmacist, red hair, student, tall, teacher, younger.

Not Fit: beautiful, brotherly, concrete, educated, feminine, masculine, messy dresser, motherly, overly specific, ugly.

Not Fit examples: Motherliness might be open to interpretation. *Beautiful* certainly is a highly subjective term. *Messy dresser* could be open to interpretation.

7. INTELLECTIVE

Any statement denoting intelligence or intellectual pursuits, or the opposite.

a. *High:*

Fit: bright, extensive knowledge, intellectual, intelligent, professor, teacher, wise.

Not Fit: aesthetic, artistic, broad-minded, experienced, good judgment, sophisticated, student, wise guy.

High, Not Fit examples: Even though intelligence may be related to *broad-mindedness,* broad-mindedness may not be used in the context of intellect. *Student* does not mean that one is highly intelligent nor does it point, necessarily, to intellectual pursuits. *Sophisticated* may refer to more superficial attitudes and external appearance. *Artistic* refers to a specific trait. *Aesthetic* need not be used in the context of high intelligence.

b. *Low:*

Fit: dumb, laborer, naive, uneducated.

Not Fit: narrow-minded, poor judgment.

Low, Not Fit examples: Narrow-mindedness is not limited to the unintelligent.

8. SELF-REFERENCE

Any statement in which the person taking the test refers directly to himself.

Fit: brother, enjoy their company, friend, I like them, I don't like them, they like me, they don't like me, personally like, sister, mother.

Not Fit: friends, brothers.

Not Fit examples: Friends could refer to the relationships among others. *Brothers* may not directly refer to self.

9. IMAGINATION

Any statement denoting subjective activity which is supplemental to or divorced from reality, or its opposite.

b. *Low:*

Fit: concrete, doctrinaire, earthy, practical, reactionary, realistic.

Not Fit: close-minded, conservative, liberal, rigid, uneducated.

Low, Not Fit examples: A lack of education does not necessarily mean that one lacks imagination. *Liberal* and *conservative* say little about imagination. One could be *rigid* or *close-minded* in the context of subjectivity divorced from reality.

10. ALTERNATIVES

The subject employs (a) *more than one description,* (b) *a qualified description suggesting the possibility of other descriptions,* (c) *a description suggesting a strong openness, or* (d) *a description suggesting little receptivity to new alternatives.*

a. *Multiple description:*
Fit: friendly and ambitious.
Not Fit: aspiring and ambitious, friendly and social.

d. *Closed to alternatives:* Understood as a more general characteristic.
Fit: always realistic, avoidant, bigoted, conservative, dogmatic, inhibited, narrow-minded, *never* angry, *no* emotions, one-track mind, rigid, status quo.
Not Fit: careful, formal, introvert, not studious, organized, prudent, realistic.

11. SEXUAL

Any direct reference to sexual behavior or implicit sexual behavior.
Fit: not physically attracted to me, engaged, going steady, interest in boys, married, sensuous, accepts my sex, not attractive sexually, sexy.
Not Fit: beautiful, female, handsome, male.
Not Fit examples: Male, female, beautiful, and *handsome* do not refer directly to sexual behavior.

12. MORALITY

Any statement denoting religious or moral values.

a. *High:*
Fit: conscientious, dependable, good, good person, honest, integrity, loyal, moral, not guilty, religious, responsible, sincere, trustworthy, truthful.
Not Fit: good personality, idealistic.
High, Not Fit examples: Idealism need not imply religious or moral concepts. *Good personality* may not refer to religious or moral values.

b. *Low:*
Fit: atheist, bad, degenerate, dishonest, disloyal, drunkard, greedy, guilty, immoral, irresponsible, lacks character, liar, morally weak, not religious, selfish, untrustworthy, weak character.
Not Fit: agnostic, alcoholic, bad personality.
Low, Not Fit examples: Alcoholism need not be related to religious or moral concepts. *Bad personality* may not refer to religious or moral values.

13. EXTERNAL APPEARANCE

Any statement describing a person's appearance which may be either more objective or more subjective.

Fit: beautiful, fat, looks old, looks young, masculine, messy dresser, meticulous, red hair, short, tall, thin, ugly.

Not Fit: older, younger.

Not Fit examples: Older and *younger* may refer only to age.

14. EMOTIONAL AROUSAL

Any statement denoting a transient or chronic readiness to react with stronger feelings such as anger, anxiety, disgust, enthusiasm, fearfulness, grief, joy, nervousness, surprise, yearning, etc.

Fit: agitated, anxious, a little anxious, cheerful, concerned, in conflict, discouraged, enthusiastic, excitable, high strung, hostile, impatient, jealous, quick tempered, sad, sentimental, spontaneous, temperamental, upset, zest for life.

Not Fit: apathetic, brat, optimistic, patient, pessimistic.

Not Fit examples: One can be *pessimistic* in one's attitude and still be rather neutral in feeling and emotion. *Patience* shows a lack of readiness to be aroused. *Apathetic* indicates the same attitude. One can be *optimistic* without being highly emotional.

16. EGOISM

Any statement denoting self importance. High egoism may be either constructive or destructive and scoring will be more liberal—not debating whether, e.g., the conceited person really is confident.

a. *High:*

Fit: authoritarian, tries to be big man, conceited, feels confident, domineering, feels comfortable with himself, respects self, self-centered, selfish, thinks he is smart, smart alec, feels superior.

Not Fit: knows what he wants to be, knows where he is going, superior, tries to be self-sufficient.

High, Not Fit examples: The question is whether one *feels superior,* not whether one *is superior. Knowing what one wants* does not imply self-importance unless one is sure it can be attained.

17. TENDERNESS

Any statement denoting susceptibility to softer feelings toward others such as love, compassion, gentleness, kindness, considerateness, or the opposite.

a. *High:*

Fit: considerate, devoted, gentle, helpful, kind, loving, a loving attitude, sweet person, sympathetic, sympathetic feelings, tender, understanding, unselfish.

Not Fit: aesthetic, altruistic, feminine, sensitive, sensitive to criticism, sentimental.

High, Not Fit examples: One can be *sensitive* without being tender. Some *aesthetic* people can be highly egocentric. *Feminine* may be associated with traits other than tenderness. *Altruism* can have a cold, administrative quality. *Sentimental* can indicate mushiness without understanding of others.

b. *Low:*

Fit: callous, cold, critical, hard, hardened, harsh, impolite, indifferent, insensitive, rejecting, rude, selfish, sour person, stern, unfeeling.

Not Fit: masculine, rough, strong.

Low, Not Fit examples: Strength and *masculinity* may or may not be associated with tenderness.

18. Time Orientation

Any statement denoting a state of mind which strongly implies an individual's future orientation and expectancy, or a past orientation and expectancy. Some descriptions may imply both orientations and cannot be scored.

a. *Past:*

Fit: pride in family background, happy childhood, *had* goals, worships the past.

Not Fit: cynical.

b. *Future:*

Fit: believes in change, *has* goals, optimistic, pessimistic, sanguine.

Not Fit: cynical.

Past, Future, Not Fit examples: Cynical may refer to past, present or future.

19. Involvement

Any statement denoting a persistent effort toward that which an individual finds more generally and internally meaningful or, restated, a high or low internal and more total commitment or dedication to and strong pursuit of an interest, occupation, way of life, philosophy, or simply the state of commitment, dedication, or lack of such.

a. *High:*

Fit: believes in change, committed, concerned with others, dedicated, deeply interested in field, egocentric, egotist, enthusiasm, an epicurean, humanitarian, insatiably curious, involved, involved with life, life has meaning, loves only self, pursues ideas, religious, zest for life.

Not Fit: compulsive, go-getter, hard worker, interested, interested in others, interested in sports, responsible, social, spontaneous.

High, Not Fit examples: Social refers to a type of activity, but not to an internal and more total commitment. *Compulsive* also refers to a type of activity, without necessarily implying more. A *responsible* person could be more externalized and conforming and not so internally committed. *Go-getter* and *hard worker* do not necessarily mean that the person has an internalized commitment, i.e., that hard work is the way to live. *Interest* is not strong enough in emphasis.

b. *Low:*

Fit: aloof, apathetic, asocial, indifferent, life is meaningless, lost, not interested in anything, nothing bothers him, stoic, uncommitted.

Not Fit: discouraged, inhibited, lacks interest, no interest in others, not spontaneous, withdrawn.

Low, Not Fit examples: A person may be *withdrawn* and still be involved and committed. *Inhibited* says nothing about one's state of commitment or lack of it. *Discouraged* could imply great involvement. *Stoic* often is used in the context of lack of involvement.

21. EXTREME QUALIFIERS

Any adjective, adverb, or phrase which makes a description extreme or suggests a high degree of the characteristic.

Fit: always, chronic, definite, hyper, never, overly, quite, too much, too possessive, too rigid, tremendous, usually, very.

22. HUMOR

Any statement specifically denoting either the ability or inability to perceive, appreciate, or express that which is funny, amusing, or ludicrous.

a. *High:*

Fit: has sense of humor, likes good jokes, knows how to laugh, witty.

Not Fit: floats along, fun to be with, good-natured, happy, happy-go-lucky, joyous, pleasant, smiles a lot.

High, Not Fit examples: Happy, happy-go-lucky, floats along, smiles a lot, fun to be with, good-natured, and *pleasant* do not specifically denote humor, although humor often is associated with these characteristics.

b. *Low:*

Fit: bitter, complaining, gloomy, glum, grave, grim, ill-humored, ill-tempered, morose, sullen, sour, unhappy.

Not Fit: sedate, serious.

Low, Not Fit examples: Serious people may have a sense of humor. A *sedate* person does not necessarily lack humor.

ALPHABETIZED LIST OF SCORED DESCRIPTIONS

abilities are mild, intellectual	7b
ability	no score
ability, lacks	4b
abrupt	2a
absent-minded	3b, 4b
abstract	7b
accept me as I am	1a, 8
accept you as you are	1a
acceptance of others	no score
accepting	no score
accepting, more	no score
accepts others	no score
achievement	2a, 5a
achievements, talk about self	2a, 5a, 16a
acquaintance, my	1a, 8
acquaintances	1a
acquainted, not well	1b
active	2a
active and fun loving	1a, 2a, 10a, 14
activities, no participation in	1b, 2b, 10d
adamant	2a, 14
adamant—closed view	2a, 10d, 14
adaptable to situations	no score
adjusted	no score
adjusted, well	no score
adjustment, social	1a
admirable, not at all times	5b, 21
advanced, intellectually	2a, 5a, 7a
adventurous	2a, 4a
adverse to phoniness	12a
aesthetic	no score
affable	1a
affected	16a
affectionate	1a, 17a
afraid	10d, 14
age	6
aggressive	1a, 2a
aggressive, not	2b
agitated	2a, 14
agreeable	1a
alert	2a
alive to the world	2a, 14, 19a
aloof	1b, 10d, 17b, 19b
aloof, rather	1b, 10d, 17b
ambition	2a, 5a
ambition, great deal of	2a, 5a, 21
ambition, less	2a, 5a
ambition, no	2b, 5b
ambition, unfulfilled	5b
ambitious, not	2b, 5b
American, good	no score
amoral	12b
amused, easily	22a
angry	2a, 14
angry easily, get	2a, 14
angry, never	10d, 21
angry under certain conditions	2a, 14
antagonism between the two of us	8, 14, 17b
antagonistic	2a, 10d, 17b
antisocial	2a, 10d, 17b
anxious	2a, 14
anxious about things	2a, 14
anxious and driving	2a, 10a, 14, 19a
anxious to help me	1a, 8, 17a
anything, not interested in	2b, 10d, 19b
apathetic about goals	2b, 18b
apathetic with life	2b, 14, 19b
apply it, have to	2a
appreciative	17a
appreciative of arts	no score
approve, don't	8
arrogant	2a, 10d, 16a, 17b
articulate	6
artistic	no score
asocial	1b, 10d, 19b

aspires to professional status	2a, 5a, 18b
assured	4a, 16a
atheist	12b, 19a
athletic	2a
athletic, very	2a, 6, 21
attention, wants	1a, 4b, 16a
attitude, critical	2a,17b
attitudes	no score
attracted to me, not physically	8, 11
attractive	13
attractive, not sexually	11, 13
authoritarian	2a, 10d, 16a
authoritarian, coldly	2a, 10d, 16a, 17b
authoritarian, rigid	2a, 10d, 16a
autistic	10d
average	no score
avoid, both are people I	1b, 2a, 3a, 8
avoid her, I don't necessarily	no score
avoids people	1b, 2a, 10d
aware	2a
awkward	6, 13
background, different family	18a
background, same family	18a
backward	7b
bad	12b
bad temper	2a, 14
balanced	3a
balanced, not	no score
balanced, well	3a
be with, like to	1a, 8
beautiful	13
beliefs, same	19a
beliefs, strong	2a, 19a
believe in similar things	no score
believe that they are always right	10d, 16a, 21
believe in equality	19a
believes in human nature	19a
belligerent	1a, 2a, 14, 17b
best friend	1a, 21
best, looking for the	no score
better person	no score
biased	10d
big guy who knows a lot	10a
bigoted	2a, 10d, 16a
bitter	2a, 14, 22b
bitter with life	2a, 14, 22b
bland	2b
blasé, very	2b, 10d, 21
blunt	2a
boastful	2a, 16a
boisterous	1a, 2a, 14
bold	1a, 2a, 16a
bored with life, seems	2b, 10d, 19b, 14
bores everyone with problems, always	21
bossy	2a, 16a
bother him, doesn't let anything	2a, 10d, 21
bouncy	2a, 14
bouyant	2a, 14
boys, interest in	11
brash	1a, 2a, 16a
brat	2a
breezy	1a, 2a
bright	7a
brilliant	7a
broad-minded	no score
broad-minded, liberal	no score
broad outlook	no score
brother	6, 8
brother and sister	6
brother and sister, because they represent	6
brotherly	1a, 17a
brown-noser	2a, 4b
bubbling	1a, 2a, 14
bubbling personality	1a, 2a, 14
bubbling with energy	1a, 2a, 14
build things	2a
bull-headed	2a, 10d
bum	5b
bumbling	2b, 3b
bureaucratic	3a, 9b, 10d

common, we don't have a lot in	8
companion	1a, 8
company, did not enjoy her	8
company, enjoy their	1a, 8, 14
compassion, no	17b
competent	3a, 4a
complacent attitude	2b
complainer, never	10d, 21
complaining	1a, 2a, 17b, 22b
complex	no score
compromises	no score
composer	5a
compulsive	2a, 3a, 10d
conceited	10d, 16a
concern for others, lacks	10d, 17b
concern for/with others	1a, 2a, 14, 17a, 19a
concern, lacks	10d
concerned, actively	2a, 14, 19a
concerned only with making money	2a, 5a, 10d, 19a
concerned over my welfare	1a, 2a, 8, 14, 17a, 19a
concerned with feelings of others	1a, 2a, 14, 17a
concerned with knowledge	2a, 7a, 19a
concerned with others	1a, 2a, 14, 17a, 19a
concrete	9b
condescending	10d, 16a
condescending attitude	10d, 16a
confidence in himself, lacks	4b
confidence, lacks	4b
confident	4a, 16a
confident, feels	4a, 16a
confidential	1a
conflict, in	3b, 14
conflict, lack of	3a
conflicts, personality	14
conforming	2b, 4b
confused	3b, 4b
congenial	1a
conscientious	2a, 3a, 12a
conservative	10d
considerate	1a, 17a
considerate, not	17b
considerate of others	1a, 17a
considerate of others' feelings, extremely	1a, 14, 17a, 21
consideration, lack of	17b
consideration, show	1a, 17a
consideration to others	1a, 17a
consistent	3a
constrained	2a, 10d
constricted	10d
constructive	2a, 3a
contact with these two is more stable, my	1a, 3a, 8
contented	2b
controlled	2a, 3a
conventional	3a, 9b
convincing, not	no score
cooperative	1a, 17a
cope with current situation, can't	4b
courteous	1a
crabby	2a, 14, 17b, 22b
creative	2a
creative, not	9b
critical	2a, 17b
critical attitude	2a, 17b
critical, helpful	1a, 2a
critical of people, too	2a, 10d, 17b, 21
crude	5b
cruel	2a, 12b, 17b
cruel, never	10d, 21
cultured	5a
cynical, somewhat	no score
curious	2a
curiosity, intellectual	2a, 7a
cynical	10d
damn, doesn't give a	2a, 17b, 19b
daring	2a, 4a

daydreamer	2b
dead (as opposed to lively)	2b, 19b
decisive	2a, 3a, 4a
decorative	13
dedicated	19a
dedicated, highly	19a, 21
deep	19a
deep, emotionally	14, 19a
deep thinkers	19a
definite	2a, 3a
degenerate	5b, 12b
degrade	17b
demanding	2a, 4b, 16a
democratic	no score
democratic, warmly	14, 17a
dense	7b
dense, slightly	7b
dependable	12a
dependent	1a, 4b
depressant	14, 22b
depressed, always	14, 21, 22b
depresses me	8, 14
desire to get ahead	2a, 5a, 18b
desires	14, 18b
desperate	14
despicable	12b
destructive	2a, 10d
destructive, others make fun of	2a, 10a, 10d, 17b
detached	2b, 19b
determined	2a
devil-may-care	2a, 4a
devoted	17a, 19a
devoted to family, very	1a, 17a, 19a, 21
different, completely	21
different family background	18a
different in respect to ideas	no score
different sex	6
different two of relationship	no score
different values to some degree	no score
difficult, can be	no score
difficult to become well acquainted with	10d
difficult to know	10d
difficult to understand	10d
difficult to work with	10d
dig him, I don't	8
dignified	5a
diligent, less	2b
direct	2a
direction, lacks	3b, 19b
discontented	14
discouraged	14
discourteous	1a, 17b
discrete	3a
disgusted by gossip	12a, 14
disgusting	14
dishonest	12b
dishonest and a drunkard	5b, 10a, 12b
dishonest, socially	12b
disinterested	10d, 19b
dislike country students	10d
dislike people	10d
dislike me	8
dislikes family	17b
disloyal	12b
disorderly	3b
disorganized	3b
disposition, good	1a
disreputable	5b, 12b
disrespect (my lack of respect)	5b, 8
dissatisfied	14
dissatisfied with work	14
distance	no score
distant	1b, 17b, 19b
distasteful	no score
distrust of people	12b, 17b
disturbed	14
dizzy-headed	3b
doctrinaire	2a, 3a, 9b, 10d
doer	2a
dogmatic	2a, 10d

Term	Score
dogmatic and very unpredictable	2a, 3b, 10a, 10d, 18b, 21
doltish	7b
domesticity, prefer	6
dominate	2a, 16a
domineering	2a, 16a
dominant	2a, 16a
doubtful	3b
down to earth	9b
dreamer	no score
dress the same	13
dresser, messy	13
dresses well	13
drink, does not	6
drinker, non-	6, 10d
drinker, serious	2a
drinking, wouldn't think of	6, 10d
drinks	6
drive in right direction	2a, 12a, 18b
drive, more	2a
driving	2a, 19a
drunkard	5b, 12b
drunkards, both are	5b, 12b
dry	2b
dry and uninteresting	2b, 10a
dull	2b, 7b
dull to talk to, rather	2b, 7b
dumb	7b
dumb, foolish	7b, 10a
dutiful	12a
dynamic	2a
eager for marriage	2a, 11, 14
earthy	9b
easier to talk to	1a
easygoing	2b
easygoing and ambitious	2a, 2b, 5a, 10a
easygoing, friendly	1a, 2b, 10a
easy to get along with	1a
easy to get along with, always	1a, 21
easy to get along with, very	1a, 21
easy to know	1a
easy to like	1a
easy to talk to	1a
easy way with people, friendly	1a, 10a
educated	5a
educated, intelligent	5a, 7a, 10a
education and intelligence, same	10a
education, good	5a
educators	5a, 6, 7a
efficient	2a, 3a
efficient, opinionated	2a, 3a, 10a, 10d, 16a
effort, makes no	1b
egocentric	10d, 16a, 19a
egotist	10d, 16a, 19a
egotistic	10d, 16a, 19a
egotistic, somewhat	10d, 16a
egotistical	10d, 16a, 19a
emotional	14
emotional problems, serious	2a, 14
emotional, very	2a, 14, 21
emotions, no	10d
empathic	1a, 2a
encouraging my efforts	1a, 3a, 8, 17a
endurance	2a
energetic	2a
energetic, more	2a
engaged	1a, 6, 11
engrossed in his career	19a
enjoy activity	2a, 14
enjoy activity and going places	2a, 10a, 14
enjoy life	2a, 14
enjoy their company	1a, 8, 14
enjoyable company	1a, 14
enjoyable personalities	1a, 14
enjoyable to be with	1a
enjoying herself, she never seems to be truly	1a, 21
enjoys everything	2a, 14, 21
enjoys new things	14
enjoys people	1a, 14

Response	Score
friendly and always happy, very intelligent and interesting to be with	1a, 2a, 7a, 10a, 14, 21
friendly and honest	1a, 10a, 12a
friendly and warm	1a, 10a, 14, 17a
friendly attitude	1a
friendly but firm	1a, 2a, 10a
friendly, industrious	1a, 2a, 5a, 10a
friendly, not	no score
friendly, outgoing	1a, 2a, 10a
friendly, sometimes	no score
friendly, tries to be	1a
friendly, very	1a, 21
friends	1a
friends, takes a while to make	no score
friends, very good	1a, 21
friendship, degree of	no score
frustrated	14
frowns a lot	6, 13, 21
full of life	2a, 14
fun	1a, 2a, 14
fun, capacity for	1a, 2a, 14
fun-loving	1a, 2a, 14
fun, lot of	1a, 2a, 14
fun, meaningful	no score
fun to be with	1a, 2a, 14
fun to work with	1a, 2a, 14
funny	1a, 22a
future, never worry about	21
generalizes beyond facts	no score
generous	12a
genteel	5a, 17a
gentle	1a, 17a
get along, we don't	8
get along with both, I feel I could	1a, 8
get things done	2a, 3a
give help when needed, will	1a, 17a
give much of their life to others, desire to	1a, 2a, 12a, 17a
given up all, has just about	12b, 19b, 21
given up much for her children	17a, 21
giver, no help	17b
gloomy	14, 22b
glory seeker	2a, 5a, 18b
glum	2b, 14, 22b
go for him, I	8, 11
goal and strives for it, sets a	2a, 10a, 18b
goal directed	2a, 3a, 18b
goal directed, more	2a, 3a, 18b
goal-minded, very	18b, 19a, 21
goal, no set	18b
goal oriented, not	18b
goals, achieve their	2a, 6, 18b
goals are set	2a, 18b
goals, definite	2a, 3a, 18b
goals, different	18b
goals, has	18b
goals, high	18b, 21
goals, lacks	18b
goals, same	18b
go-getter	2a, 4a
going steady	1a, 6, 11
good	12a
good disposition	1a
good education	5a
good family, from a	5a
good friends, very	1a, 21
good grades, school work is hard but he makes	2a, 5a, 6, 10a
good guy	1a
good-humored	1a, 22a
good-humored, not	22b
good job	5a
good listener	1a, 2b
good-natured	1a
good personality	no score
good salesmen (especially of themselves)	1a, 2a, 16a
good self-appraisal	no score
good self-evaluation	no score
good sense of humor	1a, 2a, 22a

good time, wants a	1a, 14
good to me, they are	1a, 8, 17a
gossipy	1a, 2a
got what they wanted	2a, 3a, 4a, 18b
gracious	1a, 17a
grades low	6, 7b
grateful	17a
grave	2b, 22b
great guy	1a, 21
great, he thinks I'm	8
greedy	2a, 12b
gregarious	1a, 2a
grim	2a, 17b, 22b
grouchy	2a, 14, 17b, 22b
guilty, not	12a
gullible	4b
guy, a neat	11
guys, good	1a
hair, red	6, 13
happiness, much less genuine	14, 21
happy	14
happy, always seems	14, 21
happy and content	2b, 10a, 14
happy, don't appear very	14, 22b
happy, extremely	14, 21
happy in their work	14
happy, industrious	2a, 5a, 10a, 14
happy, interested	14
happy, less	14
happy, makes me	1a, 8, 14
happy nature	14
happy, not	14, 22b
happy, not as	14
happy, not very	14, 22b
happy, seem unusually	14, 21
happy, sensibly friendly	1a, 3a, 10a, 14
happy, very	14, 21
happy with status	5a, 14
happy-go-lucky	14, 19b
happy-go-lucky by comparison	14, 19b
hard	2a, 17b
hardheaded	2a, 10d
hard to get acquainted with	10d
hard to get along with	10d
hard to know	10d
hard to like	10d
hard to understand	10d
hard workers	2a, 5a
hardened	2a, 17b
hard working	2a, 5a
harsh	17b
harsh, often	17b, 21
has sex appeal	1a, 11
hateful	2a, 14, 17b
hates the out-of-doors	6, 14
hates to see anyone smoke	14
haughty	5a, 16a
have own way, has to	2a, 10d, 16a, 17b, 19a
healthy	6
healthy, mentally	no score
heavy	no score
help everyone, wants to	1a, 17a, 21
helpful	1a, 17a
helpful and fun	1a, 2a, 10a, 14
helpful, not	17b
helpful person	1a, 17a
helpless	2b, 4b, 10d
helps me, she	1a, 8, 17a
helps others	1a, 17a
herself, likes to talk about	1a, 2a, 16a
high strung, very	2a, 14, 21
his way, only	10d, 16a, 21
himself, interested in	10d, 16a
himself, looks out for	4a
himself, only thinks of	10d, 16a, 21
history, important family	18a
history, unimportant family	18a
homebody	1b
honest	12a

honest, evasively	12b
honest, intellectually	7a, 12a
honest with me	12a, 18a
hostile	2a, 14, 17b
hostile attitude	2a, 14, 17b
hot-tempered	2a, 14
human life, sense of	no score
humanitarian	12a, 17a, 19a
humble	no score
humor	1a, 2a, 22a
humor, almost no sense of	22b
humor, good sense of	1a, 2a, 22a
humor, has	1a, 2a, 22a
humor in life, sees no	22b
humor, lacks	22b
humor, seems to lack a sense of	22b
humor, sense of	1a, 2a, 22a
humor, small	22b
humor, very good sense of	1a, 2a, 21, 22a
humored, good-	1a, 22a
humorous	22a
humorous, jovial	1a, 10a, 14, 22a
hurts some people because of his brusqueness	1a, 2a, 5a, 17b
husband	6, 8
hypochondriac	6, 16a, 19a
hypocrite	12b
hypocritical	12b
I.Q., high	6, 7a
ideal, too	3a, 21
idealistic	no score
ideals, high	19a
ideals, strong	2a, 19a
ideas, avoids	2a, 7b, 10d
ideas, can't get new	9b, 10d
ideas, different in respect to	no score
ideas fluctuate	3b
ideas, likes new	no score
ideas, odd	no score
ideas, pursues	2a, 4a, 18b, 19a
ideas, set	2a, 10d
ignorant	7b
ignore important matters	2a, 10d
ill at ease	4b, 14
illiterate	5b, 7b
imaginative	no score
imagination, no	9b
immature	4b
immature in duties	4b
immaturity	4b
immediately, does things	2a
immoral	12b
impassive	10d, 17b
impatient	2a, 14
impersonal	10d, 17b
impersonal and objective, appropriately	no score
impolite	17b
impose their ideas upon you	1a, 2a, 17b, 19a
impractical	no score
impress others, wishes to	4b, 5a
impress people, try to	5a, 16a
impressed by money	5a
impulsive	2a, 3b
in love	1a, 6, 11, 14, 17a
inactive	2b
inadequate, feels	4b
inarticulate	6, 10d
incentive	2b, 5b, 19b
incompetent	4b
inconsiderate	17b
inconsiderate of others	17b
inconsistent	3b
indecisive	2b, 3b, 4b
indifferent, perpetually	2b, 17b, 19b, 21
indefinite	2b, 3b
independence, wants	4a, 18b
independent	2a, 4a
independent kind	2a, 4a, 10a, 17a

independent, more	2a, 4a	intelligent, not	7b
indifference, a cold	2b, 10a, 17b, 19b	intelligent, rather	7a
indifferent	2b, 17b, 19b	intelligent, very	7a, 21
indifferent, tends to be	2b, 17b, 19b	intense, very	2a, 14, 21
indifferent, very	2b, 17b, 19b, 21	interest in boys	11
individualist	2a, 4a, 16a	interest in sports	6
individualistic, more	4a	interest lies in literature	6
indoor type	no score	interested	no score
industrious	2a, 5a	interested in himself	10d, 16a
inefficient	3b	interested in me	1a, 8
inferior	5b	interested in others	1a
inferior feeling around opposite sex	11	interested in self	10d, 16a
inferior, feels	4b	interested in scientific knowledge	7a
inferior to her, thinks that they are	10d, 16a	interested in scientific things, more	3a, 19a
inferiority complex	4b	interested in their work	6
influenced by ideas, easily	2b, 4b	interested in themselves	10d, 16a
informal	3b	interested in anything, not	2b, 10d, 19b
inhibited	4b, 9b, 19b	interesting	2a
inhibited, not socially	1a	interesting, if exasperating	2a, 14, 10a
inhibited, socially	1b, 10d	interesting, nice	1a, 2a, 10a
initiative, full of	2a, 4a, 21	interesting person, very	2a, 21
initiative, lack of	2b, 4b, 5b	interesting, seems	2a
initiative, lacks	2b, 4b, 5b	interesting to me, not extremely	8, 21
innerdirected	4a	interests, same	no score
innerdirected, more	4a	interests, similar	no score
insecure	4b, 14	interests similar to theirs, I have	8
insecure, basically	4b, 14	internally oriented	16a
insensitive	10d, 17b	intolerant	2a, 10d
insightful	no score	introvert	1b
insightful, stable	3a, 10a	involved	19a
insincere	12b	involved with life	2a, 19a
insincerity	12b	irrational	3b
instructors	6, 7a	irresponsible	12b
integrity	2a, 3a, 12a	irritable	1a, 2a, 14, 17b
integrity of motives	2a, 3a, 12a	jealous	14
intellect, lack of	7b	job, good	5a
intellectual	5a, 7a	joke on himself, can take	4a, 22a
intelligence, high	7a	jokes a lot	1a, 10a, 22a
intelligent	7a		
intelligent and successful	5a, 7a, 10a		
intelligent, less	7a		

jokes, doesn't catch on to	22b
joking	1a, 2a, 22a
joking, silly	1a, 2a, 10a, 19b, 22a
jovial	1a, 14
joyful	1a, 2a, 14
judgment, good	3a, 4a
judgment, poor	4b
just	12a
kept, well	13
kid around with people	1a, 2a, 22a
kind	1a, 17a
kind to me	1a, 8, 17a
kind, very	12a, 17a, 21
knew well	8, 18a
know as well, do not	8
know closely, she is difficult to	10d
know it all	10d, 16a
know own mind	4a
know what he wants, doesn't	3b, 4b
knowledge, extensive	7a
knowledge, interested in scientific	7a
knowledge, less thirst for	7a
knows himself	4a
knows what he wants	2a, 3a, 4a 18b
laborer	6, 7b
lacks background	18a
ladies	5a, 6
lady who I know, just a	6, 8
laugh, can	2a, 22a
laugh, knows how to	2a, 22a
laugh off disturbances in life	14, 22a
law, thinks her word is	2a, 10d, 16a
lax	2b, 3b
laziness	2b, 5b, 19b
lazy	2b, 5b, 19b
lazy at times	2b, 5b, 19b
lazy but friendly	1a, 2b, 5b, 10a, 19b
lazy, no ambition	2b, 5b, 10a
leader, a	1a, 2a, 4a, 5a

learn, can't	7b, 10d
lethargic	2b, 19b
levelheaded	3a
liar	12b
liberal	no score
liberal ideas, very	21
liberal, irrationally so	3b, 10d
life, free to live own	4a
life, open-ended	no score
like, everyone seems to	1a, 21
like me	1a, 8
like me, they don't	8
like people mix well in group	1a, 10a
like personally	8
like sociology	6
like them, I	8
like them, I don't	8
like to be with	1a, 8a
like to kid around with people	1a, 2a, 22a
like to make something nice for others	1a, 2a, 17a
like to operate a farm	6
likable	1a
likable in some respects	1a, 10d
liked by all, well	1a, 2a
liked by others, very well	2a, 14
liked, well	1a, 21
likes good jokes	22a
likes outdoors	no score
likes people	1a
likes the good old days	18a
limited	10d
limited in horizons	10d
listener, good	1a, 2b
literature, interest lies in	6
lives in Chicago	6
live my own life, lets me	8
lively	2a, 14
lives from day to day	3b
lives in small world	10d
logical	3a
lonely	1b, 14
loner	1b, 10d

narrow-minded	10d
natured, good	1a
neat	3a, 13
neat, very	3a, 13, 21
negative	17b
negativistic	2a, 17b
nervous	2a, 14
nervous energy	2a, 14
nervous, more	2a, 14
nervous, very	2a, 14, 21
nervousness	2a, 14
neurotic	no score
never wanted for anything	2a
nice	1a
nice guy, just a	1a
nice income for family, wants	5a, 17a, 18b
nice, sometimes too	21
nice to wife, not too	1a, 17b
nice, very	1a, 21
no, always say	10d, 21
nonconforming	2a
nonintellectual	7b
nonmoody	3a
non-profound	7b
non-public orator	6
nonreligious	12b
nosy	2a
nothing in common	21
notice everything	2a, 21
nurturant	1a, 17a
objectionable	no score
objective	no score
obnoxious	2a
obnoxious in crowds	1a, 2a
obstinate	2a, 10d
occupation, same	6
odd	no score
oddball	no score
odd in appearance	13
odd menial jobs, can do only	4b, 6, 7b
offensive	14
old, looks	13
older	6
older, because they are	6
old-fashioned	10d, 18a
on the beam	3a
one-sided opinions	10d
one-track mind	2a, 3a, 10d
open	no score
open feelings	14
open-hearted	17a
open-minded	no score
open-mindedness	no score
open to self	no score
open, very	21
opinionated	2a, 10d
opinions, has few	no score
opportunistic	2a, 12b
opportunities, has	6, 18b
opposite (score to opposite of contrasting description)	
optimistic	18b
organized	3a
organized, very	3a, 21
oriented, externally	5a
oriented, internally	16a
original	no score
others, interest in	1a
others, interested in	1a
others, likes to make something nice for	1a, 2a, 17a
others, no interest in	1b, 10d, 17b
outer-directed	4b
outgoing	1a, 2a
outgoing, not	1b
outgoing personality	1a, 2a
outlook	no score
outlook, good	no score
outlook, healthy	no score
outlook, narrow	10d
outlook, poor	no score
out-of-doorsish	no score
outside activity, no interest in	10d
outspoken	1a, 2a
outspoken, less	1a, 2a
outstanding	5a
overbearing	2a, 16a, 17b

present, lives for	no score
pretense, maintains a	4b
pretentious	5a, 16a
pricks	2a
priestly	5a
primal emphasis	18a
problems, has	no score
problems, has few	no score
problems, same	no score
procrastinates	4b, 10d
profession, dedicated to	5a, 19a
profession to be dedicated to, no	6
professional	5a
professional man	6
professor	5a, 6, 7a
profound	7a, 19a
profound in thought	7a, 19a
progressive	2a, 18b
prompt	2a, 3a
proud	16a
prudence	3a
prudent	3a
purpose, has	2a, 18b
purpose in life, lesser degree of	18b
purpose in life, strong	2a, 4a, 18b, 19a
purpose, lacks	3b, 19b
purposeful	2a, 18b
push herself, always tries to	2a, 21
pushover	2b, 4b
put things off	10d
put things off, not	2a, 4a
queer	no score
questionable	no score
quick-tempered	2a, 14
quiet	2b
quiet, good control	2a, 2b, 3a, 10a
quiet, good-humored	1a, 2b, 10a, 22a
quiet in presence of elders	1a, 2b, 5a
quiet, submissive	2b, 10a
quit, doesn't	2a
radical	2a, 10d, 19a
radical in opinions	2a, 10d, 19a
ranches	6
rash	2a, 3b
rational	3a
reach either of them, does not seem able to	8, 10d
reactionary	9b, 10d, 18a
reacts in terms of self	10d, 16a
reads a lot	6
realist	4a, 9b
realistic	4a, 9b
realistic, completely	4a, 9b, 10d, 21
reason with, can	no score
reason with, cannot	2a, 10d
reasonable	no score
rebellious	2a, 14
reckless	2a, 3b
recognition, need for	4b, 5a
refined	5a
refuse to worry about unimportant matters	2a, 10d
regret for her unhappiness, feeling of	14
regret the past	14, 18a
rejecting	2a, 10d, 17b
related, not	6
relationship, different	no score
relative, because it represents a	6
relatives	6
relaxed	2b
reliable	12a
religion, same	12a
religious	12a, 19a
religious, not	12b
religious notions	12a
religious, very	12a, 19a, 21
represents a male	6
reputable	5a
resentful	14
reserved	1b, 2b

reserved, more	1b, 2b
resigned	2b
resourceful	2a, 4a
resourceless	4b, 10d
respect (my respect toward them)	5a, 8
respect each other	5a
respect for others, lack of	1a, 5b, 10d, 17b
respect for them, my	5a, 8
respect, lack of	5b
respected	5a
respectful	1a, 5a
respects others	5a
respects self	4a, 16a
responsible	12a
responsible, not	12b
responsibilities, has	6
responsibilities, has no	4b
responsibility, accepts	12a
responsibility, lack of	12b
responsibility, more sense of	12a
responsibility, much	12a, 21
responsive	1a, 2a
responsive, not	1b, 2b, 10d
reticent	1b, 2b
retiring	1b, 2b
right, always	2a, 21
right, the feeling that he is always	16a, 21
rigid	2a, 10d
risky	2b
romanticist	9a
rough	17b
rude	17b
ruthless	2a, 12b, 17b
sad	14, 22b
sad, always looks	13, 21
sad but proud	10a, 14, 16a
salesman (especially of himself), good	1a, 2a, 16a
same age bracket, she doesn't fall into the	6
sanguine	14, 18b
sarcastic	2a, 17b
sarcastic, rather	2a, 17b
satisfied	2b, 10d
satisfied with life, not	10d, 14
satisfied with life, unselfish	2b, 10a, 10d, 17a
saying what he really feels, never seems to be	3b, 10d, 21
scandalmonger, petty	1a, 12b
scatterbrained, a bit	3b
scheduled	3a
schemer	2a, 3a
scheming	2a, 3a
school, didn't finish high	6
scornful of others	2a, 10d, 17b
searching	2a, 18b
seclusive	1b, 10d
secretive	1b
secure	4a, 16a
secure, seems	4a, 16a
security, lack of	4b
security, lack of mental	4b, 14
seeks others actively	1a, 12a
self-abasing	no score
self-appraisal, good	no score
self-centered	10d, 16a, 19a
self-centered, too	10d, 16a, 21
self-centered, very selfish	12b, 16a, 17b, 21
self-confident	4a, 16a
self-confidence, lacks	4b
self-conscious	4b, 14
self-control	2a, 3a, 4a
self-disciplined	2a, 3a, 4a
self-evaluation, good	no score
self, high opinion of	16a
self-interest	16a
self, interested in	10d, 16a
selfish	12b, 16a, 17b
selfish, sometimes	12b, 16a, 17b
selfless	1a, 17a
self, open to	no score

self-oriented, spoiled	1a, 10a, 10d, 16a, 19a
self, preoccupied with	10d, 16a, 19a
self-protective	2a, 4b, 10d
self, reacts in terms of	10d, 16a
self, respects	4a, 16a
self-sufficient	2a, 4a
self, sorry for	4b, 14
self, thinks for	2a, 4a
self, uncertain of	3b, 4b
semipessimistic	18b
sensible	3a, 4a
sensible, smart	3a, 7a, 10a
sensible, truthful	3a, 10a, 12a
sensitive	no score
sensuous	11, 14
sentimental	14
sentimental and orderly	3a, 10a, 14
serious	2a
serious-minded	2a
serious, never	19b, 21
serious, overly	3a, 10a, 14
serious, too	2a, 21
seriously, takes everything	2a, 21
service to their country	2a, 12a
set in way(s)	2a, 10d
sets high goals	2a, 5a, 18b
settled	2b, 3a
sex	11
sex, accepts my	8, 11
sex, different	6
sex, same	6
sex appeal, has	1a, 11
sexy	11, 13
shaky	3b, 4b
shallow	19b
sharp	no score
sharp-tempered	2a, 14
shiftless	2b, 4b, 5b, 19b
short	6, 13
shouts her feelings	2a, 14
show off	1a, 2a, 16a
shy	1b, 10d
sick	6
sickly	6
side, looks at positive	no score
sides, can see both	no score
similarity, age	6
simple	no score
simple-minded	7b
sincere	12a
sister	6, 8
sisterly	1a, 17a
skeptical	2a, 17b
skilled, manually	6
sloppy	3b, 13
slovenly	3b, 13
slow	2b
slow-minded	2b, 7b
slow to determine his wants in life	2b
sly	12b
smart	7a
smart aleck	2a, 16a
smile a lot	1a, 2a, 6, 13, 21
smile on face—fun person, almost always has a	1a, 2a, 6, 10a, 13, 14
smile on face, has	1a, 6, 13
smiling, always	1a, 2a, 6, 13, 21
smoke	6
smooth	no score
smooth with people, not as	3b
smug	4a, 16a
snob	16a
snobbish	16a
snobbish, conceited	10d, 16a
sober	2a
social	1a
social climber	1a, 2a, 5a
social organization	1a, 3a
social, very	1a, 21
sociable	1a
soft	2b

Term	Score
soft, quiet	2b, 10a
soft-spoken	1a, 2b, 17a
solemn	2a, 22b
solves many problems	2a, 3a, 4a
sophisticated	5a
sophistication	5a
sophistication, lacks	5b
sorrowful	14, 22b
sorry for self	4b, 14
so-so, feels	no score
sour	14, 17b, 22b
speaks without thinking	1a, 2a, 3b
speaker, intelligent and concise	1a, 2a, 3a, 7a, 10a
speaker, public	6
specific, overly	9b, 21
speech, easy	1a, 2b
spendthrift	2a
spoiled	1a, 16a
spontaneous	14
sports, interested in	6
stable	3a
stable, has common sense	3a, 4a, 10a
stable, quite	3a, 21
stacked, she's	11, 13
stand me, can't	8
standard, follow their	2a, 3a
standards, low moral	12b
stands his ground	2a, 4a
started in business at age 40, just getting	2a, 6
static	10d
status quo	10d
staunch defenders of their ideas	2a, 4a, 16a, 19a
stays to herself	1b, 10d
steady	3a
stern	2a, 17b
stern, very	2a, 17b, 21
stilted	2a
stimulating	1a, 2a
stimulating active mind	1a, 2a
stingy	2a, 10d
stodgy	2b
stoic	2b, 17b, 19b
straight	no score
straight-laced	2a, 3a, 10d, 12a
straightforward	2a, 12a
straightforward in speaking	1a, 2a, 10a, 12a
strict	2a, 3a, 10d, 12a
strict about little things	2a, 3a, 10d, 12a
strict moral code	3a, 10d, 12a
striving	2a, 5a, 18b
striving, always	2a, 5a, 18b, 21
striving for better things in life	2a, 3a, 18b
strong	2a, 4a
strong beliefs	2a, 19a
strong character	2a, 4a
strong ideals	2a, 19a
strong purpose in life	2a, 4a, 18b, 19a
strong-willed	2a, 4a
structured	3a
stubborn	2a, 10d
stubborn, very	2a, 10d, 21
stuck-up	10d, 16a
student	6
student, excellent	2a, 6, 7a, 21
student, high school	6
studious	2a, 5a, 7a
studious, not	no score
study, doesn't	7b
study very hard, does not	2b
stuffy	5a, 10d
stupid	7b
submissive	2b
submit when proved wrong, will	2a
success in family and occupation	1a, 2a, 5a
successful	5a
successful businessman	2a, 5a

successful (educated)	5a, 5b, 7a, 7b, 10a
successful in career	2a, 5a
successful in own eyes	5a, 16a
successful in personal relations	1a, 2a
successful in teaching	2a, 7a
successful in his work, very	2a, 5a, 21
successful, not	5b
suggestible	2b, 4b
superficial	10d, 19b
superior	5a
superior, acts	2a, 16a
superior, feels	16a
superior to others, feels that he is	16a
superiority, air of	16a
superiority, feels his	16a
sure of himself, too	4a, 16a, 21
surface thinker	19b
suspicious	1b, 10d
sweet	1a, 17a
sympathetic	1a, 17a
tactful	17a
tactless	17b
tactless and blunt	2a, 10a, 17b
talented	no score
talented, both very	21
talented, musically	6
talented, not as	no score
talk about others, likes to	1a, 2a
talk of self, less prone to	1a
talkative	1a, 2a
talker, excessive	1a, 2a, 21
tall	6, 13
teach, couldn't	8
teacher, because it doesn't represent a	6
teacher, intelligent, excellent	6, 7a, 10a, 21
teacher, math	6, 7a
teacher, poor	6
temperamental	2a, 14
temper, loses	2a, 14
tempered, quick-	2a, 14
tender	1a, 14, 17a
themselves, interested in	10d, 16a
theoretical	7a
theoretician, creative	2a, 7a
thin	6, 13
things, immediately does	2a
think a lot of me, seems to	1a, 8
think for themselves	4a
think I'm average, they	8
think they're smarter than they are	7a, 16a
thinker, plodding	2b
thinker, poor	7b
thinks for self	2a, 4a
thinks he is smart	16a
thinks of other people a great deal	17a, 21
thinks of the other person	17a
thinks people are machines	17b
thinks people are trying to get the best of him	10d
thinks very much of his wife	1a, 17a, 21
thoughtful	3a, 17a
thoughtful, calm, works toward goals	2a, 2b, 3a, 10a, 18b
thoughtless	3b, 17b
thoughtless of others	17b
threatening	2a, 14, 17b
thrifty	2a, 3a
tidy	3a, 13
tolerant	2a
touch-of-the-poet	no score
tramp	5b
travel, doesn't like to	6
treats everyone equally	1a, 21
tried to stay out of his company	1b, 2a
tries hard	2a

tries to be one of the boys	1a, 2a
tries to please	1a, 2a, 17a
troublemaker	2a
trouble, tends to cause	2a
trouble with family, lot of	2a, 14, 21
true	12a
trustworthy	12a
truthful	12a
try anything for fun, likes to	2a, 14
try new things, likes to	2a, 21
try to do everything at once, likes to	2a, 19a, 21
two-faced	12b
typical boy	no score
ugly	13
unaccepting	10d
unadjusted	no score
unambitious	2b, 5b
unappreciative	17b
unassuming	no score
unaware	2b
uncertain	3b, 4b
uncertain of future	3b, 18b
uncertain of self	3b, 4b
uncomfortable socially	1a
uncomfortable stare feeling	14
uncomplaining	2b
unconcerned	10d, 17b, 19b
undecided	no score
undecided about future	2b, 18b
undependable	12b
understand him, don't	8
understand me, can't	8
understanding	1a, 17a
understanding, lack	17b
understanding of children	1a, 17a
understanding, not	17b
understanding, very	1a, 17a, 21
understood, can be	no score
undisciplined	3b
undogmatic	no score
uneducated	5b, 7b
uneducated (no high school)	5b, 6, 7b
unfair	12b
unfair, very	12b, 21
unfeeling	10d, 17b
unfeminine, somewhat	no score
unfriendly	no score
ungrateful	17b
unhappy	14, 22b
unhappy at home	14
unhappy, usually	14, 21
unhelpful	17b
unimaginative	9b
uninclined, mechanically	6
unintelligent	7b
unintelligent and partly happy	7b, 10a, 14
uninterested	2b, 10d, 19b
uninterested in life	2b, 10d, 19b
uninteresting	no score
unkind	12b, 17b
unlearned	5b, 7b
unorganized	3b
unpopular	1b
unpractical, completely	21
unpredictable	3b, 18b
unreasonable, is	2a, 10d
unrealistic	10d
unsatisfied	14
unselfish	17a
unsettled	2a, 3b
unsettled, very, with no real responsibility	2a, 3b, 10a, 14, 21
unsociable	1b
unsocial	1b
unsophisticated	5b
unstable	3b
unsuccessful	5b
unsuccessful at everything	5b, 21
unsuccessful, feels	5b
unsuccessful, very	5b, 21

unsure	3b, 4b
unsure of her role to play	3b, 4b
unsure of himself	3b, 4b
unsure of own life	3b, 4b
unsympathetic	17b
unthoughtful	17b
untrustworthy	12b
upset	2a, 14
upset, easily	2a, 14, 21
upset, easily get	2a, 14, 21
upward-and-onward type	2a, 5a, 18b
uses people for own ends	2a, 12b, 17b
uses people for survival	2a, 4b
value of money, no sense of	3b
values, abstract	no score
values chosen at expense of prestige	12a, 19a
values, concrete	9b
values, have a good sense of	12a
values (in my estimation), poor sense of	8, 12b
values, respects only one's own	4a, 16a
values, sacrifices for prestige	5a, 12b
values, same	no score
values to some degree, different	no score
values, well developed	3a, 19a
variation, no	3a
variety in activity	2a
variety of past occupations	6
views biased	10d
views, similar	no score
vitality	2a
vivacious	1a, 2a, 14
vocation, ideal	no score
wants best for me	8
wants his own way all the time	2a, 16a, 21
wants things now	2a
wants to be waited on	2b, 4b, 16a
warm	1a, 14, 17a
warm, but lost in depth	3b, 14, 17a
warm, motherly	1a, 10a, 14, 17a
warm personality, very	1a, 14, 17a, 21
warm, very	1a, 14, 17a, 21
warmth toward people	1a, 14, 17a
weak	2b, 4b
weak character	2b, 4b, 12b
weak, morally	2b, 12b
wealth, wants material	5a, 9b, 18b
wealthy	5a, 6
went to college	5a, 6
wide	no score
wide-eyed	7b
wife	6, 8
wild	2a, 3b
willed, strong-	2a, 4a
willing to share ideas of others	1a
willingness to accept opinion of others	1a
willingness to accept what he had	2b
wisdom, intellectual	5a, 7a
wise	7a
wit, ready	1a, 2a, 7a, 22a
withdrawn	1b, 10d
witted, quick-	2a, 7a
witted, sharp-	2a, 7a
witty	1a, 2a, 7a, 22a
witty, intellectually	7a, 22a
women, both are	6
work, does not like to	2b
work, interested in his	6
work, no interest in	2b, 10d
work with hands, both like to	6
worked while she was in college	2a, 6

APPENDIX C

Content Norms For Better-Adjusted Students

Content Mean Scores of Better-Adjusted Males and Females at Rep Test 1

	1a	1b	2a	2b	3a	3b	4a	4b	5a	5b	6	7a	7b
12 M	5.0	.6	5.8	3.1	1.1	1.1	.6	1.2	1.0	.8	.4	1.2	.9
18 F	5.2	.4	7.1	2.8	1.5	1.1	1.5	1.5	1.6	.6	.5	1.0	.5

	8	9b	10d	11	12a	12b	13	14	16a	17a	17b
12 M	0	0	1.8	0	1.6	1.8	.1	2.3	1.2	1.9	1.8
18 F	.3	.5	3.1	0	1.3	1.0	.3	3.7	1.7	2.1	2.3

	18a	18b	19a	19b	21	22a	22b	10a
12 M	0	.4	1.0	.9	.6	.4	.2	0*
18 F	.1	.6	1.3	2.1	2.1	.4	.4	1.9

* One BA 12 male scored 22 and was deleted.

APPENDIX D

Computer Program For Scoring Role Construct Repertory Test Grid

John A. Gifford
University of Missouri

The following computer program can be used by inexperienced as well as experienced programmers as a quick and relatively easy method for scoring a modified grid form of the Role Construct Repertory Test (Rep Test). This modified Rep Test, as described by Landfield, accounts for range of convenience of personal constructs. Using this program for obtaining FIC(c) and FIC(p) values is a relatively simple matter and it can be used for grids of varying sizes, providing they do not exceed fifteen rows and/or fifteen columns. The output from this program will be in the form of two matrices on separate sheets of paper, each with the subject's name and each appropriately labeled as either "Row Comparisons" or "Column Comparisons." If the value in any cell of an output matrix is based upon unmatched grid values (1–2 or 2–1 combinations), that value will be preceded by a negative sign. Unsigned values in an output matrix are positive and are based upon matched grid values (1–1 or 2–2 combinations). The computer will automatically make the necessary adjustments for any excess number of mutual exclusions as suggested by Landfield's Rep Test scoring modification (1967).

The program is written in Fortran IV computer language and therefore should be compatible with any computer that will accept that language. The lines in the program beginning with a "C" are not necessary, but are included to define symbols and operations. Using the program requires three steps. They are as follows:

1. Check with an operator of the computer to be used in order to obtain a description of the system control cards used for that specific computer system. There are usually several special cards at the beginning, at least one before the data cards and several cards at the end of the data deck. Note: While there are other kinds of input media—paper tape, magnetic tape, etc.—this description assumes the use of cards, but can easily be applied to other input media as well.
2. Punch the program on cards using one card for each line. The system control cards mentioned in step one must also be punched and inserted in appropriate places.

3. Punch the data cards including the following information:
   a. The name of the person who completed the grid on one card, not to exceed thirty-two spaces beginning with Column 1.
   b. The size of the grid being evaluated is to be punched on the next card, with the numbers of rows in spaces 1 and 2 and the number of columns in spaces 3 and 4 (i.e. 15 by 15 would be 1515; 8 by 10 would be 0810; or a 9 by 7 would be 0907). It is important that spaces 1 and 2 contain only the row size and spaces 3 and 4 contain only the column size.
   c. The rest of the data cards contain the grid symbols and each card must contain all of the symbols from a given row and no more. The grid symbols are punched only on the even numbered spaces beginning with space number 2, thus skipping a space before each symbol. The cards must be in order with Row 1 (top row) of the grid first and the last row (bottom row) of the grid last in the card deck. The grid symbols used are *1, 2,* and *0;* the zero being substituted for all "*N*'s" and "?'s" on the grid.

   Note: See the sample data deck diagram for clarification.

When these three steps are completed the program is ready for the computer. While this may appear complex, after one trial it will probably be unnecessary to refer to this description again. In fact, since the control cards and basic program cards can be re-used, it will only be necessary to complete step 3 above (punching grid data cards) when evaluating other grids. An inexperienced person should be able to punch the data cards in less than fifteen minutes.

Sample Data Deck

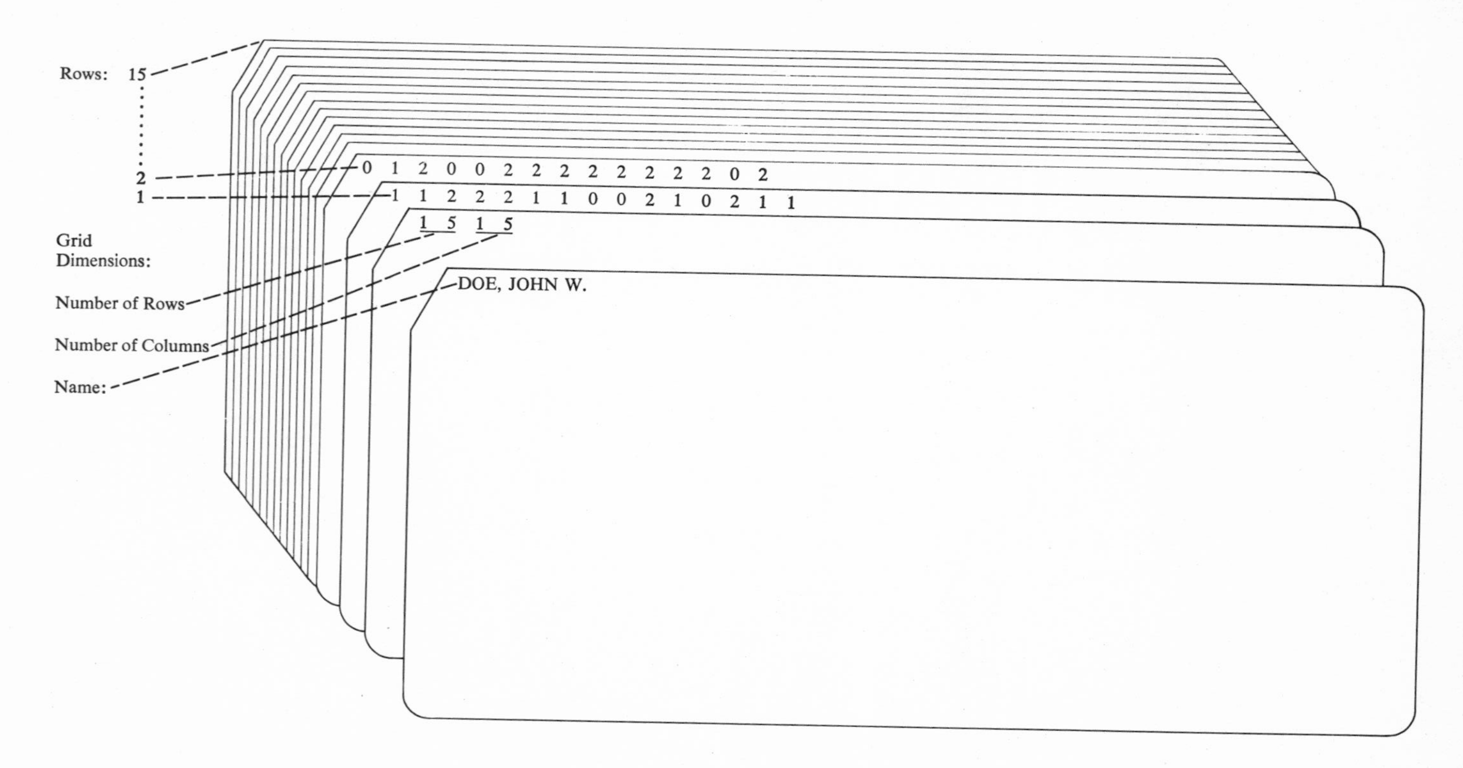

```
FORTRAN IV G LEVEL 1, MOD 3          MAIN          DATE = 69164          09/10/54
        C              LANDFIELD TRICHOTOMOUS OVERLAP RATIO MATRIX
        C
        C              PROGRAM WRITTEN IN FORTRAN IV
        C              NR=NUMBER OF ROWS
        C              NC=NUMBER OF COLUMNS
        C              NN(I,J)=ORIGINAL GRID MATRIX(INPUT)
        C              GRID CELLS MUST HAVE 1 OR 2 FOR VALUE OR 0
                      1FOR NEITHER OR QUESTION
        C              KK(I,K)=ROW COMPARISON MATRIX(OUTPUT)
        C              LL(J,L)=COLUMN COMPARISON MATRIX(OUTPUT)
        C              ME=MUTUAL EXCLUSIONS (0-0 COMBINATIONS)
        C              LK=MATCHED VALUES (1-1 OR 2-2 COMBINATIONS)
        C              NA=UNMATCHED VALUES (1-2 OR 2-1 COMBINATIONS)
        C              ME ADDED TO NA OR LK WHICHEVER IS GREATER OR
                      1TO NA IF NA AND LK
        C              2 IS SUBTRACTED FROM AN ME OF 10 OR MORE
        C              1 IS SUBTRACTED FROM AN ME OF 7, 8, OR 9
        C              ARE EQUAL
0001                   DIMENSION NN(15,15), R(15), C(15), KK(15,15), LL(15,15), NAME (8)
0002                   DATA KK,LL/450*0/
0003                   DIMENSION NUMBRS(15)
0004                   DO 10 I=1,15
0005          10       NUMBRS(I)=I
0006                   READ(5,9)NAME
0007           9       FORMAT(8A4)
        C              BEGIN WITH SIZE OF MATRIX CARD
0008                   READ(5,1) NR, NC
0009           1       FORMAT(2I2)
0010                   DO 100 I = 1, NR
0011         100       READ(5,2)(NN(I,J),J = 1,NC)
```

```
0012          2    FORMAT (15I2)
        C          BEGIN ROW COMPARISONS HERE
0013               NV = NR - 1
0014               DO 200 I = 1, NV
0015               KI = I + 1
0016               DO 200 K = KI, NR
0017               ME = 0
0018               LK = 0
0019               NA = 0
0020               DO 250 J = 1, NC
0021               IF(NN(I,J).EQ.NN(K,J).AND.NN(K,J).EQ.0)  ME=ME+1
0022               IF(NN(I,J).EQ.NN(K,J).AND.NN(K,J).NE.0)  LK = LK + 1
0023        250    IF(NN(I,J).NE.NN(K,J).AND.NN(K,J).NE.0.AND.NN(I,J).NE.0)NA=NA+1
0024               IF(ME.GE.10)ME=ME-2
0025               IF(ME.GE.7.AND.ME.LE.9)ME=ME-1
0026               IF(NA.GE.LK)KK(I,K)=-(NA+ME)
0027               IF(NA.LT.LK)KK(I,K)=LK+ME
0028        200    CONTINUE
0029               WRITE(6,6)NAME
0030          6    FORMAT(1H1,12X,8A4//20X, 'ROW COMPARISONS'/)
0031               WRITE(6,7)(NUMBRS(I),I=1,NR)
0032          7    FORMAT(1H0,5X,15I5)
0033               WRITE(6,11)
0034         11    FORMAT(/)
0035               DO 300 I=1,NR
0036        300    WRITE(6,8)I,(KK(I,J),J=1,NR)
0037          8    FORMAT(I4,2X,15I5)
        C          BEGIN COLUMN COMPARISONS HERE
0038               NZ = NC-1
0039               DO 400 J = 1, NZ
0040               LJ = J+1
```

```
0041           DO 400 L = LJ, NC
0042           ME = 0
0043           LK = 0
0044           NA = 0
0045           DO 450 I = 1, NR
0046           IF(NN(I,J).EQ.NN(I,L).AND.NN(I,L).EQ.0)ME=ME+1
0047           IF(NN(I,J).EQ.NN(I,L).AND.NN(I,L).NE.0)LK=LK+1
0048      450  IF(NN(I,J).NE.NN(I,L).AND.NN(I,L).NE.0.AND.NN(I,J).NE.0)NA=NA+1
0049           IF(ME.GE.10)ME=ME-2
0050           IF(ME.GE.7.AND.ME.LE.9)ME=ME-1
0051           IF(NA.GE.LK)LL(J,L)=-(NA+ME)
0052           IF(NA.LT.LK)LL(J,L)=LK+ME
0053      400  CONTINUE
0054           WRITE(6,3)NAME
0055        3  FORMAT(1H1,12X,8A4//20X, 'COLUMN  COMPARISONS'/)
0056           WRITE(6,4)(NUMBRS(I),I=1,NC)
0057        4  FORMAT(1H0,5X,15I5)
0058           WRITE(6,11)
0059           DO 500 I=1,NC
0060      500  WRITE(6,5)I,(LL(I,J),J=1,NC)
0061        5  FORMAT(I4,2X,15I5)
0062           STOP
0063           END
```

Row Comparisons

	1	2	3	4	5	6	7	8	9	10	11	12	13	14	15
1	0	−4	−10	8	−6	−7	−6	6	−7	9	−10	−9	−10	−7	−9
2	0	0	−7	−5	−8	10	−8	11	7	7	5	−7	−6	−8	−5
3	0	0	0	−5	8	−8	8	−9	5	−5	8	9	9	11	7
4	0	0	0	0	−6	−6	−6	−5	−9	6	−10	−7	−7	−6	−8
5	0	0	0	0	0	−8	15	−10	−4	−6	11	11	11	12	10
6	0	0	0	0	0	0	−8	11	5	7	8	−7	−8	−9	7
7	0	0	0	0	0	0	0	−10	−4	−6	11	11	11	12	10
8	0	0	0	0	0	0	0	0	6	9	−6	−10	−10	−11	−7
9	0	0	0	0	0	0	0	0	0	−8	−6	6	7	5	−6
10	0	0	0	0	0	0	0	0	0	0	−7	−10	−10	−7	−8
11	0	0	0	0	0	0	0	0	0	0	0	11	11	10	13
12	0	0	0	0	0	0	0	0	0	0	0	0	13	12	12
13	0	0	0	0	0	0	0	0	0	0	0	0	0	12	10
14	0	0	0	0	0	0	0	0	0	0	0	0	0	0	9
15	0	0	0	0	0	0	0	0	0	0	0	0	0	0	0

Column Comparisons

	1	2	3	4	5	6	7	8	9	10	11	12	13	14	15
1	0	8	−8	−6	−9	8	9	−7	−5	−9	−8	−6	−8	10	−8
2	0	0	9	10	10	10	−8	10	7	11	7	−7	11	10	−8
3	0	0	0	10	12	12	−9	9	7	13	9	−6	12	7	−9
4	0	0	0	0	12	7	−9	7	6	10	−5	−6	11	10	−9
5	0	0	0	0	0	9	−11	7	5	11	8	−7	10	9	−11
6	0	0	0	0	0	0	8	9	7	12	11	6	11	7	−8
7	0	0	0	0	0	0	0	6	5	−8	9	7	−7	−7	11
8	0	0	0	0	0	0	0	0	12	11	9	−6	11	6	6
9	0	0	0	0	0	0	0	0	0	9	7	−4	10	4	5
10	0	0	0	0	0	0	0	0	0	0	9	−5	14	7	−8
11	0	0	0	0	0	0	0	0	0	0	0	6	8	−6	−7
12	0	0	0	0	0	0	0	0	0	0	0	0	−5	−8	8
13	0	0	0	0	0	0	0	0	0	0	0	0	0	7	−7
14	0	0	0	0	0	0	0	0	0	0	0	0	0	0	−8
15	0	0	0	0	0	0	0	0	0	0	0	0	0	0	0

APPENDIX E

Brief Description of Clients

LONGER-TERM CLIENTS (LT 24)

LT 1, male, had seen a psychiatrist previously. His therapist described him as having deep-seated hostility toward the whole world and himself. *LT 2,* female, was apathetic but was still questioning whether she should quit tranquilizers and face her psychological problems. *LT 3,* female, was described as depressed, dependently immature, and self-conscious. *LT 4,* male, was chronically nervous, admitted to a drinking problem, and expressed concern over an auto accident while drinking. He also had been seen by a psychiatrist. *LT 5,* female, suffered from sleeplessness and weight loss. *LT 6,* male, was a kleptomaniac. *LT 7,* male, complained of physical weakness, although he was average in size and strength. *LT 8,* female, was fearful and confused in relationships with others, and particularly so with boys. She was described as childish. She stated that her mother warned her about talking too much, swimming, and flying in airplanes. *LT 9,* male, complained of abnormal fears and feelings and blamed his neurotic parents. *LT 10,* male, was despondent, feeling unable to hold to any line of action. He also described himself as a marital failure. *LT 11,* male, complained that he kept pulling his eyebrows and eyelashes. *LT 12,* female, suffered guilt over past homosexual behavior. She indicated many confusions in relationships with others, especially her parents. *LT 13,* male, was frantically searching for additional supplies of tranquilizers. *LT 14,* male, complained of insomnia and loss of interest in studying. *LT 15,* female, complained of general confusion. *LT 16,* male, stated that he felt "as though I'm sitting back and waiting for the world to blow up." *LT 17,* male, was unable to complete sexual relations. *LT 18,* female, felt extreme self-consciousness and nervousness. *LT 19,* male, complained that he would spend an hour thinking about how long it would take to go from one place to another. *LT 20,* female, daydreamed at least three hours a day. She also had nightmares which caused her to perspire and shake. She reported a theme of brother and sister being smashed. *LT 21,* female, was described as depressed but well organized. She constantly ruminated over the dynamics of her problems. *LT 22,* female, suffered from extreme shyness, especially with peers. *LT 23,* male, complained of mild auditory hallucinations and academic difficulties. *LT 24,* female, had no specific problem, but was concerned with one's meaning to one's self.

PREMATURELY TERMINATING CLIENTS (PT 13) ASSIGNED TO LONGER-TERM THERAPY

PT 1, female, was suffering from a grief reaction over the death of a boy-friend. She also was quite immature and feared entering an adult world. *PT 2,* male, complained of physical weaknesses which had no organic basis. *PT 3,* female, experienced periods of depression. *PT 4,* male, was unable to study, generally seemed confused, and talked about sexual value conflicts. *PT 5,* female, had dependency conflicts and distrusted boys. *PT 6,* male, feared academic failure and disappointing his parents. *PT 7,* female, complained of emotional instability, tiring easily, and little self-confidence. *PT 8,* female, complained of an inability to control her eating and sexual behavior. She continued to date a repulsive boy when she had no problem getting dates. One of her family has been diagnosed as schizophrenic. *PT 9,* female, talked about conflicts with her father and her inability to express her emotions. *PT 10,* male, had a history of emotional instability and psychiatric care. He experienced his first "nervous breakdown" at the age of twelve. *PT 11,* male, complained of marital problems and epileptic seizures. *PT 12,* female, described herself as self-condemning, complained of prolonged mood swings, and feared dying in her sleep. *PT 13,* female, experienced long periods of depression set off by small incidents. She expressed the feeling that life was meaningless. Her views of friendship were idealized and she felt isolated from others. She expressed great hostility toward everyone. She stated that mother only talked about money and death.

EIGHTEEN VARIABLE-TERM CLIENTS (FROM VT 36)

VT 2, female, stated her problem as overdependency, feeling that her boy-friend as well as others perceived her as an anchor around their necks. *VT 4,* male, complained of an inability to concentrate. *VT 6,* male, a withdrawn, very anxious and inhibited boy, experienced difficulty in expressing himself. *VT 8,* male, felt apart from others and was beginning to reject his compulsive achievement pattern. *VT 10,* female, described a weird experience of crawling under the pews during a chapel service. *VT 13,* male, complained of decreasing interest in school at midterm. He also was apprehended for window peeping. *VT 15,* female, a senior, complained of depression which seemed related to breaking up with a boyfriend and anticipatory anxiety over her vocational future. *VT 17,* male, talked about his lack of social experience. *VT 19,* female, was described as poorly organized with nothing to care for or work toward. *VT 22,* male, experienced difficulties because of his hot temper. *VT 24,* male, described his problems as a mental block against studying and not getting along with the fellows. *VT 26,* female, focused on her excessive emotional involvement with the opposite sex. *VT 28,* male, suffered from bleeding ulcers. *VT 29,* female, presented an ill-defined problem related to future goals and a career; however, the underlying problem seemed to be guilt over sexual involvement with three boys. *VT 30,* female, complained of an uncontrollable temper and anxiety which bordered on a panic reaction. *VT 33,* female, was unable to establish friendships easily or relate to groups. *VT 34,* male, cried for the first time since he was a child. The therapist described him as constantly preoccupied with analyzing himself and others. *VT 36,* female, discussed value conflicts she was having with her parents.

REFERENCES

Affleck, D. C., & Mednick, S. A. The use of the Rorschach test in the prediction of the abrupt terminator in individual psychotherapy. *Journal of Consulting Psychology,* 1959, *23,* 125–126.

Bannister, D. Psychology as an exercise in paradox. *Bulletin of the British Psychological Society,* 1966, *19,* 63, 21–26.

Bannister, D., & Mair, J. M. M. *The evaluation of personal constructs.* London & New York: Academic Press, 1968.

Baugh, L. J. Functionally independent construct score as a function of role construct repertory test heterogeneity. Unpublished master's thesis, University of Missouri, 1968.

Berg, I. A., & Collier, J. S. Personality and group differences in extreme response sets. *Educational and Psychological Measurement,* 1953, *13,* 164–169.

Bieri, J. Cognitive complexity-simplicity and predictive behavior. *Journal of Abnormal and Social Psychology,* 1955, *51,* 263–268.

Bieri, J. Complexity-simplicity as a personality variable in cognitive and preferential behavior. In D. W. Fiske and S. Maddi (eds.), *Functions of varied experience.* Homewood, Illinois: Dorsey, 1961.

Bonarius, J. C. J. Research in personal construct psychology. In Brendan Maher (ed.), Progress in experimental personality research. London & New York: Academic Press, 1965.

Bonarius, J. C. J. Personal constructs and extremity ratings. *Heymans Bulletins,* Institute of Psychology, Groningen, The Netherlands, June, 1968.

Bonarius, J. C. J. Fixed role therapy: A double paradox. *British Journal of Medical Psychology,* Sept., 1970, *43,* 213–219.

Carson, R., & Heine, R. Similarity and success in therapeutic dyads. *Journal of Consulting Psychology,* 1962, *26,* 38–43.

Crockett, W. H. Cognitive complexity and impression formation. In B. A. Maher (ed.), *Progress in experimental personality research,* New York & London: Academic Press, 1965.

Cromwell, R. L. & Caldwell, D. R. A comparison of ratings based on personal constructs of self and others. *Journal of Clinical Psychology,* 1962, *18,* 43–46.

Danforth, W. J. An internal consistency study of conceptual organization within personal construct theory. Unpublished doctoral dissertation, University of Missouri, 1968.

Edwards, L. *Statistical analysis*. New York: Rinehart, 1946.

Farson, R. E. Introjection in the psychotherapeutic relationship. *Journal of Counseling Psychology,* 1961, *8,* 337–343.

Fiedler, F. E., Dodge, J., Jones, R. E., & Hutchins, E. B. Interrelations among measures of personality adjustment in nonclinical populations. *Journal of Abnormal and Social Psychology,* 1958, *56,* 345–351.

Fjeld, S. P., & Landfield, A. W. Personal construct consistency. *Psychological Reports,* 1961, *8,* 127–129.

Frank, J. D., Gliedman, L. H., Imber, S. D., Nash, E. H., & Stone, A. R. Why patients leave psychotherapy. *American Medical Association's Archives of Neurology and Psychiatry,* 1957, *77,* 283–299.

Fromm-Reichmann, F. Notes on the personal and professional requirements of a psychotherapist. *Psychiatry,* 1949, *12,* 361–378.

Gerler, W. Psychotherapy as a function of client-counselor similarity. Unpublished doctoral dissertation, University of Illinois, 1958.

Halpern, H. M., & Lesser, L. N. Empathy in infants, adults, and psychotherapist. *Psychoanalysis and the Psychoanalytic Review,* 1960, *47,* 32–42.

Heilbrun, A. B. Male and female personality correlation of early termination in counseling. *Journal of Counseling Psychology,* 1961, *8,* 31–36.

Hiler, E. W. An analysis of patient-therapist compatibility. *Journal of Consulting Psychology,* 1958, *22,* 341–347.

Hinkle, D. N. The change of personal constructs from the viewpoint of a theory of implications. Unpublished doctoral dissertation, The Ohio State University, 1965.

Hollingshead, A. B., & Redlich, F. *Social class and mental illness: A community study*. New York: John Wiley, 1958.

Hunt, D. E. Studies in role concept repertory: Conceptual consistency. Unpublished master's thesis, The Ohio State University, 1951.

Hunt, R. G. Conceptual congruity among psychiatric patients and staff. *Psychological Reports,* 1961, *9,* 53–54.

Imber, S. D., Frank, J. D., Gliedman, L. H., Nash, E. H., & Stone, A. R. Suggestibility, social class, and acceptance of psychotherapy. *Journal of Clinical Psychology,* 1956, *12,* 341–344.

Isaacson, G. I. A comparative study of the meaningfulness of personal and common constructs. Unpublished doctoral dissertation, University of Missouri, 1966.

Isaacson, G. I., & Landfield, A. W. The meaningfulness of personal and common constructs, *Journal of Individual Psychology,* 1965, *21,* 160–166.

Karst, T. O., & Trexler, L. D. Initial study using fixed role and rational emotive therapy in treating public-speaking anxiety. *Journal of Consulting and Clinical Psychology,* 1970, *34,* 360–366.

Katz, M. M., Lorr, M., & Rubenstein, E. A. Remainer patient attributes and their relation to subsequent improvement in psychotherapy. *Journal of Consulting Psychology,* 1958, *22,* 411–413.

Kelly, G. A. Alternatives. Unpublished lecture presented at Purdue University, May 20, 1952.

Kelly, G. A. *The psychology of personal constructs.* New York: W. W. Norton, 1955, Vols. I and II.

Kessel, P., & McBrearty, J. Values and psychotherapy: A review of the literature. *Perceptual and Motor Skills,* 1967, *25,* 669–690.

Landfield, A. W. The extremity rating revisited within the context of personal construct theory. *British Journal of Social and Clinical Psychology,* 1968, *7,* 135–139.

Landfield, A. W. Grid relationship scoring used with a Rep Test modification. *Psychological Reports,* 1967, *21,* 19–23.

Landfield, A. W. Meaningfulness of ideal, self and other on client and therapist constructs. *Psychological Reports,* 1965, *16,* 605–608.

Landfield, A. W. A personal construct approach to suicidal behavior. Unpublished manuscript, 1969.

Landfield, A. W. Rep Tests on five alcoholics. Unpublished data, 1967.

Landfield, A. W. Self predictive orientation and the movement interpretation of threat. *Journal of Abnormal and Social Psychology,* 1955, *51,* 434–438.

Landfield, A. W., Danforth, W., & Baugh, L. Functionally independent construction (FIC): Studies of consistency. *Psychological Reports,* 1968, *23,* 337–338.

Landfield, A. W., & Nawas, M. M. Psychotherapeutic improvement as a function of communication and adoption of therapists' values. *Journal of Counseling Psychology,* 1964, *11,* 336–341.

Landfield, A. W., Nawas, M. M., & O'Donovan, D. Improvement ratings by external judges and psychotherapists. *Psychological Reports,* 1962, *11,* 747–748.

Landfield, A. W., Nawas, M. M., & O'Donovan, D. A quarter century in the life of a university mental hygiene clinic. *College Health,* 1963, *12,* 202–207.

Landfield, A. W., Stern, M., & Fjeld, S. P. Social conceptual processes and change in students undergoing psychotherapy. *Psychological Reports,* 1961, *8,* 63–68.

Lemcke, F. Some aspects of change process in personal construction systems. Unpublished doctoral dissertation, The Ohio State University, 1959.

Levy, L. H. Personal constructs and predictive behavior. *Journal of Abnormal and Social Psychology,* 1956, *53,* 54–58.

Levy, L. H. *Psychological interpretation.* New York: Holt, Rinehart & Winston, 1963.

London, P. *The modes and morals of psychotherapy.* New York: Holt, Rinehart & Winston, 1964.

Maher, B. Personality, problem solving, and the einstellung effect. *Journal of Abnormal and Social Psychology,* 1957, *54,* 70–74.

Maher, B. (ed.) *Clinical psychology and personality: The selected papers of George A. Kelly.* New York: John Wiley, 1969.

Mair, J. M. M. & Crisp, A. H. Estimating psychological organization, meaning, and change in relation to clinical practice. *British Journal of Medical Psychology,* 1968, *41,* 15–29.

Mendelsohn, G. A. Client-counselor compatibility and the effectiveness of counseling. Unpublished manuscript, University of California, Berkeley, 1968.

Mitsos, S. B. Personal constructs and the semantic differential. *Journal of Abnormal and Social Psychology,* 1961, *62,* 433–434.

Nawas, M. M., & Landfield, A. W. Improvement in psychotherapy and adoption of the therapist's meaning system. *Psychological Reports,* 1963, *13,* 97–98.

O'Donovan, D. Polarization and meaningfulness in 6,300 value judgments. Unpublished manuscript, 1964.

O'Donovan, D. Rating extremity: Pathology or meaningfulness. *Psychological Review,* 1965, *72,* 358–372.

Oliver, D., & Landfield, A. W. Reflexivity: An unfaced issue in psychology. *Journal of Individual Psychology,* 1962, *18,* 114–124.

Osgood, C. E., Suci, G. J., & Tannenbaum, P. H. *The measurement of meaning.* Urbana, Illinois: University of Illinois Press, 1957.

Ourth, L., & Landfield, A. W. Interpersonal meaningfulness and nature of termination in psychotherapy. *Journal of Counseling Psychology,* 1965, *12,* 366–371.

Pepinsky, H. B., & Karst, T. O. Convergence: A phenomenon in counseling and psychotherapy. *American Psychologist,* 1964, *19,* 333–338.

Persons, R. W., & Pepinsky, H. B. Convergence in psychotherapy with delinquent boys. *Journal of Counseling Psychology,* 1966, *13,* 329–334.

Resnick, J., & Landfield, A. W. The oppositional nature of dichotomous constructs. *The Psychological Record,* 1961, *11,* 47–55.

Rhys, E. (ed.) *The fables of Aesop and others.* London: J. M. Dent & Sons, Ltd., 1913.

Rogers, C. R. *Client-centered therapy.* Boston: Houghton Mifflin, 1951.

Rosencranz, H. Role of perceptions of significant others by older persons. Proceedings of the 7th International Congress of Gerontology, Vienna, Austria, 1966.

Rosenthal, D. Changes in some moral values following psychotherapy. *Journal of Consulting Psychology,* 1955, *19,* 431–436.

Runkel, P. J. Cognitive similarity in facilitating communication. *Sociometry,* 1956, *19,* 178–191.

Strickland, B. R., & Crowne, D. P. Need for approval and the premature termination of psychotherapy. *Journal of Consulting Psychology,* 1963, *27,* 95–101.

Teichman, M. Interrelationships among perceived family roles of neurotic and well adjusted students. Unpublished manuscript, 1970.

Tippett, J. S. A study of change process during psychotherapy. Unpublished doctoral dissertation, The Ohio State University, 1959.

Tuma, A. H., & Gustad, J. W. The effects of client and counselor personality characteristics on client learning in counseling. *Journal of Counseling Psychology,* 1957, *4,* 136–143.

Tyler, F. B., & Simmons, W. L. Patient's conceptions of therapists. *Journal of Clinical Psychology,* 1964, *20,* 122–133.

Varble, D., & Landfield, A. W. Validity of the self-ideal discrepancy as a criterion measure of successful psychotherapy—a replication. *Journal of Counseling Psychology,* 1969, *16,* 150–156.

Weisskopf-Joelson, E. The present crisis in psychotherapy. *The Journal of Psychology,* 1968, *69,* 107–115.

Welkowitz, J., Cohen, J., & Ortmeyer, D. Value system similarity: Investigation of patient-therapist dyads. *Journal of Consulting Psychology,* 1967, *31,* 48–55.

Zax, M., & Klein, A. Measurement of personality and behavior changes following psychotherapy. *Psychological Bulletin,* 1960, *57,* 435–448.

NAME INDEX

SUBJECT INDEX

PRINTED IN U.S.A.